Diakonia Studies

Diakonia Studies

Critical Issues in Ministry

JOHN N. COLLINS

OXFORD
UNIVERSITY PRESS

OXFORD
UNIVERSITY PRESS

Oxford University Press is a department of the University of Oxford.
It furthers the University's objective of excellence in research, scholarship,
and education by publishing worldwide.

Oxford   New York

Auckland   Cape Town   Dar es Salaam   Hong Kong   Karachi
Kuala Lumpur   Madrid   Melbourne   Mexico City   Nairobi
New Delhi   Shanghai   Taipei   Toronto

With offices in

Argentina   Austria   Brazil   Chile   Czech Republic   France   Greece
Guatemala   Hungary   Italy   Japan   Poland   Portugal   Singapore
South Korea   Switzerland   Thailand   Turkey   Ukraine   Vietnam

Oxford is a registered trademark of Oxford University Press
in the UK and certain other countries.

Published in the United States of America by
Oxford University Press
198 Madison Avenue, New York, NY 10016

© Oxford University Press 2014

Library of Congress Cataloging-in-Publication Data
Collins, John N. (John Neil), 1931–
Diakonia studies : critical issues in ministry / John N. Collins.
pages cm
Includes bibliographical references and index.
ISBN 978–0–19–936757–3 (hardcover : alk. paper)—ISBN 978–0–19–936758–0 (updf)—
ISBN 978–0–19–938461–7 (online content)   1. Pastoral theology—History.   I. Title.
BV4207.C655 2014
262'.14—dc23
2014000013

1 3 5 7 9 8 6 4 2
Printed in the United States of America
on acid-free paper

*To my wife Carolyn
and our daughter and son
Catherine and John
with love and deepest gratitude*

Contents

PART THREE: *Toward Ministry for the Twenty-First Century*

Preface

THE STUDIES IN this volume have prehistories of four kinds. Some have been published in theological journals (Chapters 1, 2, 6, 11–13); some are extracts from published (but not necessarily widely read) books (Chapters 4, 5, 7–10); one (Chapter 14) is a reworked public lecture previously unpublished; and one (Chapter 3) is having its first airing. Previously published material may have been lightly edited.

The contents page shows that the papers are gathered into three groups: (1) ideas and values associated in theology since at least the 1930s with the ancient Greek term *diakonia*; (2) the different ideas and values that ancient Greeks associated with the term; and (3) what the ancient Greek ideas and values can contribute to making ministry effective within churches that are in crisis early in the twenty-first century.

The project is not so much ambitious as utilitarian, if I may use a term brought to mind by the bicentenary as I write of the birth of Charles Dickens. As awareness of shifts in the understanding of *diakonia* becomes more widespread, readers who do not have access to my research volume of 1990, *Diakonia: Re-interpreting the Ancient Sources*, and others who do but are disinclined to work their way through the linguistic detail and long argumentation there, will find the essentials and some further significant developments here. The latter mainly concern how I understand a re-interpretation of *diakonia* to be greatly advantageous for the workings of the church today.

My engagement in the semantics of *diakonia* began in September 1971. My thesis on the matter was examined at the University of London in 1976. The book *Diakonia: Re-interpreting the Ancient Sources* did not appear until 1990 after a postdoctoral life raising young children, the purchase of a family home in Melbourne, and the teaching in high schools that helped pay for it.

Southern hemisphere summer vacations in 1990 and 2000 combined happily with two northern winter fellowships to provide opportunities to write *Are All Christians Ministers?* (1992) at the Institute for Ecumenical and Cultural Research in Collegeville, Minnesota, and *Deacons and the Church* (2002) at the Deacon Samariterhemmet in conjunction with the theology faculty of the University of Uppsala and at the warm and generous invitation of its dean, Professor Sven-Erik Brodd.

Sadly, the latter book contributed to the already widespread misconception that *diakonia* is mainly about deacons. More sadly, the former book, which aimed to expound the view that *diakonia* was an expression of the essential character of ministry, either was not read at all or divided opinion when it was. In one view, the argument of the book was "at best pedantic, at worst moot" (*National Catholic Reporter*, April 23, 1993) while in another view the thrust of the book was "to recover the radical newness of the New Testament vision" (*Commonweal*, December 3, 1993). Let it be said that I would not attempt to recycle the book under its 1992 title in the wildly different context of ministerial theology today.

Hence the utilitarian approach here. Having been born in the year Wilhelm Brandt published *Dienst und Dienen im Neuen Testament* (1931), but wanting still to help release ministry in the church from the narrow constraints of "a servant model" put upon it by that linguistic study, I have excused myself from the tedium of developing a newly constructed apologia for *diakonia* and have turned instead to making a collection of what I consider to be effective earlier writings. I would like to think that they will appear attractive to a younger and, I hope, broader range of readers. Each paper is self-sufficient. The reader can begin anywhere. And no one has to read from cover to cover.

For a snap preview of how deeply the "servant model" is set in modern perceptions of Jesus of the gospels, the new reader may find the following short extract helpful. It sets up a theological scenario that my research and the following publications have sought to dismantle. It originates from a peak period for the modern paradigm of *diakonia* when Gerhard Lohfink, writing in 1982 as professor of New Testament at the University of Tübingen, published "What Kind of Community did Jesus Intend?" (*Wie hat Jesus Gemeinde gewollt?*). This appeared in English two years later under the anodyne title *Jesus and Community*, where we read (47):

He did not allow his disciples to wash his feet, but performed for them this service which was part of the meal (John 13:1–20). He was in their midst as one who served (Luke 22:27). He did not come to let himself be served, but to serve (Mark 10:45).

Jesus' words about *service* are part of the most widely attested tradition which stems from him. . . . That Jesus did not let himself be served but rather himself served others—presumably not only at the Last Supper—must have impressed his community of disciples so deeply that they later termed their own offices *diakonia,* services.

That was 1982. The target audience in 1990 for my volume of linguistic research comprised principally those who were theologically and vocationally engaged under this German banner of *Diakonie* understood as service to people. As a consequence, I was nonplussed when no German review of the book appeared.

Ten years later, it was some surprise that Hans-Jürgen Benedict blew the whistle with his sensational article (to translate the title), "Does the Claim of Lutheran *Diakonie* Rest on a Misinterpretation of the Ancient Sources? John N. Collins' Investigation of *diakonia*." Inside three years, the University of Heidelberg's *Diakoniewissenschaftliches Institut* published a collection of papers appraising the research. Further developments of dialogue and debate are recorded in some of the present studies.

Hans-Jürgen Benedict had noted in his article that my stated objective had been a "futile" exercise from the start. In a later paper, he instanced that even in the case of his explosive article it was four years before a colleague in his own academic institute in Hamburg—one dedicated to education in *Diakonie*—"condescended" to take notice of his dramatic exposure. Throughout those years the institute's copy of *Diakonia* remained unaccessed on the library's shelves.

Another ten years later, in France, a similar situation elicited the following expression of grievance in *Revue d'éthique et de théologie morale* (March 2012) from Mathias Nebel of L'Institut catholique de Paris—indeed from the faculty named after the revered Jean Rodhain, founder of *Secours catholique* and advocate of a French theology of *diaconie*:

How could we reach such a situation? What twists were able to deceive a whole generation of theologians on a term that bears such a theological load nowadays? How is it that such a deeply flawed interpretative habit now rules the day and presents us with a new theological idea that we are not supposed to contest?

In this process we see once more the extent to which our own cultural context controls the way we read our texts: this context simply blocks access to any other meaning we may need to pursue.

Even more remarkably, in August 2013, after the manuscript of this book was already in the hands of the publishers, Dr Esko Ryökäs informed me from Finland of the publication of Dr Anni Hentschel's study of New Testament ecclesiology under the title *Gemeinde, Ämter, Dienste* (Community, Offices, Ministries). Its relevance here is clear from the second study in this collection being a positive evaluation of Dr Hentschel's earlier major investigation *Diakonia im Neuen Testament* (2007). Her new book's blurb announced that the author "opens on the issue of what this word [*diakonia*] means" before moving into the central ecclesiological passages of the New Testament and coming up with what the blurb named "extremely interesting results." An outline of these I append to the second study below but suggest here that, whatever of some differences in emphasis and detail between us, our two current studies contribute to the resolution of critical issues that for decades now have disturbed and distorted ecclesiological investigations and pastoral policies.

One part of the hermeneutical problem would seem to be that vernaculars themselves constitute barriers to transferring theological ideas between language groups. The English/German barrier may be furnished with regular checkpoints in the form of translations of many leading German books, but, strangely, traffic reduces to a trickle in the reverse cycle. Things may be changing with the high level of competence in English within the current generation of German theologians.

Within anglophone theology itself, however, other barriers also exist. These are not of a linguistic kind. They are either of a denominational kind as in the Protestant/Roman Catholic divide or, more broadly, as in a low/high church division. Relevant here is the existence of a unique intra-church divide within the Roman Catholic academe, especially in the United States. The divide is determined in the main by theological pedigree, this relating to stances taken in regard to the interpretation of the Second Vatican Council. Terms like "liberals" and "restorationists" often headline reports of the situation. In the matter of *diakonia* the divide is particularly awkward to straddle. A ministerial culture newly described on the basis of first-century biblical data has little to offer advocates whose priority is to refurbish for the twenty-first century a sixteenth-century amalgam of biblical, imperial, feudal, and counter-Reformation ecclesiologies. Nor, on the other side, within a liberal environment, is a new ministerial culture likely to develop on ground which one mistakenly suspects of having been seeded with elements of exclusivity and absolutism. Thus, more than once a "repressive" character has been ascribed to ecclesiological tendencies in my writings (G. Goosen, *Pacifica*, June 1993).

This larger discourse is not engaged here. The collection invites a tighter engagement with *diakonia* itself, with exposure to whatever it implies. Not surprisingly, readers will discover that, like many another disparate collection, this one is marked by a level of repetition. I believe, however, that readers of collections come to them mainly for the bits they want. If they are to read those bits well, they will need to be informed about the main point at issue because this constitutes the viewpoint from which I am conducting each of my reflections. Thus, I regularly remind readers of theological misconceptions that have arisen from misunderstandings of what *diakonia* meant to ancient Greeks.

The preceding short guide to useful reading applies especially to the seven studies in the first and third sections of the collection. The seven in the middle section, on the other hand, require no such pre-schooling. Chapter 4 is a headlong romp through those parts of ancient Greek literature where authors felt the urge to draw on the rather rare words within the *diakon-* group. With the exception of Chapter 6, the rest of the middle section provides nontechnical accounts of how early Christian writers used *diakon-* words in relation to different aspects of Christian living and of responsibilities within Christian communities. The sources for papers published previously are listed at the end.

For closer engagement with the Greek text under analysis, readers would need to consult the volume *Diakonia: Re-interpreting the Ancient Sources*. This remains available in a 2009 reprint as well as online at *Oxford Scholarship/Religion*. Readers should note that in relation to two passages of the New Testament (1 Cor. 12:4–6; Acts 6:1–6) my later comment improves greatly upon what I attempted in the research volume of 1990, and these revised opinions are represented in studies here.

I sincerely thank publishers and editors who have taken on my work in previous years and now have supported republication here. In order of presentation these include Kari Latvus, former editor of *Diakonian tutkimus*, Helsinki; Tom Weterings of *Ecclesiology* published by Koninklijke Brill NV, Leiden, in association with the Department of Theology and Centre for the Study of the Christian Church, whose director, Dr Paul Avis, has been highly supportive of my work for many years; David Lovell of

David Lovell Publishing, Melbourne, original publisher of my 1992 book *Are All Christians Ministers?*; Professor James McLaren of the Melbourne campus of Australian Catholic University, co-editor of *Australian Biblical Review*; Tom Longford of Gracewing, Leominster, UK, publisher of *Deacons and the Church* (2002); and Bernadette Gasslein, interim editor of *Worship*, Collegeville, Minnesota, after the death in mid-2013 of longtime editor Kevin Seasoltz, OSB, with whom I had enjoyed a long and helpful association.

Timing of other developments has been intriguing. The date 1931 has already been noted for its beginnings. Forty-one years later marked the beginning of my research as well of the life of my now colleague in research, Dr Hentschel. Forty-one further years saw the publication both of my own study of *diakonia* (1990) and of Dr Hentschel's two investigations in the same area (2007, 2013) as well as notice of the acceptance for publication of the studies in this volume. The latter, I am happy to record, has been under the aegis of the same editor within Oxford University Press in New York, Ms Cynthia Read, whose ready ear and professionality I admire. Less intriguing but inspiring and simply heartwarming are the support and friendship I have experienced from scholars not already mentioned. These include Professor Bart Koet of Tilburg; Professor Kjell Nordstokke, Oslo; Dr Kari Latvus, Helsinki; and Deacon Ninni Smedberg, director of Vårsta Diakonigård, Härnösand, Sweden, who, as onetime strategist for deacons in the Church of Sweden and on the basis of our chance 1997 meeting at an international conference on the diaconate in Bressanone, Italy, began familiarizing me with the lively and ever reflective Nordic deacon enclaves. My experiences among them and their colleagues I continue to cherish.

Collaboration has not been so close as such connections might suggest, nor have they produced the larger outcomes that I may have anticipated or hoped for. With the present publication my objective remains as it has long been, and that is to make my initial reflections on ministry more easily accessible to new audiences and to stimulate further much needed discussion and debate. In this my sentiment is one with that of Dr Hentschel, who declared at the end of her current volume: "The present study sees itself as a contribution to a pressingly urgent discussion about fundamental issues of how we are to understand office and community in the New Testament and the early church"—I would simply add: "and in the churches today."

PART ONE

Diakonia from the Nineteenth Century to Today

I

From Διακονία to Diakonia Today: Historical Aspects of Interpretation

A Morality Tale About Translating Biblical Text

In 1532 Thomas More published the first three volumes of his "Confutation" of William Tyndale's New Testament. More was still Chancellor of King Henry VIII of England. Tyndale was a Catholic priest who had smuggled his translation from the European continent into England. There the books were hunted down and burned by the Bishop of London.

Tyndale's translation had appeared in 1526, and was the first translation of the New Testament from Greek into English. Thomas More did not thank Tyndale for this. More called Tyndale "a hell-hound in the kennel of the devil . . . a drowsy drudge drinking deep in the devil's dregs . . . discharging a filthy foam of blasphemies out of his brutish beastly mouth."[1]

The intensity of these feelings arose from what had been going on in central Europe during the first decades of the Lutheran challenge to the church. Thomas More was uncontrollably angry at how Tyndale's translation represented what the New Testament had to say about the church and its operations. A particular complaint was that Tyndale translated the Greek *ekklesia* as "congregation," not as "Church" with a capital C.

Tyndale was equally unhappy—although he was more temperate in his language—with "how they [the church of his day] stablish their lies with falsifying the scripture."[2]

---

1. David Daniell, *William Tyndale: A Biography* (New Haven/London: Yale University Press, 1994), 277.

2. Ibid., 272.

The scripture, of course, was the Latin Vulgate, which the church had been using across Europe for over a thousand years. Tyndale was accusing the churchmen of twisting the translation to fit the model of church they already had.

A classic instance of "twisted" translation is the Vulgate's version of what to do in the case of serious illness (James 5:14). The Vulgate read: "Inducat presbyteros ecclesiae," which the official Roman Catholic Rheims version of 1582 translated: "Let him bring in the priests of the church." In 1526 Tyndale translated the Greek: "Let him call for the seniors of the congregation"; in 1534 he changed "seniors" to "elders".

Tyndale professed himself less preoccupied with how we name the functionaries in English. His priority was to understand their function. In addressing his reader, he observed drily, "Whether ye call them elders or priests, it is to me all one: so that ye understand that they be officers and servants of the word of God."[3] In other words, preachers and not just Mass priests or Chantry priests.

The Rheims version was twisting the translation of the Greek to fit the model of church: "priests" and "church" instead of "elders" and "congregation."

One moral of this story is that translators of the Bible cannot install a firewall against the virus of mistakes. A second lesson is that churches do not advertise their exposure to the virus of erroneous translation.

Outline

The following historical sketch traces the steps by which, from the nineteenth century onward, scholars and church leaders introduced errors into the lexical description of the small group of Greek words in the New Testament that are main designations of ecclesial ministry in general and of the ministry called diaconate in particular. The words—*diakonia* and associated terms—were once unremarkable, but the sketch reveals how new meanings wrongly accrued. These misinterpretations were to the detriment of both exegesis and ecclesiology. We begin with the sample case of Phoebe and move on to that of the diaconate. In this case, nineteenth-century innovations begin to impact on the lexical values of the title "deacon" and of cognate Greek terms. The survey concludes with

---

3. David Daniell, *Tyndale's New Testament. Translated from the Greek by William Tyndale in 1534* (New Haven/London: Yale University Press, 1989), 10.

notice of the newly emerged consensus regarding a re-interpretation of *diakon-* words that requires, in its turn, a rethinking of the whole question of what in central European countries is named *diaconia/Diakonie* today.

Phoebe

The *diakon-* terms have been inextricably involved with contemporary discussion and debate regarding the diaconate. The reason is obvious. All languages maintain an explicit connection with these terms by reason of the name they have given to the church officer known in English as the deacon. In the protracted controversies following upon the Reformation in relation to the ministries of bishops and priests, where was this other minister of the historical church?

In the first published English translation of the New Testament, William Tyndale was happy to write plainly about "deacons" at Phil. 1:1: "Paul...to all the saints...with the bishops and deacons" and at 1 Tim. 3:8. At Rom. 16:1, where the same Greek word *diakonos* applies to Phoebe, Tyndale wrote of her as "a minister of the congregation."

The Roman Catholic Rheims version also balked at calling Phoebe a deacon, naming her "our sister, who is in the ministry of the church." In this, however, Rheims was taking a lead from the curious circumlocution in the Vulgate: "quae est in ministerio ecclesiae." The Authorized Version (AV) wrote simply "a servant of the church," a designation Phoebe retained through the 1881 Revised Version (RV) until 1946 when the Revised Standard Version (RSV) introduced the strikingly novel designation, "our sister Phoebe, a deaconess of the church." In the New Revised Standard Version (NRSV) of 1989, "deaconess" becomes "deacon," although a footnote offers the alternative translation "minister."

Phoebe, of course, is a unique case, as a woman in an early Christian literary context which elsewhere does not apply a technical term of office to any woman. So why should the title "deacon" come to be applied to her in the NRSV of 1989? This designation is very puzzling so early in the institutional evolution of the Christian community. My own view is that Paul is writing a commendatory note for Phoebe as the "delegate" of the church of Cenchreae to the communities in Rome.[4] In designating her "deacon" at the end of the twentieth century, however, could there have been vested

---

4. John N. Collins, *Diakonia: Re-interpreting the Ancient Sources* (New York: Oxford University Press, 1990), 223–25.

ecclesial interests at work like those which led Thomas More—against Tyndale's best instincts—to demand the presence of "priests" at the bedside of the sick mentioned by James (5:14)?

Deacons and the Reformation

The churchmen of the sixteenth and seventeenth centuries who so earnestly debated the relative merits of "priest" and "presbyter" had virtually no problem with the existence of officers called deacons.

Among Roman Catholics, deacons remained a symbolic appendage within the hierarchical arrangement. The status of the diaconate as an official part of the church's order was religiously represented in liturgical functions reserved on more solemn occasions for the deacon. On such liturgical occasions, however, the deacon's role was normally performed by a priest vested in a deacon's robes. The diaconate itself was merely a brief transitory stage on the way to the higher ranking of priesthood—perchance of episcopacy.

Among reformed churches a much more pragmatic regime was quickly in place. These churches perceived deacons to have a clear role as officers of charity. In *Institutes* iv.iii.9, Calvin enunciated this: "...although the term *diakonia* has a more extensive meaning, Scripture specially gives the name of deacons to those whom the Church appoints to dispense alms, and take care of the poor...Their origin, institution, and office, is described by Luke (Acts 6:3)."[5]

In neither the Roman Catholic nor the Protestant situation did these arrangements expose any sensitive theological principle for the opposition to attack. The Protestants, however, could at least claim that they had made something real of an original Christian institution, whereas the Roman Catholics had allowed it to atrophy.

Demise and Restoration

Within a century or two, however, changing social and economic conditions increasingly delivered social welfare into the administration of the state, and even the Protestant deacon mostly lost his distinctive role.[6]

---

5. John Calvin, *Institutes of the Christian Religion*, vol. 2, trans. Henry Beveridge (London: James Clarke, 1962), 322.

6. Elsie Anne McKee, *Diakonia in the Classical Reformed Tradition and Today* (Grand Rapids, MI: Eerdmans, 1989), 62–64; Jeannine E. Olson, *One Ministry Many Roles: Deacons and Deaconesses through the Centuries* (St Louis: Concordia, 1992), 130–34, 185–86.

The attempt in the sixteenth century to restore a functional diaconate had been driven by a conviction that scripture required the church to be so ordered. The prescription was recognized in the directions on bishops and deacons in 1 Tim. 3, while the identification of the role as an office of charity was read from the institution of the Seven in Acts 6—though there was disagreement as to whether the Seven were deacons.[7]

With the virtual demise of this office by the early nineteenth century, a dramatically different role of scripture in the understanding of the diaconate began to unfold. This has had broad ramifications not only for the modus operandi of the diaconate across the churches today but also for a revised estimation of the nature of ecclesial ministry itself.

Initiatives within German Lutheranism taken in the 1830s by Johann Hinrich Wichern and the Fliedners, Theodor and Friederike,—to mention only these revered names—saw the creation of communities of men and especially of women who were dedicated exclusively to the works of charity so desperately needed in the wake of social dislocations created by industrialization and the Napoleonic wars.

Nineteenth-century Servant Model

The development brought the terminology of deacons, deaconesses, and diaconate back into circulation. It also brought a sharper focus to bear on the few passages in the New Testament that spoke of deacons. Associated with this was closer attention given to passages that speak of the works of mercy. In turn, this attention spilled over into a high level of interest in the semantic values of the *diakonia* words themselves. This occurred in regard to the other ninety-eight instances of *diakonia* terms in the New Testament that do not designate deacons at all.

By the 1930s, Lutheran and Reformed diaconal operations stemming from the nineteenth-century foundations had grown enormously in central and northern Europe and had traveled with migrants to North America in particular.

Accompanying the broadening of diaconal undertakings and the geographical spread of the diaconal institutions was the strong growth of a distinctively modern diaconal spirituality. In essence, this centered on the servant roles of the deacon and deaconess in their meeting the needs of the

---

7. Elsie Anne McKee, *John Calvin on the Diaconate and Liturgical Almsgiving* (Geneva: Droz, 1984), 139–58.

disadvantaged. The basic scriptural paradigm supporting the spirituality was that of Jesus of Nazareth as the one "who came not to be served but to serve" (Mark 10:45), where "serve" is a Greek *diakon-* term. Deacons and deaconesses sought to make their own the saying of Jesus: "I am among you as one who serves" (Luke 22:27). Here again a *diakon-* term is used.

Diakonia Among the Scholars

The nineteenth century was a period of intense scholarship in the matter of words. This was so in regard to vernaculars like English and to classical Greek and Latin. The Greek lexicon of Liddell and Scott, which first appeared in 1843, built upon the German 1819 Passow and Hase's 1831 French edition of Henri Estienne's *Thesaurus* of 1572.

While this was going on, views about the semantics of *diakonia* ruffled no feathers. In Liddell and Scott, we read that the verb *diakoneō* meant— among a few other things—to "minister, do service" (note the latter expression); the abstract noun *diakonia* meant "service," "attendance on a duty" (again, notice the latter); and the common noun *diakonos* meant "servant," "messenger," "attendant or official" in a cult (note the two latter: "messenger," "official"), and, of course, the Christian "deacon."

Over the next hundred years little more was to be heard of *diakonia*, certainly not at any level of disputation. Some semantic refinement did occur here and there, and this was because scholars observed a certain obscurity around the origins and character of these rather rare words.

At this point I cannot help remembering what the pathbreaking English lexicographer, Dr Samuel Johnson, had to say about assumptions affecting investigations into "ancient tongues, now immutably fixed." Dr Johnson observed that the learned results might yet be "inadequate and delusive."[8]

With such a possibility in mind, Richard Chenevix Trench, who had initiated the creation of the *Oxford Dictionary of the English Language*, was one who chose to meet this kind of challenge in his *Synonyms of the New Testament* (originally 1854). A few pages of the ninth edition of this book included observations on the so-called synonyms of the Greek "servant" terms: *therapōn, doulos, diakonos, oiketēs*, and *hypēretēs*.[9]

---

8. E. L. McAdam and George Milne, *Johnson's Dictionary. A Modern Selection* (London: Macmillan, 1982), 29.

9. Richard Chenevix Trench, *Synonyms of the The New Testament*, 9th edn (London: Macmillan, 1880), 30–34.

Of Trench's comments, those on *doulos* and *diakonos* are of interest in the context of early Christian Greek and the predominant understanding today of *diakonia*. The leading difference Trench noted between *diakonos* and *doulos* was that "*diakonos* represents the servant in his activity *for the work* ... not in his relation, as that of the *doulos* ... *to a person*."[10] In illustration he cited Eph. 3:7, Col. 1:23, and 2 Cor. 3:6: "God has qualified us to be ministers of a new covenant."

Trench was drawing on Phillip Carl Buttmann's *Lexilogus*, a work of 1818 that saw five editions in English translation between 1835 and 1861. Buttmann derived *diakonos* from διώκειν ("to run"), and says it "properly means *the runner*; whence *a messenger, a servant*." He added that "the word is always retaining the free and honourable idea implied in the original word."[11]

This idea of "the free and honourable" is strikingly emphasized by Buttmann. He derives the idea from the association—lost in time—of the messenger god Hermes with the two terms *diakonos* and its older relative *diaktoros*. So strong in the two *diak-* words is the root semantic value of "the free and honourable" that it resurfaces—according to Buttmann—in the German word *Diener* (standard term for "servant"). Given the modern story of the German *Diener* and *Dienst* words in ecclesiology—not to mention in connection with the diaconate—this ancient correlation with *diakon-* as "free and honourable" is remarkably ironic.

Buttmann wrote, "The same honourable meaning which διάκονος has in Greek, existed in old German in the word *Degen*" (to be distinguished from the modern *Degen*, "dagger");[12] this in turn was the old Frankish *thegan*, and I add that in English it was "thane": Macbeth was "thane of Cawdor," which was not honor enough for him, although as a Scottish title it made him a "lord" who "held lands from the king and ranked with the son of an earl."[13]

---

10. Ibid., 32.

11. Phillip Carl Buttmann, *Lexilogus, or A Critical Examination of the Meaning and Etymology of Numerous Greek Words and Passages* ... trans. and ed. J. R. Fishlake, 5th edn (London: John Murray, 1861), 233; Collins, *Diakonia*, 89–95.

12. Buttmann, *Lexilogus*, 233, note 4.

13. *Shorter Oxford English Dictionary on Historial Principles*, 5th edn, vol. 2 (Oxford: Oxford University Press, 2002), 3229. Apart from the concept referenced above, I note definition no. 1 of this "Old English ... Old High German" term: "A servant, a minister, an attendant, a disciple esp. of Christ."

Writing an early book on deaconesses in 1861, John Saul Howson also drew on Buttmann: "The derivation does not point, as is often thought, to laboring and slaving in the dust, but rather to the notion of alacrity and willing activity.... The *diakonos* is never properly a slave."[14]

The Modern Turnaround of Diakonia

In today's predominant understanding of *diakonos*, a semantic shift has occurred in the direction opposite to that indicated by Buttmann and Trench. The perception of *diakonos* has moved from a servant "for the work," in Trench's phrase, to a servant "for the person."

We see this even in Howson, who translated *diakonia* by "help." He found that "help" corresponds "precisely" with the Greek. Writing, then, about deaconesses, he recorded his Victorian view that "Woman's work is helping work." And he saw this as corresponding to woman's nature as established in Eve, who, according to the AV of 1611 (and even the RV of 1885), was made by God to be Adam's "help meet" (Gen. 2:18). This biblical allusion supported Howson's teaching that "Whenever helping work is to be done, the woman is in her place."[15]

This stance that woman has a natural affinity for helping is largely attributable to the nineteenth-century romantic view of woman being the sex that possesses, as Howson wrote, "delicate tact, patience, cheerfulness, a gentle hand, a quick eye." In 1842, the Strassburg pastor Franz Heinrich Härter gave similar expression to the suitability of women as deaconesses; they were "not domineering but given to helping others... in a gentle and undemonstrative spirit."[16]

Howson also noted how the Germans had recognized "the truth" of this equivalence between *diakonia* and "help," "which," as he wrote, "the Germans have made their own by adopting the word '*Diakonie.*'"[17] That was in 1862. In 1856, Theodor Fliedner of Kaiserswerth had presented a paper in Berlin at the Monbijou conference of 1856, in which he argued for

---

14. John Saul Howson, *Deaconesses or The Official Help of Women in Parochial Work and in Charitable Institutions* (London: originally Quarterly Review 1860, enlarged for Longman, Green, Longman, 1862; Elibron Classics Replica edition, 2005), 15.

15. Howson, *Deaconesses*, 15.

16. Herbert Krimm, ed., *Quellen zur Geschichte der Diakonie*, vol. 2 (Stuttgart: Evangelisches Verlagswerk, 1963), 359; Collins, *Diakonia*, 9.

17. Howson, *Deaconesses*, 16.

the incorporation of such *"Diakonie"* into the church order as the church's diaconate (*Diakonat*). But Fliedner understood the meaning of *"Diakonie"* as something more than "helping." It was "an office of servant love: ein Amt der dienenden Liebe."[18]

A Servant Love

The idea of *diakonia* as a beneficent service of a loving kind was thus present within the deaconess movement from the beginning. It is also registered in comments by nineteenth-century lexicographers of Christian Greek, although not as constituting the whole semantic profile of the *diakon-* words. In the book *Diakonia*, I noted how Hermann Cremer shifted from Trench's emphasis on the notion of the work itself to that of the relationship arising from the work.[19] Contrasted with *doulos*, Cremer wrote, "In *diakonos* the main reference is to the service or advantage rendered to another." The phrase *diakonein tois hagiois* in reference to the collection for Jerusalem (Rom. 15:25), he described as "a beautiful expression for compassionate love towards the poor within the Christian fellowship."[20]

J. H. Thayer's widely used revision of the *Grimm's Wilke's Clavis Novi Testamenti*[21] also provided occasional references to deacons who are "to take care of the poor and the sick" (1 Tim. 3:10,13), including "collecting or bestowing benefactions" (Acts 12:25) and "distributing of charities" (Acts 6:1; 2 Cor. 9:13). In addition, however, he recorded denotations closer to Trench, whom Thayer includes in an additional note: *diakonia* as *"ministering, especially of those who execute the commands of others"*; *diakonein* as *"render ministering offices to"* (Philem. 13); and *diakonos* as *"one who executes the commands of another."*

---

18. Theodor Fliedner, "Gutachten'die *Diakon*ie und den *Diakon*at betreffend'" (1856) in N. Friedrich, C-R. Müller, and M.Wolff, eds, *Diakonie pragmatisch: Der Kaiserswerther Verband und Theodor Fliedner* (Neukirchen-Vluyn: Neukirchener Verlag, 2007), 28–54, citing 34.

19. Collins, *Diakonia*, 94.

20. Herbert Cremer, *Biblico-Theological Lexicon of New Testament Greek*, 4th English edn, trans. (Edinburgh: T & T Clark, 1895), 177, 179. Text accessible at http://bluehost.levendwater.org/books/cremer_lexicon_nt_greek/index.htm.

21. J. H. Thayer, *A Greek-English Lexicon of the New Testament being Grimm's Wilke's Clavis Novi Testamenti* (Edinburgh: T & T Clark, 1885).

In spite of such occasional glances toward Trench's emphasis on the work, under the growing influence of the deaconess movement—with its constant focus on *diakonia* as a service of love to the disadvantaged—the lexical understanding of the *diakon-* words received its defining twist in 1931 through the study of Wilhelm Brandt, *Dienst und Dienen im Neuen Testament.*[22]

Brandt's intervention is what led to the present widespread confusion within the theology of diaconate and, indeed, of ministry. The confusion may not be immediately evident to the practitioners of *Diakonie* within the Lutheran tradition. In fact, its impact has been rather more direct on theologies of ministry that have developed since the 1960s within Roman Catholic and Episcopal churches.[23] These theologies also include quite a variety of diaconates, each of which has struggled to arrive at a definitive sense of diaconal identity with consequent loss of efficacy of the diaconate in these churches.

The Consolidation of Diakonia

The service Brandt described in this book was a specifically Christian *diakonia* deriving from the character of the service Jesus extended to all. Thus, within ancient Christian usage, *diakonia* was, in Brandt's description, "a plain helping activity, a service rendered to the neighbour—not a service as rendered to the master whom one serves...not service from the perspective of obedience, but in relation to the neighbour."[24]

The phrase "not a service as rendered to the master whom one serves" severs the last connection with the historical lexicography. Instead of a focus on "the servant in his activity *for the work*," the servant is now irretrievably bonded to the recipient of the service. For Brandt, the term "is one of those words that suppose a 'Thou': not a 'Thou' to whom I could establish a relationship as I choose but a 'Thou' before whom I place myself as a servant/*diakonōn*."

The central sayings of Jesus about *diakonia*, Luke 22:27 and Mark 10:45, are about—in Brandt's words—a "life that is full of helping activity

---

22. Wilhelm Brandt, *Dienst und Dienen im Neuen Testament* (Gütersloh: Bertelsmann, 1931).

23. Collins, *Diakonia*, 11–41; "Ordained and Other Ministries: Making a Difference," *Ecclesiology* 3.1 (2006), 11–32, also in this volume as Chapter 12.

24. Brandt, *Dienst und Dienen*, 71.

for every human need, and the death that crowns these helping activities." Service or *diakonia* of this character is the mark of his messiahship: "the Christ serves."[25]

Fortuitously, Brandt's study became available as a ready new resource for H. W. Beyer as he prepared his entry on the *diakon-* terms for the second volume of Kittel's *Theological Dictionary of the New Testament* (TDNT). This appeared in 1935. It did not appear in an English translation until nearly thirty years later.[26]

Beyer's description and theological evaluation of *diakonia* has far out-stripped any simple application to the identity and role of deaconesses and deacons. In many languages, especially those of central Europe, *diakonia* is recognized as an ancient and original Christian construct bearing pro-found theological and ethical values.

Nowhere has this shift been so marked and intrusive as within the German Lutheran and Reformed traditions where the original Greek term *diakonia* enshrines all the values associated with Beyer's description of *diakonia* as "any loving assistance rendered to the neighbour...the very essence of service, of being for others, whether in life or death."[27]

Like Brandt, Beyer asserted that a development is observable in early Christian usage of the *diakon-* words. At the basic level of meaning— "service at table"—Christians simply replicated standard usage or basic meaning within Classical and Hellenistic Greek usage. But as applied to the activity of Jesus, the words were placed within an increasingly ethical and then theological frame of reference. Thus, at Matt. 25:44 the *diakon-* word,

25. Ibid., 80. Twenty years later, Brandt (1894–1973) reflected upon how the *diakon-* terms had fared in the Christian story. Writing in 1953 under the title "Der Dienst Jesu/[Jesus' Service]" in a paper introducing a collection of fifteen studies of "Diakonie" across the Christian era, Brandt observed: "Certainly these *diakon-* terms transmitted by the gospels were known in contemporary non-Christian literary sources. Within Christianity, however. they initiated a history and shaped a tradition. In this it is fascinating to see how in the course of church history these words were interpreted in different ways, how church author-ities, who should have been embodying the meaning of the terms in their activities, gave different expressions to them, but also how these terms nonetheless constantly stimulated activities of helping the needy to the extent that across a turbulent history they provided a unity and continuity to the church's 'Diakonie.'" See H. Krimm, ed., *Das Diakonische Amt der Kirche*, 2nd edn (Stuttgart: Evangelisches Verlagswerk, 1965), 15–60, citing 15.

26. H. W. Beyer, "διακονέω, διακονία, διάκονος," *Theological Dictionary of the New Testament*, ed. G. Kittel, trans. and ed. G. W. Bromley, vol. 2 (Grand Rapids, MI: Eerdmans, 1964), 81–93. The acronym here is TDNT; TWNT is the German acronym.

27. Ibid., 86.

Beyer wrote, "comes to have the full sense of active Christian love for the neighbor and as such it is a mark of true discipleship of Jesus."[28]

Further to this ethical sense, however, is the theological value attaching to the statement of the Son of Man at Mark 10:45. Here the service of the Son of Man expresses a unique level of care. Beyer puts it thus:

> διακονεῖν is now much more than a comprehensive term for any loving assistance rendered to the neighbor. It is understood as full and perfect sacrifice, as the offering of life which is the very essence of service, of being for others, whether in life or in death. Thus the concept of διακονεῖν achieves its final theological depth.[29]

Diakonia and Ecclesiology

Once this evaluation began circulating among mid-twentieth-century theological schools and, especially, in influential ecumenical centers, extensive and radical rewriting of the theology of ministry in general and of the diaconate in particular got under way.

Within New Testament scholarship, the most influential voice was and remains that of Eduard Schweizer,[30] echoed in the popular and effective communicator of the 1960s Robert McAfee Brown: "In the early church everything that led to the upbuilding of the *Christian* community was *diakonia*, service, ministry. Every Christian participated in this *diakonia*, so every Christian was a servant, a 'minister.'"[31]

As applied radically to the theology of church office, Ernst Käsemann's estimation of *diakonia* among the *charismata* (1 Cor. 12:4–6) has had far-reaching effects.[32] As a result of being endowed through baptism with

---

28. Ibid., 85.

29. Ibid., 86.

30. Eduard Schweizer, *Church Order in the New Testament*, trans. F. Clarke (London: SCM, 1961), 171–180; "Ministry in the Early Church," *The Anchor Bible Dictionary*, vol. 4, ed. D. N. Freedman (New York: Doubleday, 1992), 835–42; "Die diakonische Struktur der neutestamentlichen Gemeinde," in Gerhard K. Schäfer and Theodor Strohm, eds, *Diakonie—biblische Grundlagen und Orientierungen*, 2nd edn (Heidelberg: HVA, 1994), 159–85.

31. Robert McAfee Brown, *The Spirit of Protestantism* (New York: Oxford University Press, 1965), 102–03.

32. Ernst Käsemann, "Ministry and Community in the New Testament," *Essays on New Testament Themes*, Eng. trans. (London: SCM, 1964), 63–94; Collins, "Ordained and Other Ministries."

the charisma of *diakonia*, "all the baptized are 'office-bearers' ... charismat-ically endowed persons who are under an obligation to serve each other to the measure of their gift."[33]

The leading voice within ecumenism was Hendrik Kraemer, whose interest was ministry of the laity, a concept powerfully supported by a conviction that "the Church *is* Ministry...the Church *is* diakonia."[34] This term *diakonia* Kraemer presented as "that profound, revolutionary word" requiring a "drastic remoulding of the [traditional ordained] ministry and of the theologians."[35]

Such estimations have determined the reconfiguration of the theology of ministry in ecumenical thinking since the report on "The Redemptive Work of Christ and the Ministry of his Church" at the Fourth World Conference on Faith and Order announced in Montreal in 1963: "A re-covery of a true doctrine of the laity has brought with it the recognition that ministry is the responsibility of the whole body and not only of those who are ordained. This recovery is one of the most important facts of re-cent church history."[36]

Reactions and Developing Consensus

Against this now long-standing *diakonic* trend in the theology of ministry, my own linguistic research has attained a certain level of recognition.[37]

---

33. Käsemann, "Ministry and Community," 123.

34. Hendrik Kraemer, *A Theology of the Laity* (London: Lutterworth, 1958), 143.

35. Ibid., 187.

36. P. C. Rodger and L. Vischer, eds, *The Fourth World Conference on Faith and Order*, Faith and Order Paper No. 42 (London: SCM, 1964), 62.

37. Hanover Report of the Anglican-Lutheran International Commission, *The Diaconate as Ecumenical Opportunity* (London: Anglican Consultative Council/Lutheran World Federation, 1996); Frederick William Danker, ed., *A Greek-English Lexicon of the New Testament and other Early Christian Literature*, 3rd edn, BDAG (Chicago and London: University of Chicago Press, 2000); Sven-Erik Brodd, "*Caritas* and *Diakonia* from a Biblical Point of View," in G. Borgegård, O. Fanuelsen, and C. Hall, eds, *The Ministry of the Deacon*, 2. *Ecclesiological Explorations* (Uppsala: Nordic Ecumenical Council, 2000), 30–69; Hans-Jürgen Benedict, "Beruht der Anspruch der evangelischen Diakonie auf einer Missinterpretation der antiken Quellen? John N. Collins Untersuchung '*Diakonia*,'" *Pastoraltheologie* 89 (2000) 343–64, now in Benedict, *Barmherzigkeit und Diakonie. Von der rettenden Liebe zum gelingenden Leben* (Stuttgart: Kohlhammer, 2008), 114–28; Paul Avis, *A Ministry Shaped by Mission* (London: T&T Clark, 2000), 105, 110–11; id., "Editorial: Wrestling with the Diaconate," *Ecclesiology* 5.1 (2009) 3–6; Church of England Faith and Order Advisory Group, *The Mission and Ministry of the Whole Church*. GS Misc 854 (London: General Synod of the Church of England, 2007), esp. ch. 2, "Ministry, the New Testament and the Church today"; Joseph

Significant here is Danker's revision of the *diakon-* terms in the third English-language edition of Bauer's lexicon of early Christian Greek. Danker replaced Bauer's page with articles on the *diakon-* terms that were of twice the length and based on the new semantic profile.

More telling, however, is probably the intervention in the same year by Hans-Jürgen Benedict. A professor at Wichern's Rauhes Haus in Hamburg, Benedict was writing from within the German *diakon*ic establishment, and chose the provocative title: "Is the Evangelical *Diakonie* founded upon a misunderstanding of the ancient sources?"[38] To this question Benedict gave an affirmative response accompanied by critical comment on the neglect of the research within German academic circles during the previous decade.

A reaction was soon forthcoming from the Heidelberg Institute of Diaconal Studies (*Diakoniewissenschaftliches Institut*) in Part I of its publication *Diakonische Konturen* dealing with *diakon*ic issues in the New Testament.[39] No fewer than four of the six studies there critically address the new semantic description of *diakonia*. Only one of these, however, seeks to challenge the basic semantic outcomes of the new research, although disagreements arise elsewhere in regard to some points of interpretation and emphasis. In contrast, Stefan Dietzel claimed that the new interpretation was fundamentally skewed as a result of my misreading of Brandt.[40] In 2009 Herbert Haslinger would draw on such reservations in

---

A. Fitzmyer, *First Corinthians*, Anchor Yale Bible (New Haven, CT: Yale University Press, 2008), 464–65; and most recently, M. Nebel, "La notion néotestamentaire de *diakonia*: une difficile reconnaissance," *Revue d'éthique et de théologie morale*, 268 (March 2012) 79–102, accessed at http://www.fondationjeanrodhain.org/IMG/.

38. Benedict, "Beruht der Anspruch" (preceding note). A few years later, Wilfried Brandt, former director of Diakoniewerk Karlshöhe, Ludwigsburg, provided a searching but less controversial assessment of the reinterpretation in "Biblische 'Diakonia' contra Evangelische Diakonie? Die Wortgruppe 'diakonia, diakonein, diakonos' im griechischen Neuen Testament, neu interpretiert durch John N. Collins," *Impuls* 3.7 (2004) 1–7, available at http://www.vedd.de/obj/Bilder_und_Dokumente/pdf-Daten/Impulse/Impuls200401.pdf.

39. Volker Herrmann, Rainer Merz, and Heinz Schmidt, eds, *Diakonische Konturen: Theologie im Kontext sozialer Arbeit*, Veröffentlichungen des Diakoniewissenschaftlichen Instituts an der Universität Heidelberg 18 (Heidelberg: Winter, 2003), including Stefan Dietzel, "Zur Entstehung des Diakonats im Urchristentum. Eine Auseinandersetzung mit den Positionen von Wilhelm Brandt, Hermann Wolfgang Beyer und John N. Collins," 136–70; Ismo Dunderberg, "Vermittlung statt karitative Tätigkeit? Überlegungen zu John N. Collins' Interpretation von *diakonia*," 171–83; Dierk Starnitzke, "Die Bedeutung von *diakonos* im frühen Christentum," 184–212.

40. Dietzel, "Zur Entstehung des Diakonats" (preceding note); see further discussion in Chapter 3 at note 32.

the *Diakonische Konturen* volume to support his own rejection of the new interpretation,[41] a position that he did not attempt to support by direct engagement with interpretation of text.[42] I note that neither Benedict nor Hentschel were persuaded by Dietzel. Indeed, Hentschel—who provided a seventy-page evaluation of the Collins re-interpretation as a preliminary to her own investigation into *Diakonia in the New Testament*[43]—asserted that Dietzel had brought to his critique of the re-interpretation an over-riding conviction in regard to the conventional German understanding of *Diakonie* as well as a failure to engage in a methodology which was se-mantic in character.[44]

In a different context, an examination of the specific relationship be-tween *diakonia* and leadership in early Christian communities, Andrew Clarke has shown a helpful sensitivity to the linguistic issues involved.[45] His first treatment addressed the semantic issues at length under the heading "Ministry or Service," providing in this a reliable précis of my re-interpretation. However, his attempt to apply to the *diakonia* of Paul the notion of "service as a dominical imperative" arising from usage in the gospels did violence to the rhetorical context of Paul's discourse and undervalued the semantic range of the *diakon-* terms. One would have to identify the process here as "illegitimate totality transfer"[46] of meaning in one context (gospel narrative) to another (rhetorical apologia). Clarke's more recent volume evidences considerable rethinking of the semantics. For example, "it has been convincingly demonstrated that [*diakonos* language] does not always or necessarily carry servile connotations";[47] indeed,

41. Herbert Haslinger, *Diakonie. Grundlagen für die soziale Arbeit der Kirche* (Paderborn: Schöningh, 2009), 17, 348–50.

42. See my review, "A German Catholic view of Diaconate and *Diakonia*," *New Diaconal Review* 2 (2009), 41–46.

43. Anni Hentschel, *Diakonia im Neuen Testament. Studien zur Semantik unter besonderer Berücksichtigung der Rolle von Frauen* (Tübingen: Mohr Siebeck, 2007), 21–89.

44. See indexed references to Dietzel in Hentschel, *Diakonia*, especially discussion relating to 43, note 136; 280, note 445.

45. Andrew D. Clarke, *Serve the Community of the Church. Christians as Leaders and Ministers* (Grand Rapids, MI: Eerdmans, 2000), 233–45; *A Pauline Theology of Church Leadership* (London: T&T Clark, 2008), 63–67.

46. This phrase, widely used in issues relating to biblical interpretation, derives from James Barr in his *The Semantics of Biblical Language* (New York: Oxford University Press), 218. The phrase points to the illegitimacy of applying to a particular occurrence of the term—irre-spective of context—senses that the term is known to carry in other contexts.

47. Clarke, *Pauline Theology*, 102.

the re-interpretation "has in large measure overturned a consensus."[48] However, Clarke remains "unpersuaded" by "attempts to detach from the *diakonia* word group the idea of service."[49]

Against the background of such hesitancy, the work of Anni Hentschel takes on greater significance. It now provides important—and, I would venture, decisively effective—scholarly support for the re-interpretation. In the sections of her *Diakonia im Neuen Testament* that are devoted to a semantic examination of Greek usage in non-Christian sources (11–89), Hentschel expressed full agreement with the semantic profile I had presented in *Diakonia: Re-interpreting the Ancient Sources*. She wrote that her examination of the sources "confirms the findings in Collins' monograph in regard to the semantic field covered by the *diakon*- terms."[50] Some points of exegesis within the New Testament are different between us,[51] but not in a way that disturbs the semantics. In particular, in the key New Testament passages underlying the traditional conceptualization of *Diakonie*, Mark 10:45 and Luke 22:27, Hentschel's reading is at one with my own long-standing interpretations.[52]

More recently, of deacons and *Diakonie*, she wrote:

> The novel connection established in the 19th century between *Diakonie* and the offices of deaconess and deacon has much weaker support in the biblical terms *diakonos* and *diakonia* than has generally been thought.[53]

This is a modest understatement, to say the least. In stronger vein, in a study focused on the early diaconate, she has written:

> It is not possible to establish that the *diakon*- words have an inherent semantic orientation towards expressing activities of a specifically charitable character, nor is there any indication of a modification to

---

48. Ibid., 100.

49. Ibid., 66.

50. Hentschel, *Diakonia*, 85.

51. Collins, "Re-interpreting *Diakonia* in Germany," *Ecclesiology* 5.1 (2009), 69–81 (see Chapter 2 in this volume).

52. Hentschel, *Diakonia*, 278, note 438; 286–89.

53. Anni Hentschel, "Diakonie in der Bibel" in L-D. K. Kottnik and E. Hauschildt, eds, *Diakoniefibel: Grundwissen für alle, die mit Diakonie zu tun haben* (Gütersloh: Gütersloher Verlag; Rheinbach: CMZ, 2008), 17–20. My translation above.

this effect in Christian usage. This holds even when the terms apply in particular instances to officially mandated activities of a charitable kind (like those carried out in the name of a community).[54]

Addressing in the same journal what Hentschel's assessment might mean for the diaconate today, Eberhard Hauschildt concluded:

> The *diakonia* of the Bible is part of the language of the community and has nothing to do specifically with the radical Christian emphasis on love of neighbour.[55]

In conjunction with evaluations resulting directly from my own work, these are judgments that mark the end of the modern consensus supporting the Brandt-Beyer lexical description of the *diakon-* terms, supported as that may be by the authority of the TDNT, most other lexicography,[56] and the main body of subsequent commentary.

Where does this leave the modern diaconate/s? In response to that inevitable question, I glance back to the pre-Kittel era when the lexicographer Cremer used the following phrases about how to understand deacons lexicographically:

> As a *term. techn.*, side by side with *episkopos*,... it denotes those who stood by the bishop (or presbyters) as helpers... the presbyters being distinct officers, the care of the churches devolved upon the deacons as their helpers. Such were the beginnings of the diaconate in the early church.[57]

Something quite similar is how I tried to explain the lexical background to the emergence in the Christian communities of members called *diakonoi*.[58]

---

54. Anni Hentschel, "Gibt es einen sozial-karitativ ausgerichteten *Diakon*at in den frühchristlichen Gemeinden?" *Pastoraltheologie*, 97.9 (2008), 290–306. My translation above.

55. Eberhard Hauschildt, "Was bedeuten exegetische Erkenntnisse über den Begriff der Diakonie für die Diakonie heute?," *Pastoraltheologie* 97.9 (2008), 307–14, citing 308.

56. With the notable exceptions of Danker (note 37 above) and *Diccionario Griego-Español*, ed. F. F. R. Adrados, vol. 5, ed. Elvira Gangutia (Madrid: Consejo supereior de invertigaciones científicas, Instituto de Filología, 1997), 984–86.

57. Cremer, *Biblico-Theological Lexicon*, 178.

58. John N. Collins, *Deacons and the Church: Making Connections Between Old and New* (Leominster, UK: Gracewing, 2002), 128–44.

These members went on in history to considerable roles in the church, not least in succeeding to those bishops to whom they had been assistants.

Conclusion

This review of historical aspects of the interpretation of the early Christian term *diakonia* has revealed a gradual change of interpretation arising in the nineteenth century under two influences. The first of these were the lexicographical initiatives taken toward ancient Greek which joined forces with the second influence in the Lutheran dedication to a modern diaconate. The scholarly lexical outcome in the earlier decades of the twentieth century was a *diakonia* of servant love. Applied to the diaconate, this interpretation had immediate relevance, but indirectly the interpretation also had a powerful effect on the understanding of church office in general. However, the two recent reassessments of the *diakon-* terms by Collins and Hentschel have established that the *diakonia* of servant love represents a basic misunderstanding of what the early Christians had in mind when they used this and cognate terms.

Ces études de mots ont une grande importance dans la science historique. Un terme mal interprété peut être la source de grandes erreurs.

Fustel de Coulanges,

Histoire des institutions politiques de l'ancienne France ... (1927⁴), 170,
cited after J. F. Niermeyer, *Mediae Latinitatis Lexicon Minus*
(Leiden: Brill, 1976), Inscription.

It is not sufficient that a word is found, unless it be so combined
as that its meaning is apparently determined
by the tract and tenour of the sentence.

Samuel Johnson
Preface to the Dictionary,
Johnson's Dictionary: A Modern Selection,
E. L. McAdam and G. Milne (1963), 19

2

Re-interpreting Diakonia in
Germany: Anni Hentschel's Diakonia
im Neuen Testament

ANNI HENTSCHEL, *DIAKONIA im Neuen Testament: Studien zur Semantik unter besonderer Berücksichtigung der Rolle von Frauen* (Tübingen: Mohr Siebeck, 2007), xiv + 498 pp. ISBN 978-3-16-149086-6 (pbk).

Anni Hentschel completed her dissertation within the New Testament department of the University of Würzburg in 2005. The book will achieve some notoriety in central Europe especially, where talk of *diakonia* has been commonplace for sixty years. Her semantic investigation opens sensationally with the following observation:

> In the German Protestant churches the loanwords *"Diakonie"* and *"diakonic"* designate commitments of a social-charitable character. However, this *diakonic* profile, so highly lauded among German Protestant churches, has its biblical roots much more in passages about love of the neighbour than in New Testament occurrences of the Greek words *diakonia* and its cognates. In reality, these words express neither lowly service nor merciful concern.[1]

The Demise of Diakonia as Lowly Service

The author's table of contents presents earlier linguistic research into the *diakonia* words conducted by five German-language scholars (Beyer,

---

1. Anni Hentschel, *Diakonia im Neuen Testament: Studien zur Semantik unter besonderer Berücksichtigung der Rolle von Frauen* (Tübingen: Mohr Siebeck, 2007), xiv, cited parenthetically throughout this chapter.

Weiser, Schweizer, Schottroff, Schüssler Fiorenza), each of whom understood *diakonia* as centering precisely on notions of lowly service and merciful concern. Hentschel knew full well the pervasive influence of such a
view within contemporary ecclesiology (p. 4) and, to create a furor among
a German audience, needed to say no more than that this view should be
discarded.

The whole Protestant church membership has understood for more
than a lifetime that *Diakonie* (the German term) is a foundational expression of lowly service and self-emptying love. Hentschel's claim will
engender unease, at the least, once the media brings the claim to the attention of the general church membership, while sections of the German
Protestant theological establishment, church administration, and pastoral
arm will voice a mixed chorus of incredulity, protest, and perhaps dismay
before this dismantling of one of the key constructs within modern
Lutheran and Reformed ecclesiology and spirituality.

English-language readers, by contrast, may well wonder what the
fuss is about. While the effects of the German interpretation of *diakonia* are undoubtedly recognizable within English-language theology of
ministry—with direct impact upon the new diaconates—*diakonia* has
never attained there the iconic status enjoyed by the central European
diakonia. In Germany alone, half a million Lutherans are on the payroll
of the *Diakonisches Werk*, the welfare agency of the German Evangelical
Churches. Both workers and clients understand that they are involved in
the loving outreach of merciful care in its varied forms. Supporting this
vast undertaking are the many theological faculties that present courses
in *diakonic* theology and pastoral practice, and leadership comes from
the *Diakoniewissenschaftliches Institut* (Institute for the Academic Study of
Diakonie)—with its strong publishing tradition—within the University of
Heidelberg.[2]

Hentschel engages no dialogue around this overriding issue, remaining content to make occasional passing reference to its existence in the
course of her exegetical exercise. Thus, concluding her reflections on Paul
as a "servant/*diakonos*" (e. g., 2 Cor. 11:23), she simply alerts readers to the
fact that "an interpretation of the *diakonia* of Paul as a service in which

---

2. The renewal of the Roman Catholic diaconate in Germany has also always drawn strongly
upon values associated with the traditional German expression *Diakonie*. Most recently,
Herbert Haslinger has incorporated these—after firmly rejecting the re-interpretation
by Hentschel and myself—in *Diakonie: Grundlagen für die soziale Arbeit der Kirche*
(Paderborn: Ferdinand Schöningh, 2009). See there 17–19, 347–50.

he humbles and sacrifices himself for the sake of the community…is no longer possible" (p. 138).

Hentschel's Pathway

What set Hentschel on this path was the work of two remaining scholars on her list, Dieter Georgi in *The Opponents of Paul in Second Corinthians*[3] (English translation and greatly expanded edition of 1986—the edition to which Hentschel refers—of the German original 1964) and the present writer in *Diakonia: Re-interpreting the Ancient Sources*.[4] She presents these two studies—the former including barely two pages of comment on *diakonia* in ancient non-Christian writers, mainly the Stoic Epictetus—as having established that the dominant semantic element within ancient usage was the notion of the commission or mandate under which people carried out activities named *diakonia*. Because my investigation had aimed to be comprehensive in regard to ancient usage, Hentschel reports (p. 23) the main lines of the semantic profile presented in my Appendix 1 on "Meanings" and proceeds to test the profile against her own readings of Plato and then Hellenistic (Dio Chrysostom, Epictetus, Lucian) and Jewish (LXX, Twelve Patriarchs, testaments of Job and Abraham, Philo, Josephus) writers closer to the era of the earliest Christian literature.

Fifty pages later, she concludes that her sampling supports in principle the features of the usage described in my reinterpretation. In the process she deflects partial criticisms of my method expressed by Dunderberg[5] (p. 38) and Dietzel,[6] (p. 41), but makes only passing reference to the article by Hans-Jürgen Benedict[7] that made a forcible statement about the German neglect of the new research and prompted the symposium in which the essays of Dunderberg and Dietzel appeared.

---

3. Trans. Harold Attridge et al. (Philadelphia: Fortress Press).

4. New York: Oxford University Press, 1990.

5. Ismo Dunderberg, "Vermittlung statt karitativer Tätigkeit? Überlegungen zu John N. Collins' Interpretation von diakonia," in V. Herrmann, R. Merz, and H. Schmidt, eds, *Diakonische Konturen: Theologie im Kontext sozialer Arbeit* (Heidelberg: Winter, 2003), 171–83.

6. Stefan Dietzel, "Zur Entstehung des Diakonats im Urchristentum. Eine Auseinandersetzung mit den Positionen von Wilhelm Brandt, Wolfgang Hermann Beyer und John N. Collins," in *Diakonische Konturen*, 136–70.

7. "Beruht der Anspruch der evangelischen Diakonie auf einer Misinterpretation der antiken Quellen? John N. Collins Untersuchung 'Diakonia,'" *Pastoraltheologie* 89 (2000), 349–64.

Detailing her support of the reinterpretation, she acknowledges the recurring notion of mediation, although her preferred emphasis is on the mandated character of the activities (p. 85). She accepts that activities associated with these words are not necessarily lowly tasks of women and slaves, that the words are not part of everyday language, and that the notion of helping cannot be established as a basic meaning. She also emphasizes that any reading of the *diakonia* words requires close and sensitive consideration of literary context, and in the end she is satisfied that early Christian usage is indistinguishable from that in the surrounding literary culture (pp. 85–87).

These preliminaries open the way to a rereading of *diakonia* in passages of the New Testament relevant to early church office. Hentschel begins with the earliest usage in Paul's references to evangelistic activity (pp. 90–184). She follows this with a much more extensive discussion of *diakonia* in Luke-Acts (pp. 185–382), then a more succinct one on the usage in Deutero-Pauline letters (pp. 383–406) and in the Didache, 1 Clement, and Ignatius of Antioch (pp. 407–32) She concludes with a substantial overview of outcomes (pp. 433–44) that complements a useful series of such overviews at the end of each section. The bibliography, although extensive (pp. 445–72), omits Manuel Guerra y Gomez, whose innovative approach merited attention, and André Lemaire, whom not many other writers fail to mention. A. D. Clarke's study of secular and Christian leadership in Corinth (1993) appears, but not his later *Serve the Community of the Church*, containing as it does pointed criticism of my reading of *diakonia* in Paul's usage.[8] Hentschel noted Frederick Danker's *Benefactor* but not his third English-language edition of Bauer's lexicon with its expanded description of *diakonia* drawn largely from my *Diakonia*. Contributions I have made since 1994, including two books and two articles dealing with *diakonia* in feminist scholarship, do not appear.

Paul as Diakonos

In depicting the character of Paul's *diakonia*, Hentschel rightly points out that numerous commentators continue to align the Greek terms with terms for servants and slaves—even, to some extent, Thiselton and

---

8. Grand Rapids, MI/Cambridge, UK: Eerdmans, 2000, 233–47. Clarke's modification of his 2000 stance vis-à-vis my reinterpretation appeared after the publication of Hentschel's study (see discussion in relation to Chapter 1, note 45 above).

Schrage (p. 92, note 8). Hence Hentschel's emphasis on restoring to the Pauline text the values arising from *diakonia* as a divinely commissioned ministry. Her insistence at this point does much to free discussion of Paul's discourse from the tangles of some earlier scholarly controversies. Indeed, not a little of the exegetical comment from which she demurs loses its urgency in light of new understandings and perspectives she introduces into the discussion as a result of appreciation of the higher values carried by *diakonia*.

For my part, I hesitate to see my reading of *diakonos* virtually identified with that of Georgi (p. 92, note 8), who sought to import into the Corinthian correspondence from a supposed Stoic usage a notion of *diakonos* as " 'envoy' ... in the sense of responsible, fateful representation and manifestation" of the Godhead. The status implied here, arising from Georgi's misreading of Epictetus, would almost dehumanize Paul while furthering Georgi's thesis of *theios anthropos*. But, in my view, Paul had something simpler in mind. He was a man of acknowledged weakness who was nonetheless receiver of the Word of God and under mandate to transfer this to the Corinthians. It is in the transference that evangelization occurs. The process is what Greeks could call *diakonia*.

In this connection, by contrast, Hentschel reads Paul's use of *diakonia* as an appeal to authority resting in his divine mandate and thus as his method of outbidding the claims of his missionary rivals in Corinth. I think, rather, that Paul had no intention of appealing to his mandate at all, and that in arguing from his *diakonia* he was, instead, asking the Corinthians to reflect upon the process that terminology implied. That is to say, Paul was playing on the capacity of the Greek terms to convey the notion of a transmission or mediation of the Word of God, and was urging the Corinthians to look into their spiritual experience (*syneidēsis*, "consciousness," 2 Cor. 4:2) to recognize what he had delivered.

Part of his agenda was that their personal acknowledgement of and witness to what they had received would then be his endorsement against any commendatory letters his rivals flaunted. I also think that it is in the contrast between an authoritative standing and a process of mediation that we find the differentiation between the two terms *apostolos* and *diakonos* (pp. 128, 133–34, 138), the former requiring commendatory letters or at least evidence of an authorized status while the other induces a confirming experience.

Diakonia in Mark 10:45 and Luke 22:27

The almost two hundred pages Hentschel next devotes to the nineteen instances of *diakonia* in Luke-Acts greatly surpass the eighty-four pages devoted to the more ecclesiologically significant Pauline usage (comprising thirty-five instances). Included here are twenty pages on Jesus "as one who serves" (22:27, *hōs ho diakonōn*) that include significant comment also on the nature of Jesus's *diakonia* at Mark 10:45 (pp. 276–81). Her German translation of the latter dovetails with the paraphrase with which I concluded *Diakonia*, and in translation reads, "The Son of Man has not come to have tasks carried out for himself but to carry out a task himself," this task being then identified as "to give his life as a ransom for many" (p. 278 [italics hers]: "nicht gekommen, um *für sich selbst Aufträge ausführen zu lassen*...sondern *um selbst einen Auftrag auszuführen*").

In this Hentschel notes the concordance with my view, and adds a point or two (p. 279) about consequences: "In Mark 10:45a Jesus is presented neither as a waiter nor as a humble neighbour-loving servant who would be motivated by such an attitude to give his life for people." Precisely this interpretation, however—attributed to Roloff by Hentschel (and by me in my *Diakonia*[9]) as significant for church office—pervades much of the literature, especially the pastoral kind represented by Christian Wessely's *Gekommen, um zu dienen*,[10] and has even been advocated by the influential lexicographers Louw and Nida: "The Son of Man did not come in order for people to serve him but in order to serve people."[11]

This Markan verse has long been established within ecumenical theology of ministry as the quintessential expression of what ecclesial ministry is.[12] When, however, Hentschel of 2007 is agreeing essentially with Collins of 1990—in the two most extensive linguistic enquiries into Mark's Greek word for "ministry"—then we have a concurrence of informed evaluation of *diakonia* that demands a reconsideration of much of the ecclesiology of these last fifty years.

---

9. Collins, *Diakonia*, 53–54.

10. Regensburg: Pustet, 2004, 246.

11. J. P. Louw and E. A. Nida, eds, *Greek-English Lexicon of the New Testament based on Semantic Domains*, 2nd edn (New York: United Bible Societies), 460, no. 35.20.

12. This contention was broadly illustrated in Part I of Collins, *Diakonia*. See also my "A Ministry for Tomorrow's Church," *Journal of Ecumenical Studies* 32.2 (Spring 1995), 159–78, esp. 170–71.

Remarkably, if we take up the annotation in the Geneva New Testament of four hundred years ago, we recognize the Hentschel-Collins understanding of Mark 10:45: "The Pastors are not called to rule, but to serve according to the example of the Son of God himself, who went before them forsomuch as he also was a Minister of his Father's will."[13]

Hentschel goes much further in her accord with my earlier lexical investigation. Important as Mark 10:45 is to the basic shape of ecclesiology, Jesus's statement after the supper in Luke 22:27 has its place (less commonly invoked) alongside it: "I am among you as one who serves [*hōs ho diakonōn*]." Too often this statement has been seen as simply endorsing the service orientation of Mark's statement. Illustrating the force of this conviction, many exegetes see Mark's statement as deriving from such a saying at the Last Supper scene. Nearly five hundred years ago, however, the less critically educated William Tyndale did at least recognize the depth with which Luke anchored *diakonia* at this point of his narrative in a table scenario, a purely literary situation delimiting the semantic range possible for the *diakon-* word. Tyndale translated—with AV later taking a lead from him—"whether is greater, he that sitteth at meate: or he that serveth? . . . I am amonge you, as he that ministreth." Tyndale's *meate* leaves no doubt as to what *service* or *ministry* is about in this scenario: it is about the waiting at tables. Tyndale could read this clearly in this context from the presence of the phrase *hōs ho diakonōn*, "like one who serves" food.

Hentschel agrees. So closely, in fact, that she too reads from the character of the *diakonia* word here the impossibility that the tradition represented in the *diakonia* of Mark 10:45 is dependent on the tradition represented in Luke 22:27. It is actually the innovative Luke who is able to transform the stark theology of Mark into a meal story of the kind that is central to Luke's narratives and thus contribute to his theology of the salvific presence of Jesus within the community as they are "at meate" (pp. 286–89).

To a major extent, then, Hentschel's investigation strongly supports the ecclesiological principle that I have long sought to expose in both the Markan and Lukan statements, namely that ecclesial ministry of a kind that is essential to the making and sustaining of a church is an activity within the church that certain individuals need to be appointed to: identified, qualified, selected, prayed over, commissioned.

---

13. *The Geneva Bible (The Annotated New Testament, 1602 Edition)*, ed. G. T. Sheppard (New York: The Pilgrim Press, 1989).

Diakonia Elsewhere in Luke-Acts

The level of concurrence in the two readings of Mark 10:45 and Luke 22:27 is noteworthy and has a bearing on tradition criticism at these points no less than on any ecclesiology deriving from it. Tradition criticism has a further and more contentious role to play in Hentschel's evaluation of the rest of Luke's usage. Much of her evaluation centers on the relationship between *diakonia* as an expression for household and table service and *diakonia* as an expression for the preaching mandate in the community. In this extended exercise, Hentschel has, to my mind, become incongruously captive to the book's subthesis. Her investigation originated in an inquiry alluded to in her subtitle, "With special attention to the role of women" (in the early Christian communities). The fact is, of course, that over the last twenty years, women theologians in particular have turned a blinding light on Luke's attitudes toward women and, unexpectedly perhaps, claim to have discovered revealing and allegedly damning indications in Luke's use of the *diakonia* words of a post-Pauline exclusion of women from ministerial roles in the community.

At the heart of argumentation to this effect is the linguistic connection between the Martha and Mary scene at Luke 10:38–42 and Acts 6:1–6. The *diakonia* that Jesus dissuaded Martha from would not be her busyness in waiting upon him but an allusion to the *diakonia* of the word that the Twelve were involved in (Acts 6:4); the latter was the same *diakonia* that leading women in Paul's communities are known to have engaged in and that the later church of Luke's generation took away from them.

The point should be made about this line of argument, however, that all the scholars involved—although writing in the 1990s—were interpreting *diakonia* without having at hand the reinterpretation published in my *Diakonia* of 1990. By working from a base where *diakonia* represented demeaning tasks reserved to slaves and women, they could forcibly draw attention to the predominance of such roles for women in the gospel narrative, while the same word in Acts took on an altogether different color and applied exclusively to men in their divinely or ecclesially designated tasks for the spread of the gospel. The contrast between the two usages could thus be used to argue for Luke's poor attitude toward women. The disparagement of Luke in this regard could hardly be more strongly expressed: "a formidable opponent" who built "oppressive dynamics" into his gospel[14] and

---

14. Jane Schaberg, "Luke," in Carol A. Newsom and Sharon H. Ringe, *The Women's Bible Commentary* (Louisville, KY: Westminster/John Knox Press, 1992), 291.

who colluded with "the phallocentric citadel"[15] and indulged "hegemonic rhetoric"[16] against women.

Altogether contrary to this line, however, my 1990 reinterpretation revealed Luke as the Christian writer with the most sensitive awareness of the place of the *diakonia* words within the Hellenistic literary world. In this light, one has the greatest difficulty envisaging Luke presenting a scene of hospitality in the house of Martha and Mary in which he had in mind— and expected his Hellenistic readers to understand—that the *diakonia* words had a reference beyond table service. In her *Double Message*—even though written without reference to the reinterpretation of 1990—Turid Seim considered that attempts to demonize Luke were "based on assumptions of a universally-diffused technical use of the *diakon-* terms" that are 'problematic.' "[17] The grounds of Seim's disquiet were, I believe, fully exposed in *Diakonia* and subsequently examined within the challenging context of the feminist readings of the Martha and Mary story.[18]

For her part, Hentschel recognizes Seim's reservations (e. g., p. 247) but appears to be unfamiliar with my post-1994 relevant writings. It would also seem that her extensive critique of Luke 10:38–42 was originally part of an earlier investigation into gender balance in early Christian communities (p. 239, note 273). Here the investigation may have been led less by semantic considerations than by a particular stream of tradition criticism dependent at this point on the ill-founded semantic orientation in Beyer's interpretation of *diakonia* in TNDT. Certainly this orientation is widely represented in feminist writings over that decade, preeminently in Schottroff, as reported also by Hentschel (pp. 16–18).

In her attempts to clarify the relationship between the Seven and the Twelve (Acts 6:1–6, pp. 318–46), within the parameters long set by a largely German scholarship, Hentschel refuses to see "the daily *diakonia*" (6:1) and the *diakonein trapezais* (6:2) as instances of *diakonia* expressing some

15. Robert M. Price, *The Widow-Traditions in Luke–Acts: A Feminist-Critical Scrutiny* (Atlanta: Scholars Press, 1997), xx.

16. Elisabeth Schüssler Fiorenza, *But She Said: Feminist Practices of Biblical Interpretations* (Boston: Beacon Press, 1992), 215.

17. Turid Karlsen Seim, *The Double Message: Patterns of Gender in Luke–Acts* (Nashville: Abingdon Press, 1994), 100.

18. John N. Collins, "Did Luke Intend a Disservice to Women in the Martha and Mary Story?," *Biblical Theology Bulletin* 28.3 (1998), 104–11; "Does Equality of Discipleship Add Up to Church? A Critique of Feminist Ekklesia-logy," *New Theology Review* 12.3 (August 1999), 48–57.

form of practical charity. Instead, consistent with her emphasis on *diako-nia* as expressing authoritative activity, she sees Luke dividing the origin-ally dual responsibility of the Twelve for "Word" and "Deed" into separate responsibilities for the Seven ("Deed") and the Twelve ("Word"). That Acts has nothing further to say of the Seven's activity in "Deed" but only in "Word" (Stephen, Philip) suggests to Hentschel that this arrangement is wholly a Lukan fiction aimed at disguising a preexistent ministry of the "Word" carried out by the Seven among the Hellenists. To canvass the ex-istence of this would be an embarrassment to Luke in his determination to reserve the "Word" to the Twelve.

To my mind, however, the problems resolve themselves when we attri-bute to *diakonia* in Acts 6:1–6 the values intended by Luke. Hentschel's sociocultural observations about Hellenists and traditional Jews already point strongly in this direction. The "daily *diakonia*" in which the Hellenist widows are overlooked is indeed an authoritative activity, as she argues, but not of a different kind from that identified in Acts 1:17, 25. It is simply a continuation of that apostolic commission among the Aramaic-speaking Jews in the temple and in house after house "every day" (5:42). The Twelve, however, just cannot cope with the demands of a "daily" bilingual ministry and respond to the Hellenists' complaint by asking them to put forward Greek-speaking preachers who might "carry out the task" in the domestic situation ("at tables") to which the Greek widows are mostly confined.[19]

Further Dissonances

The odd thing is that in Hentschel's other exegetical comment—carried out with the same dispassionate scholarship—she takes conclusions from some points of the scripture significant for ecclesiology that are likewise different from the conclusions the same data led me to.

The points of difference occur principally at 1 Cor. 12:4–6, Phil. 1:1, and Eph. 4:12. The readings at 1 Corinthians and Ephesians share a common semantic element. In each instance, Hentschel recognizes a generic com-mission in the *diakonia* such that the *diakonia* among the gifts (1 Cor. 12:5) pertains to the whole body and bespeaks a commission to the whole mem-bership; I attempted a solution of this kind in *Diakonia*, and Hentschel

---

19. John N. Collins, *Are All Christians Ministers?* (Collegeville, MN: Liturgical Press, 1992), 35–40; *Deacons and the Church: Making Connections Between Old and New* (Leominster, UK: Gracewing, 2002), 47–58.

records my shift to understanding the *diakonia* here as specific to the evangelizers.[20] Similarly, for Hentschel the *diakonia* in "the equipment of the saints" (Eph. 4:12) is the commission of all members to the work of building up the body. Each of these readings I would contest. At the same time they are not part of a tendency to extend the specifically evangelistic *diakonia* to all members of the community and thus do not destabilize the Pauline supposition of a specifically evangelical mandate different in kind from any mandate shared by all believers.

The roles of the "episkopoi and *diakonoi*" of Phil. 1:1 Hentschel presents, respectively, as leaders of communities—such as heads of house-churches—and commissioned preachers. The latter would be after the manner of—indeed, are possibly to be identified with—the collaborators Paul mentions at Phil. 4:2–3, a group that includes women (pp. 172–78). Yet in this evaluation Hentschel again departs from her carefully enunciated methodology of reading *diakonia* within its context. Across ancient Greek usage, only with the later emergence of the Christian denotation "deacon" is the term *diakonos* used as a titular designation for a person in a stable office. All agree that that can hardly be the denotation here.

Further, as I argued initially and as Hentschel frequently points out— even in the context of this discussion (p. 177)—the term *diakonos* always looks back to a person, persons, institution, or physical dependency from whom or from which the term receives the individuation of its signification. In this instance, that element of the semantics appears to be an open-and-shut case. In *episkopoi* we have a term clearly designating persons with superior public responsibilities. In such a context, the term *diakonoi* that Paul closely associates with *episkopoi* inevitably points to a relationship that expresses functional subordination. Hentschel, by contrast, arrives at a designation that makes *diakonos* a simple technical term for a commissioned preacher, a term shorn of its characteristic reference to the commissioning authority. Even when, later in history, the term does attain the status of the technical term "deacon," the reference to "bishop" is still semantically inscribed within it. Appeals to commentators like Georgi (p. 176, note 420) and Dunn (p. 175, note 418) hardly help Hentschel's case because they wrote with only partial appreciation of the usage, while the tentative observations of Bartlett (p. 175, note 417) hardly add up to a

---

20. Collins, *Are All Christians Ministers?*, 120–36; "Ministry as a Distinct Category among Charismata (1 Corinthians 12:4–7)," *Neotestamentica* 27.1 (1993), 79–91; "God's Gifts to Congregations," *Worship* 68.3 (May 1994), 242–49; *Deacons and the Church*, 82–84.

criticism of my position. Is it possible, rather, that in her comparatively brief discussion of the *diakonoi* in Phil. 1:1, as perhaps in regard to her very extensive investigation of *diakonia* in Luke 10/Acts 6, Hentschel's evaluation has been influenced by her earlier agenda of establishing public roles for women in early Christian communities (as in her interpretation of Phil. 4:2–3)?

Conclusion

This book closes a long chapter in the modern story of *diakonia*. *Diakonia* began to emerge as a distinctive and innovative Christian idea in the initiatives of the Fliedners and their colleagues in relation to the deaconess movement in Germany of the 1830s. The idea acquired theological credentials a century later with the scholarship of Wilhelm Brandt and Hermann Beyer, and in the post–World War II decades took center stage in movements of church renewal, the birth of the World Council of Churches, and the process of the Second Vatican Council. From the 1960s–80s, *diakonia* contributed fundamentally to a redeveloped theology of ministry that impacted deeply upon ecclesiology. My own revisionist study, *Diakonia: Re-interpreting the Ancient Sources*, may have questioned the theological legitimacy of much that went under the name of *diakonia* in the preceding sixty years, and may have been noticed by individuals here and there, but had minimal influence on movements and institutions. With the publication of Anni Hentschel's study, a second scholarly voice has insisted that the reinterpretation of *diako*nia in 1990 was essentially correct, that the New Testament has to be read differently from the way its modern translators have presented *diakonic* ideas. As a consequence, theology of church and ministry needs to explore and accommodate ideas that may not sit conveniently within contemporary patterns of thought and practice.

Hentschel's book is all the more significant in that the author has not been content simply to adopt a new semantic profile of *diakonia* that she came across in an earlier publication. She has done something more definitive than this. She reopened the files of nearly a dozen Classical and Hellenistic writers of Greek for the purpose of testing the new semantic profile against her own rigorous examination of the ancient rhetoric. Perhaps the study presents signs that Hentschel was drawn into this process later rather than early in her study, when her focus was more narrowly on the place of women in early Christian ministry. This could well have made untoward demands on her chosen methodology, but the situation indubitably adds to the integrity of the work because the proofing of the new semantic approach convinced Hentschel that she could not invoke *diakonia* without a similarly rigorous rereading of those sections of the New Testament where *diakonia* contributed to ecclesiology.

In spite of the handful of interpretations already noted (1 Cor. 12:5, Eph. 4:12, Phil. 1:1, Acts 6:1–4), the overall agreement between the two readings is profound not only in their semantic alignment but in the foundational ideas they expose at crucial points. The most important of these are Mark 10:45 and Luke 22:27, while the passages most relevant to a theology of pastoral ministry are those about *diakonia* in Paul's own apostolate, especially 2 Cor. 2–6. On the other hand, of considerable interest rather than importance, is our agreement on *diakonia* usage in relation to Rom. 15:25 and other passages about the Collection for Jerusalem, as well as in the parallel usage in Acts 11:29 and 12:25. Our congruent readings here illustrate the inadequacy of attempts to introduce caritative elements into the semantic makeup of *diakonia* in such contexts.

I repeat that Hentschel's stance is genuinely independent of mine. In the course of her exegesis, she makes scant reference to my work but forces a path through the standard scholarship to establish a reading that meets the requirements of academic method. That the two readings should stand at the end so closely together is a remarkable testament to the long-hidden and much too lightly ignored rhetorical and theological value of this small word group. We will await responses within German theology and ecclesiastical administration with interest. Meanwhile, the serious business of what *diakonia* means for church and theology is not yet determined.

Additional Note

A. Hentschel, *Gemeinde, Ämter, Dienste: Perspektiven zur neutestamentlichen Ekklesiologie* (Neukirchen-Vlujn: Neukirchener Verlagsgesellschaft, 2013). pp ix-254

The first section of Dr Hentschel's recent study of *Community, Offices, Ministries* in the New Testament carries the title (translated): "*Diakonia* as the Key Term in New Testament Ecclesiology and Ethics." The first statement of her foreword advises us: "*Diakonie*—over the last 200 years there

can hardly be a term that has so deeply marked the Protestant churches."
Illustrating this situation are comments in the Preface to the present
book (in relation to Brandt and Lohfink) and discussions in the preceding chapter (see on Howson and Fliedner) and throughout the following
chapter. Given that all this has been based on a misunderstanding of the
underlying Greek term *diakonia* and that, consequently, a rewriting of
the theological implications of *diakonia* would be necessary, Hentschel
informs us that she was not of a mind to get involved. However, the wide
discussions prompted by her 2007 volume (reviewed above) suggested
that scholarship needed clarification on the relevant biblical passages
themselves.

Semantically, Hentschel's readings continue to align themselves closely
with my own—with one exception. This applies to her understanding that
in early Christian usage the noun *diakonos* can appear as a self-standing
titular designation of "preacher" or "evangelizer." This would apply, for example, to Phoebe (Rom. 16:1). Similarly, the verb *diakoneo* can of itself designate preaching and other functions of leadership, as in the case of the
women disciples in Mark 15:41. My own reading of such passages in such
senses would require much clearer contextual indicators than Hentschel
appears to provide, although Hentschel does indeed emphasize elsewhere
(pp. 20–23) the importance of context in the more precise determination
of instances of the terms.

On the other hand, in relation to the semantic range of the *diakon*-
terms, Hentschel appears to allow considerably more scope than on previous occasions for the concept of mediation to emerge in the process
especially of delivering the Word of God (e. g., pp. 48–49; 54–56). Even
so she is mindful that no single concept can be identified as underlying
the usage (p. 61) so that in German (as in English) no one term can adequately represent the range of meanings to which the Greek term can
give expression.

Exegetically, Hentschel reveals approximately the same level of com-
patibility with my own readings as illustrated in this chapter. Thus we are
not in full accord on our understanding of the differentiation within the
giftedness of the church (1 Cor. 12:5), the specific identity of the *diakonoi*
at Phil. 1:1 (or even 1 Tim. 3:8–13), or the nature of the *diakonia* in Acts 6:1.

One new point of difference is in relation to the nature of the *diakonia*
performed by the royal attendants in the parable of the judgment (Matt.
25:45). Routinely cited as the classic illustration of *diakonia* as "loving
service to those in need" (the German *Diakonie*), the instance—to my

knowledge—has not previously been examined by Hentschel. Here she reads the Greek not as expressing helping activities as specifically benevolent but as specifically designating them as a responsibility: "When have we seen you hungry...and not felt required to carry out our duties." As noted elsewhere, I read the verb here ("when did we not *serve* you") as simply an instance of courtly language appropriate for an address to a king.

The demands that the subtleties of the Greek usage can put on the interpreter are in evidence with Hentschel's frustration at uncertainties attending the interpretation of *diakonia* at the high point of ecclesiology in Eph. 4:11–12 (p. 144). Is it "the saints" of 4:12 or the designated teachers of 4:11 to whom "the work of *diakonia*" (4:12) is committed? Her preference ultimately is the saints (p. 145). My own attitude at this juncture has perhaps been partly influenced by my experience of difficulties generated within the lurking parti pris of much German exegetical engagement—not that any of this shows in Hentschel's measured approach. In this instance, however, it seems to me that German discussion of the identity—and the historical phases of the activity—of the functionaries listed at 4:11 is bedeviled by the inclusion of *diakonos* (mentioned by the ancient author earlier at 3:7) among the titles of those authoritatively engaged in delivery of the heavenly message. *Diakonos* in this document, however, is no such word. It is not just another title. At a comparatively later era, when *diakonos* does designate the deacon, a professional character attached to the term. In this earlier Ephesian discussion, however, *diakonos* has no place in a list of designations for publicly acknowledged officers. The function of the term at 3:7 ("the gospel of which I became a *diakonos*") is purely rhetorical but carries a powerful message because it identifies Paul as the holder of the role of mediating the timeless "mysteries" known previously only to God. Every rhetorical aspect of chapters 3–4 reflects an awareness of the dimension introduced to the discourse by the appeal to the *diakon-* term at 3:7 and expressly invoked once again by the cognate *diakon-* term at 4:12. Only the publicly commissioned functionaries of 4:11 could have been understood as being engaged in the same *diakonia* of mystery as had engaged the person named Paul.

Elsewhere in Hentschel's study, the range of agreement includes the nature of Paul's own historical evangelizing activity when expressed as "diakonic" and the nature of the mission of the Son of Man when expressed as "diakonic" (Mark 10:45). At these critical points, our level of agreement is surely significant in relation to Hentschel's overriding concern, which is the reinvigoration of ministry in the church. She sees her study (p. 230) as "a contribution to a pressingly urgent discussion about fundamental issues in our understanding of office and community in the New Testament and in the early church."[21]

---

21 See also A. Hentschel, "Frauendienst-Frauenamt: Zur Frage nach einem Diakonissenamt im Neuen Testament" in J.-C. Kaiser and R. Scheepers, eds, *Dienerinnen des Herrn: Beiträge zur weiblichen Diakonie im 19. und 20. Jahrhundert* (Leipzig: Evangelische Verlagsanstalt: 2010), 38–56.

3

The Problem with Values Carried by Diakonia/Diakonie in Recent Church Documents

The Emergence of Diakonia/Diakonie

The following paragraph from a web page of the Evangelical Church of Germany (EKD) describes the term *Diakonie*:

> *Diakonie* is the social work of the Evangelical Churches. Because faith in Jesus Christ and an active love of the neighbour must go together, *diakonic* organisations deliver many forms of service to men and women. They help people in need and in unjust social situations. They also seek to remove the cause of such distress. "*Diakonie*" derives from the Greek word for "service."[1]

This Greek word is basically *diakon*, with endings in *-ia* for "service," *-os* for "servant," and *-ein* for "to serve"; each of these endings changes according to requirements of sentence structure in ancient Greek.

In Germany, The *Diakonic* Work *(das Diakonische Werk)* is a charitable organization whose members include the twenty-two Lutheran, Reformed, and United regional churches (of German *Länder* or states) that make up the EKD, commonly referred to in English as Lutheran churches. Also belonging to the organization are a number of Free Protestant churches and over eighty professional associations (medical, psychiatric, etc.). More than 450,000 people work full or part time in 27,000 independent institutions of various sizes.

---

1. http://www.ekd.de/diakonie/45618.html (accessed September 12, 2010), my translation.

For these people and for the EKD at large, the term *Diakonie* is a constant reminder of the selfless love taught by Jesus in such gospel passages as Luke 10:25–37, the story of the Good Samaritan. This selfless love is thought of as *Diakonie* because in some other passages where the Greek word *diakon-* occurs, the gospels appear to speak of "serving" others. Jesus himself states that he came "to serve (*diakon-*) and give his life as a ransom for others" (Mark 10:45). Special inspiration for engaging in service of this kind is taken from the image of the judgment of the nations when those on the left of the king say to him, "When was it that we saw you hungry or thirsty or a stranger...and did not take care of you?" (Matt. 25:44). Here, "take care of" is more often translated as "serve"; in the Greek, the verb is *diakon-*.

In the organization of most churches—from the earliest times—one of the leaders has been known by a title clearly related to the *diakon-* words. This person is of course the deacon (German *Diakon*). Accordingly, much theology of the modern diaconate and the spirituality associated with it have been deeply affected by values that have accrued around the *diakon-* words. These words signaled an ecclesial ministry to others in selfless love. This slant on the diaconate began to develop with the first stirrings of the modern diaconate within the EKD and generated there the emergence of the neologism *Diakonie*.[2]

As the deacon movement spread and the works of *Diakonie* multiplied, so too did interest in the theological reach of the Greek word *diakonia*. In the course of the rapid development of scholarly biblical method in the early twentieth century, one study of worldwide influence was the multivolume *Theological Dictionary of the New Testament* initiated in Germany in the 1930s by Gerhard Kittel. The pages in that dictionary by Hermann W. Beyer on the *diakon-* words presented *diakonia* as "the symbol of all loving care for others" and "a mark of true discipleship of Jesus." As applied to Jesus in Mark 10:45, "to serve" is "much more than a comprehensive term for any loving assistance rendered to the neighbour"; rather, it expresses the notion of "full and perfect sacrifice, as the offering of life which is the very essence of service, of being for others, whether in life or in death."[3] In

---

2. An early instance of the term occurs in a proposal to a church council by Theodor Fliedner in his "Gutachten 'die Diakonie und den Diakonat betreffend' (1856)," in *Diakonie pragmatisch*, ed. Norbert Friedrich, Christine-Ruth Müller, and Martin Wolff (Neukirchen-Vluyn: Neukirchener Verlag, 2007), 25–54.

3. H. W. Beyer, *TDNT* 2 (1964), 92, 85–86.

the second half of the twentieth century, writings on the relevance of these dictionary meanings to the task of reappraising the nature of the church's ministry and authority have been voluminous.[4]

One aspect of the present-day conventional semantic profile of the Greek *diakon-* words demands closer attention. This is the supposition that the rich theological and powerful ethical values now attributed to the words in the New Testament derive exclusively from usage within the early Christian communities. For this convention to be effective within especially ecclesiology we have to suppose that in pre-Christian usage the *diakon-* words had been—in Eduard Schweizer's description—"entirely unbiblical and non-religious and never include[d] association with a particular dignity or position."[5] In a much-cited passage from *The Church*, Hans Küng added, "*Diakonia* means an activity which every Greek would recognise at once as being one of self-abasement."[6] In fact, because early Christians felt a need to avoid any current terms that expressed "a relationship of rulers and ruled," they felt obliged "to develop a new word," namely, "*diakonia*, service": "Jesus, however, gave this notion of service a radically new meaning."[7] Thomas O'Meara, probably the most influential North American Roman Catholic voice in the theology of ministry, emphasized that *diakonia* was an "ordinary Greek word for serving."[8] In particular, the term did not suggest the "sacral"[9] but was part of "a language-event" through which "the church fashioned a language that disclosed its way of life."[10] The new terminology looked toward "a theological reappreciation of every church role...as inescapably one of service."[11]

---

4. For overviews of such developments, see my *Diakonia: Re-interpreting the Ancient Sources* (New York: Oxford University Press, 1990, reprinted 2009), 1–72, and "Ordained and Other Ministries: Making a Difference," *Ecclesiology* 3.1 (2006), 11–32 (in this volume, as Chapter 12).

5. Eduard Schweizer, *Church Order in the New Testament*, Eng. trans. (London: SPCK, 1961), 174 (21c).

6. Hans Küng, *The Church*, Eng. trans. (Garden City, NY: Image Books, 1976; original German and Eng. trans., 1967), 498.

7. Ibid., 497–98.

8. Thomas O'Meara, *Theology of Ministry*, 2nd edn (New York: Paulist Press, 1999), 64.

9. Ibid., 74.

10. Ibid., 75.

11. Ibid., 64.

Cardinal Ratzinger Addressing the Roman Synod of Bishops, 1990

The impact of this pervasive but originally German conceptualization of the *diakon-* terms in early Christian writings was striking. The scope of the impact may be measured by the strong reaction against it in Joseph Cardinal Ratzinger's October 1990 address opening the Synod of Bishops on the formation of priests.[12] A synod on such a topic was itself evidence of the crisis in pastoral ministry that is today a talking point in every Roman Catholic parish. In the late 1980s, the Vatican was seeking a solution to the failing supply of ordained ministers, and the synod's objective was to to revamp the training offered to candidates for the priesthood.

Cardinal Ratzinger began by expressing strong criticism of developments within the theology of priesthood in the post-conciliar period. "The Catholic model of priesthood," he observed, had entered "a profound crisis," evidenced by the great numbers of resignations from the priesthood and "the dramatic decline in new priestly vocations." However, the situation could not have arisen, he proposed, if "this ministry had not become dubious from within." Ratzinger identified the essential contributors to this inner doubt as the ascendancy in the modern period of "the old Reformation-era arguments combined with the findings of modern exegesis," the latter also being Protestant in character.

The issues came down to the introduction of a new "terminology," whereby the essentially sacerdotal and cultic character of the Roman Catholic priesthood had been obscured.[13] Protestant "philological considerations" had made it "indisputably clear" to Catholic theologians "that the teaching of Trent concerning the priesthood had been formulated on false assumptions."[14] The crucial issue for Catholic theologians was the perception that "the nascent Church named her developing ministries, not with a sacral, but with a profane vocabulary," thus opening up a "purely functional" theology

---

12. Joseph Cardinal Ratzinger, "On the Essence of the Priesthood," *Called to Communion: Understanding the Church Today*, Eng. trans. (San Francisco: Ignatius Press, 1996), 105–31. See original: "Vom Wesen des Priestertums," *Zur Gemeinschaft gerufen: Kirche heute verstehen* (Freiburg im B.: Herder, 1991, reprinted 2005), 101–28.

13. Ibid., 106–107.

14. Ibid., 109.

of ecclesial roles and limiting these to proclamation of the Gospel and "the ministry of love."[15]

The last phrase is a clear reference to the German *Diakonie* already described,[16] and Ratzinger was deploring the deleterious effect the German understanding of the term had had upon the modern churchwide perception of the Roman Catholic priesthood. He made the linguistic nature of the issue explicit in a note criticizing the Protestant claim that early Christians adopted "profane vocabulary" for ecclesial roles. Ratzinger did not enlarge on his thinking here, although the issue was crucial to his argument. He wrote simply, "This opinion [i. e., *diakon-* terms are 'profane vocabulary'], which is current in modern exegesis, has recently been energetically contested—especially in relation to the semantic field *Diakonia, diakonein, etc.*"[17]

Die Collins-Debatte

Ratzinger's rejection of the semantic values attaching to the German tradition of *Diakonie* seemingly passed unnoticed. "*Diakonic*" values continued to be identified as those of loving service. A decade later, however, a shift of opinion was occurring in some quarters in regard to the reliability of the lexical description presented in Kittel's *Theological Dictionary of the New Testament*. In fact, German-language discussion of *Diakonie* and the diaconate began mentioning "the Collins debate" to reference fundamental differences between conventional understandings of the Greek *diakon-* words and the re-interpretation of these words first published in my research volume of 1990.[18] The German phrase *die Collins-Debatte* originated in connection with a lecture I presented at the Evangelische Fachhochschule in Ludwigsburg in June 2005.[19] The

---

15. Ibid., 106–107. The German for the latter phrase is "der Dienst der Liebe," "Vom Wesen," 103.

16. "Der Dienst der Liebe" and "der Liebesdienst" are standard synonyms for *Diakonie*.

17. The reference provided by Ratzinger was to my dissertation at the University of London in 1976, "*Diakonein* and Associated Vocabulary in Early Christian Tradition." The published reworking of this thesis (note 4 above) did not appear until July 1990. How Cardinal Ratzinger came to access the thesis itself remains mystifying to me, but the published volume would have greatly strengthened the linguistic—if not necessarily the theological—case he wished to make at the Roman Synod.

18. See note 4.

19. "Dazwischengehen. Die Rekonstruktion eines neuen Diakoniebegriffs aus den neutestamentlichen Quellen" (unpublished).

press release for this occasion announced, "Eine internationale Debatte zu: *Diakonia*[20]—*Diakonie*—*Diakon/innen*,"[21] and named the topic, "The Biblical Foundations of the Diaconal Office."[22]

The institute's yearbook duly noted "a vigorous controversy."[23] The novelty of the situation was evident in the headline of the weekly Württemberg church paper: "Is *Diakonie* a big mistake? How an Australian Catholic forces a rethink of the Evangelical Church's social work."[24] An introductory note to the article alluded to the "shock" the new linguistic findings were causing within *Diakonie*.[25] Several weeks later, Professor Annette Noller of the Fachhochschule, who had been both the debate's host and a member of the debating panel, contributed a reassuring article to the newspaper entitled, "The foundations of *Diakonie* are not shaking."[26] Here she initiated some critique of the new interpretation in the interests of maintaining the legitimacy of concepts that had gone into the making of *Diakonie* over the previous 160 years.

Independently of the Ludwigsburg event, an earlier and more incisive German initiative supporting the re-interpretation of *diakonia* had been a forthright publication by Hans-Jürgen Benedict, a professor at Hamburg's

---

20. The Greek term that, with its cognates, occurs one hundred times in the New Testament in reference to pastoral activities in the early churches in Acts and the Epistles as well as to household tasks in gospel narratives.

21. *Diakonie* is the German neologism deriving from the Greek *diakonia; diakon/innen* represents two German terms for the male and female deacons who form the foundational body of social workers within *Diakonie*.

22. "Eine kontroverse Debatte der biblischen Grundlagen des diakonischen Amtes wollen Prof. Dr. John Neil Collins aus Melbourne / Australien, Dr. Wilfried Brandt, Direktor der Karlshöhe i[m].R[uhestand], und Prof. Dr. Annette Noller, E[vangelische] F[ach]H[ochschule] Reutlingen-Ludwigsburg, am Donnerstag, 30. Juni 2005, führen."

23. Jahresbericht 04/05, 9 (www.efh-reutlingen-ludwigsburg.de): "Lösten eine heftige Kontroverse aus..."—although for my part, after I had read my German script, participation in the German exchanges was limited.

24. M. Ernst Wahl, "Diakonie, ein grosser Irrtum? Wie ein Australischer Katholik die evangelische Sozialarbeit zum Nachdenken zwingt," *Evangelisches Gemeindeblatt für Württemberg* 29 (July 17, 2005) Thema der Woche.

25. "seine Erkenntnisse, die innerhalb der Diakonie für Aufregung sorgen..."

26. "Die Grundlage der Diakonie wankt nicht: Gedanken zur diakoniewissenschaftlichen Diskussion um John Collins," *Ev. Gemeindeblatt* 34 (August 24, 2005), again "theme of the week." My response to this article was in English and did not appear in the newspaper: Five years later, in an extensive paper on the history of the diaconate, Dr Noller acknowledged the new semantic profile of diakon- terms provided by Collins and Hentschel, but proceeded to base the historical diaconate upon a reading of Acts 6:1–6 which neither of them supports but which for her legitimizes the new office as one of neighbourly love ("Amt der Nächstenliebe.") See "Die Geschichte des Diakonats in evangelischer Perspektive," Impuls I/2011, 7–47, citing 13. Accessed at http://www.vedd.de/.cms/111 on April 13, 2013.

Rauhes Haus, the nineteenth-century home of Johann Hinrich Wichern, founder of the Inner Mission of the Evangelical Church and champion of *Diakonie*. Benedict explained that he had first been made aware of the existence of a re-interpretation of *diakonia* at a Finnish conference in 1998 that had been addressed by Kjell Nordstokke, currently professor at *Diakonhjemmet* University College in Oslo.[27] His curiosity aroused, Benedict made a close study of the new research and in 2000 published a skillful précis of the research.[28] He lightheartedly characterized the task of drawing attention to the new information as "pouring a little water into the wine of *diakonic* self-satisfaction" in Germany.[29] He concluded his review, however, on a much more sober note. The new research, he wrote, "effectively brings into question the dominant *diakonic* line of thinking [in Germany] which brooks no opposition; the new research removes the possibility of identifying Christian existence with humble and benevolent service, and it leaves us to confront once more the question of what...this *diakonia* is."[30]

In laying down such a challenge to German theologians and church leaders, Benedict did not hesitate to direct a sharp criticism against German scholarship for a decade-long neglect of new research that undercut a core value of the Evangelical Church.[31]

In response to this in-house critique, the University of Heidelberg's Academic Institute for *Diakonie* published a collection of essays two years later under the title *Diakonische Konturen*, Part I of which contained three

---

27. Nordstokke's recent publication evidences continued support of the reinterpretation of *diakonia*; see *Liberating Diakonia* (Trondheim: Tapir Akademisk Forlag, 2011). Chapter 2, "Theoretical Framework of the Science of Diakonia," is based on the lecture in Lahti, Finland, which evoked the strong reaction from Benedict noted above. Chapter 3 is an article arising from a joint presentation by us in Sigtuna, Sweden (January 2000), and subsequently co-authored by Nordstokke and myself for the Swedish church paper *Svensk Kyrkotidning* 96 (March 17, 2000): "Diakoni—teoria—praxis," 107–111 (text in English). See more at note 33.

28. "Beruht der Anspruch der evangelischen Diakonie auf einer Missinterpretation der antiken Quellen? John N. Collins Untersuchung 'Diakonia,'" *Pastoraltheologie* 89 (2000), 343–64, reprinted in id., *Barmherzigheit und Diakonie: Von der rettenden Liebe zum gelingenden Leben* (Stuttgart 2008), 114–28, and in Volker Herrmann and Martin Horst, eds, Studienbuch Diakonik, vol. 1: *biblische, historische und theologische Zugänger zur Diakonie* (Neukirchen-Vluyn: Neukirchener Verlag, 2006, 2nd edn 2008), 117–33.

29. Benedict, "Beruht der Anspruch," 351.

30. Ibid., 363.

31. Ibid., 352. This criticism he expressed more trenchantly in the first thesis of his paper at the 2005 Rummelsberg conference (see note 37).

evaluations of *Diakonia: Re-interpreting the Ancient Sources*[32] and one theological reflection upon it. This last was again by Benedict,[33] who engaged in what the editors of the collection called the necessary further explorations of diaconate in the light of the research.[34]

Benedict continued his advocacy of the new interpretation at the Rummelsberg conference of October 2005. The conference primarily aimed to locate the extensive educational activities across the German *diakonic* training and research institutes within the Bologna process of European further education. An undercurrent, however, was the issue of how to interconnect the traditional diaconal initiatives of the churches within the new theological framework created by the re-interpretation of *diakonia*. The invitational brochure announced the theme of the conference as "The Professional Identity of Deacons," and invited participants to reflect on the following situation (translated):

What is a deacon? What will characterise this profession in the future? In former years only a few could give clear answers to these

32. Volker Herrmann, Rainer Merz, Heinz Schmidt, eds, *Diakonische Konturen: Theologie im Kontext sozialer Arbeit*, Veröffentlichungen des Diakoniewissenschaftlichen Instituts an der Universität Heidelberg 18 (Heidelberg: Winter, 2003), including Stefan Dietzel, 'Zur Entstehung des Diakonats im Urchristentum. Eine Auseinandersetzung mit den Positionen von Wilhelm Brandt, Hermann Wolfgang Beyer und John N. Collins,' 136–170; Ismo Dunderberg, "Vermittlung statt karitativeTätigkeit? Überlegungen zu John N. Collins' Interpretation von *diakonia*,' 171–183; Dierk Starnitzke, 'Die Bedeutung von *diakonos* im frühen Christentum,'184–212. In his more recent study, *Diakonie in biblischer Orientierung* (Stuttgart: Kohlhammer, 2011), Starnitzke significantly increases the emphasis he places on differentiating between Pauline usage, where he accepts my semantic description, and usage in gospel narrative, where he reverts to the service values supporting the traditional German conceptualization of *Diakonie*. The two usages are clearly different, but neither evidences a caritative dimension. Reservations expressed by Starnitzke, Dunderberg, and especially by Dietzel cannot be discussed here but are dismissed by Hentschel, *Diakonia im Neuen Testament*, 21 (n. 57, 58), 280 (n. 445).

33. H.-J. Benedict, "Die grössere Diakonie: Versuch einer Neubestimmung in Anschluss an John N. Collins," *Diakonische Konturen*, 127–35. In his Rummelsberg paper, "Diakonie als Dazwischengehen," 134 (see note 37 below), Benedict acknowledged the grounds of my reservations about his attempt to extend the semantic range of *diakonia* in "Die grössere Diakonie." Nordstokke (note 27 above) tends to something similar in delimiting the signification to the "prophetic" role of the church in society ("Prophetic Diakonia," 49–53; "Theoretical Framework," esp. 37). This obstructs our ability to appreciate the multifaceted usage of *diakon-* terms in the New Testament. Nebel's attempt in the second half of his paper (Chapter 1, note 37 above) to present "une relecture de la notion de diaconie à la lumière de l'avènement en Jésus Christ du règne du Roi-Messie attendu par Israël" also fails here. The *diakon-* terms remain essentially of indeterminate semantic value until an author evokes a context that provides particularity.

34. Einleitung, *Diakonische Konturen*, 9.

questions, but because of recent developments the question has become more difficult. The Australian theologian John N. Collins has
brought into question the traditional understanding of the biblical
term *diakonia*.

In this context, the first working session addressed "the biblical
foundations of the professional self-understanding of deacons and the
outcomes for diaconal praxis." The first contribution on this theme, by
Folker Siegert, sought to deepen the spirituality of *diakonic* praxis within
the traditional framework of the German *Diakonie*. In the course of these
reflections, Siegert's paper made some oblique connections with the new
research.[35] The second presentation, by Benedict, was typically lively and
closely aligned with the tenor of the new research that he had introduced
to German theology in 2000. He expressed the view that had German theology acknowledged the research earlier, the large volume of the 1990s,
Diakonie: biblische Grundlagen und Orientierungen,[36] "would have to have
been thoroughly revised."[37] His final comment, however, was that the
German term *Diakonie* is so deeply enshrined in German spiritual aspirations that to change it would be to deprive the church of "the freedom to
develop fully the ecclesiological implications of the *diakon-* words." To this

---

35. Surprisingly, the opening lecture by Folker Siegert ("Biblische Grundlagen der
kirchlchen Diakonie") did not engage the conference's leading question. The lecture developed exclusively within the conventional framework of German *Diakonie*, thus avoiding
engagement with the basic semantic and exegetical issues raised by the re-interpretation
while still managing to make a number of critical comments on the reinterpretation.
I cannot take up the details here, but do note that Siegert's advocacy of Estienne/Stephanus
(p. 21) appears to overlook the close attention given to this seventeenth-century lexicon
within the context of ancient (e. g., Pollux) and contemporary (e. g., Georgi) scholarship
in *Diakonia: Re-interpreting the Ancient Sources* (see 93, 169–73, and index). Siegert's paper
appeared with other conference papers in Rainer Merz, Ulrich Schindler, Heinz Schmidt,
eds, *Dienst und Profession: Diakoninnen und Diakone zwischen Anspruch and Wirklichkeit*
(Heidelberg: Winter, 2008), 16–30, presumably without opportunity to take account of
Hentschel, *Diakonia im NT* (2007).

36. Gerhard K. Schäfer and Theodor Strohm, eds, *Diakonie—biblische Grundlagen und
Orientierungen*, 2nd edn (Heidelberg: HVA 1994, originally 1990).

37. H.-J. Benedict, "Diakonie als Dazwischengehen und Bauftragung. Die Collins-Debatte
aus der Sicht ihres Anstossgebers," *Barmherzigkeit und Diakonie*, 129–37, citing 130. This
paper did not appear with those of Siegert and other participants at the Rummelsberg conference in *Dienst und Profession* but in Benedict's own later *Barmherzigkeit* collection (above,
n. 28).

thought he added, "We hear the objections and choose the freedom to do things differently."[38]

Anni Hentschel was not so politic. Introducing a handbook on *Diakonie* with a reflection on "*Diakonie* in the Bible," she concluded:

> In the 19th century the concept of '*Diakonie*' was introduced as the foundation for the offices of deaconesses and deacons. This concept owes much less to biblical terminology, however, than people thought. Judged from the perspective of biblical sciences, a number of errors of interpretation occurred. Some of these, we must say, were 'productive' mistakes in that they contributed in practice to a strengthening of love of neighbour. Nevertheless, the idea that *Diakonie* should develop in its practitioners a special kind of humble service and self-denial is far from what the biblical text means.[39]

Answering a question she posted as the title of an academic paper in 2008, "In the early church did a diaconate exist that was characterized by charitable service?," Hentschel's response was a definitive negative.[40]

Roman Catholic Reception of the Re-interpreted Diakonia

Other than Cardinal Ratzinger's grateful reception of the re-interpretation of *diakonia* at the Roman Synod of 1990, there is little evidence, outside

---

38. Ibid., 134. Dutch editors announced a similar policy on introducing the large collection *Diaconie in beweging: Handboek diaconiewetenschap*, H. Crijns et al., eds (Kampen: Kok, 2011): "In this book we propose to proceed on the understanding of the term 'diaconate/ diaconia' as the church's response to people in need...starting from the idea that such service constitutes an essential part of what being church is. And Collins agrees with this, although he would not use the term *diakonia* for it." (p. 13, my translation) Nonetheless, in the long second chapter of this volume, Bart Koet expounds my understanding of the Greek term: "Exegetische kanttekeningen over *diakonia* in het Nieuwe Testament: Leren of doen?," 69–96. More understandable is the approach adopted by Heinz Rüegger and Christoph Sigrist in *Diakonie—eine Einführung: Zur theologischen Begründung helfenden Handelns* (Zurich: TVZ, 2011) 81–82, who restrict use of the terms *Diakonie/diakonisch* to designating institutions and activities so named in Germany but without implying that what those terms connote represents what the ancient Greek *diakon-* terms express.

39. Anni Hentschel, "Diakonie in der Bibel," in Klaus-Dieter K. Kottnik and Eberhard Hauschildt, eds, *Diakoniefibel: Grundwissen für alle, die mit Diakonie zu tun haben* (Gütersloh: CMZ Gütersloher Verlag, 2008), 17–20, citing p. 20 (my translation).

40. Anni Hentschel, "Gibt es einen sozial-karitativ ausgerichteten Diakonat in den frühchristlichen Gemeinden?" *Pastoraltheologie* 97.9 (2008), 290–306.

of book reviews,[41] of other expressly Roman Catholic interest in or advocacy of the re-interpretation. One may have expected that the novel appeal in the Second Vatican Council's Latin documents—particularly in *Lumen gentium*—to a notion called *diakonia/diaconia* would have sparked sustained exploration of the relevance of the re-interpretation of this term to ecclesiology. There the bishop's office is called "verum... servitium quod in sacris Litteris 'diaconia' seu ministerium significanter nuncupatur." The translation on the Holy See's web page reads, "A true service, which in sacred literature is significantly called *'diakonia'* or ministry."[42] In ecclesiological writings, Roman Catholics have largely confined comment on *diakonia* to promoting ethical[43] or churchwide[44] dimensions of ministry or—and especially—to theological and pastoral perspectives of the renewed diaconate. In some instances, the latter has been part of an attempt to enrich the theology through the re-interpretation,[45] but other comment overwhelmingly focuses on the lowly loving service represented in the German notion of *Diakonie*.

Indeed, resistance to disturbing the German model has been quite apparent.[46] The most striking instance has been the "Historico-Theological

---

41. See reference to reviews by Jerome Murphy O'Connor, Jerome H. Neyrey, and Timothy Radcliffe, among others, in my "A Ministry for Tomorrow's Church," *Journal of Ecumenical Studies* 32 no. 2 (Spring 1995), 159–78, esp. 166–68.

42. Why "significanter"? The German has the same ("bezeichnenderweise") and translates both "servitium" and "diakonia" by "dienen/Dienst," the preferred German terms in modern times for all church "office/s" (earlier "Amt/Ämter") and ecclesial activities. German lacks the Latin-based "ministry" terms. The Spanish has "con toda propriedad"; the French, "expressément."

43. Thus, Hans Küng, *The Church*, Eng. trans. (Garden City, NY: Doubleday Image Books, 1976), 495–502.

44. Thus, Thomas F. O'Meara, *Theology of Ministry*, rev. edn (New York: Paulist Press, 1999), 62–65, 171.

45. Richard R. Gaillardetz, "On the Theological Integrity of the Diaconate," in Owen F. Cummings, William T. Ditewig, and Richard R. Gaillardetz, *Theology of the Diaconate: The State of the Question* (New York: Paulist Press, 2005), 67–97; Bart J. Koet, "Diakonie ist nicht nur Armenfürsorge. Neuere exegetische Erkenntnisse zum Verständnis von Diakonie,"in C. Gramszow and M. Sander-Gaiser, eds, *Lernen wäre eine prima Alternative: Religionspädagogik in theologischer und erziehungswissenschaftlicher Perspektive* (Leipzig: Evangelische Verlaganstalt, 2008), 303–18; Ralf Miggelbrink, "Die 'verschiedenen Dienstämter' (LG, 18) und die Einheit des Ordo: Zum Spezifikum des diakonalen Amtes," in Klemens Armbruster and Matthias Mühler, eds, *Bereit wozu? Geweiht für was? Zur Diskussion um den ständigen Diakonat* (Freiburg: Herder, 2009), 204–21.

46. Thus, Thomas Söding, "'Nicht bedient zu werden, sondern zu dienen' (Mk 10:45): Diakonie und Diakonat im Licht des Neuen Testaments" in *Bereit wozu?* 30–62 (contrast with Miggelbrink [preceding note] in the same volume); Herbert Haslinger, *Diakonie: Grundlagen für die soziale Arbeit der Kirche* (Paderborn: Schöning, 2009), see esp. 348–50; Christian Wessely, *Gekommen um zu dienen: Der Diakonat aus fundamental*

Research Document" published in 2003 after a decade-long investigation by the International Theological Commission.[47] The report opened its consideration of the diaconate in the New Testament under the heading "Difficulties in Terminology" but was wholly silent about the semantic research published in 1990 in *Diakonia: Re-interpreting the Ancient Sources*, drawing instead on eight German-language resources both older and more recent, including H. W. Beyer, and strongly endorsing the philological views of Eduard Schweizer.

What really surprises is the terminological volte-face evident in the homiletic uses to which Pope Benedict XVI put the German *Diakonie*. At the November 20, 2010 consistory creating twenty-four cardinals, Pope Benedict reflected upon the Gospel reading for that occasion, Mark 10:32–45. In an early reference to "the icon of Jesus...who did not come to be served, but to serve," Pope Benedict evoked the image of the Messiah's "style of life" as "the basis of new relationships...and a new way of exercising authority." Such phrasing already suggests the values of the German *Diakonie*, and the reference becomes explicit as the homilist moves to the contention that "the criterion of greatness and primacy according to God is not dominion but service," adding at this point that "*diakonia* is the fundamental law of the disciple and of the Christian community." This *diakonia* shows its authentic character in "the logic of bending down to wash the feet, the logic of service, the logic of the Cross."[48] This pattern is indeed the mirror image of the logic of H. W. Beyer, for whom, as we

theologisch-ekklesiologischer Sicht (Regensburg: Pustet, 2004), 13; 246–47; Walter Kasper, "The Diaconate," *Leadership in the Church*, Eng. trans. (New York: Crossroad Publishing Company, 2003), 13–44; Stefan Sander, *Das Amt des Diakons: Eine Handreichung* (Freiburg: Herder, 2008) 31–32 (p. 32: "overriding attitude/*alles bestimmende Grundhaltung*"; the book's subtitle identifies the office as "helping; assistance").

47. *From the Diakonia of Christ to the Diakonia of the Apostles*, International Theological Commission Historico-Theological Research Document, Eng. trans. (Chicago: Hillenbrand Books, 2003). For information on the two committees engaged in this project, see *La civiltà cattolica* 154 no. 3663 (Feb. 2003), 253–336, *Nota preliminare*, 253. Introducing the German translation of the document, Gerhard L. Müller, a member of the second committee, stated that "Christian existence is participation in the Diakonia that God himself has exercised towards humankind in Christ" and that "it is most incisively described as service to people" (my translation); see G. L. Müller, ed., *Der Diakonat—Entwicklung und Perspektiven* (Würzburg: Echter, 2004), 7.

48. Text of Pope Benedict's homily from *Zenit.org*. Similarly, in the first year of Pope Francis's papacy, at his first ordination of bishops on October 24, his homily advised: "The bishop must strive to serve rather than to rule, according to the Master's commandment: 'Whoever would be great among you must be your servant.'...Always serving, always." Eng. trans. available at http://www.vatican.va/holy_father/francesco/homilies/2013.

saw above, *diakonia* expresses the notion of "full and perfect sacrifice, as the offering of life which is the very essence of service, of being for others, whether in life or in death."

While Pope Benedict's usage here is in striking contrast to the usage he preferred in his address to the Roman Synod of 1990, it echoes the notion of *diakonia* embedded in his first encyclical, *Deus caritas est*. Introducing Part 2 of the encyclical on "*Liebesdienst*" ("this service of charity"), Pope Benedict immediately invokes the terminology of *Diakonie* and develops its full dimension as "an *ordered* service to the community" (20, my emphasis). This he sees embodied in the work of the Seven in Acts 6, who perform their "*diakonia*" as a "ministry of charity" that becomes "part of the fundamental structure of the Church" (21). *Diakonia* thus envisaged becomes part of the church's "deepest nature" alongside the proclamation of the Word of God (*kerygma-martyria*) and the celebration of the sacraments (*leitourgia*) (24). In a book-length study of the encyclical, Heinrich Pompey recognized here the unprecedented character of this papal endorsement of *diakonia* understood as "caritative *Diakonie*."[49]

Essential to the authenticity of the *diakonia* of the individual Christian, Pope Benedict later observes, is the personal character of the service, this again closely echoing the sentiments in H. W. Beyer's presentation, who in turn drew upon his own mentor, Wilhelm Brandt, in stating that *diakonia* "presupposes a Thou, and not a Thou towards whom I may order my relationship as I please, but a Thou under whom I have placed myself as a *diakonōn* [servant]."[50] Pope Benedict XVI expressed this sentiment as follows (34):

> My deep personal sharing in the needs and sufferings of others becomes a sharing of my very self with them: if my gift is not to prove a source of humiliation [for the recipient], I must give to others not only something that is my own, but my very self; I must be personally present in my gift.

Addressing the hierarchy of England and Wales in May 2008 on the subject of Pope Benedict XVI's encyclical, Cardinal Cordes—then

49. Heinrich Pompey, *Zur Neuprofilierung der caritativen Diakonie der Kirche: Die Caritas-Enzyklika "Deus caritas est." Kommentar und Auswertung* (Würzburg: Echter, 2007), 129.

50. Beyer, *TDNT*, 85, citing Wilhelm Brandt, *Dienst und Dienen im Neuen Testament* (Gütersloh: Bertelsmann, 1931), 71

president of the Pontifical Council *Cor Unum* for Human and Christian Development—drew upon this citation to support his own proposition that "whoever dedicates himself to *diakonia* thus takes on the opposite of reputation, power, and rank that leaders and political entities claim for themselves."[51] Such a comment points back to a deeper connection with the German (Evangelical) tradition. The website of *Cor Unum* states that its activities include the "promotion and encouragement of theological reflection among Pastors in order to strengthen *the Christian roots of Charity*; the Encyclical Letter *Deus caritas est* has a special place in this area."[52] This citation takes on greater significance in light of the German-language page, which translates the preceding italicized phrase as "die christlichen Wurzel der *Diakonie.*"

No wonder, then, that on the occasion of spiritual exercises for members of *Cor Unum* in December 2010, the website issued the invitation to "Responsibles [sic] of the Church's *Diakonia.*" The term appears also in the invitations in French, Italian, and Spanish; in the German version, however, the phrasing is "those with responsibilities for *the church's services to the neighbour* (Dienste am Nächsten)." In April 2011, the preacher to the papal household, Raniero Cantalamessa, chose charity as the theme of his Lenten addresses, the fourth of which he devoted specifically to the theme of service under its New Testament guise of *diakonia.*[53]

Given such patronage—indeed, such dominance—of a theological concept hardly older in Roman Catholic discourse than the Second Vatican Council itself, we are not to be surprised that in 2010 the French Bishops Conference should have announced a three-year pastoral program named *Diaconia 2013.* Nor ought we to be surprised that the main inspiration for the initiative is identified as Pope Benedict XVI's encyclical *Deus caritas est.*[54] Influential as well was a publishing event closer to home in the

51. http://www.zenit.org/article-22486?l=english. In writing an introduction to the Festschrift presented to Cardinal Cordes upon his retirement, Pope Benedict extended a warm expression of thanks to the cardinal for insights he had provided into *caritas* in conversations between the two while Pope Benedict was preparing to write the encyclical.

52. http://www.vatican.va/roman_curia/pontifical_councils/corunum/corunum_en/profilo_en/istituzione_en.html. Italics added. See the German text of the introduction at the *Cor Unum* website under "Publications."

53. Raniero Cantalamessa, "Love Must Be Active: The Social Relevance of the Gospel," as reported by ZENIT news, April, 8, 2011, http://www.zenit.org/.

54. See the address by the president of the National Council for Solidarity, Bishop Bernard Housset of La Rochelle/Saintes, "Diaconie et solidarité: du témoinage au service," *Diaconat Aujourd'hui* 151 (August 2010).

aspirational book *So Tight a Link: When Love of God Becomes Diaconia* by the Etienne Grieu of the Jesuits' faculty of theology in Paris,,[55] nor should we overlook the precedent established in Belgium where the bishops organized "the year of *Diaconia*" in 2003.[56]

Ecclesiologist Alphonse Borras of the Catholic University of Louvain-la-Neuve made apparent his misgivings about the French initiative. Borras has written extensively and sympathetically on the diaconate but, confronted with the concept of *Diaconia 2013* (in September 2011), he had difficulty coming to grips with what "this famous *diaconia*" might mean. The expression is new in "church jargon" and "alien to the usage of the vast majority of catholics," and different groups within the church can make what they want of it.[57]

A sense of theological uneasiness, not to mention impatience, arises here. Borras's words bring to mind the no-nonsense outburst from the eloquent Claude Bridel who had the same sense of something being out of place. His lines from 1971 concluded the first chapter of my 1990 *Diakonia*, which had offered, under the title "The Latter-Day Servant Church," a critique of the newfound theological values of *diaconia* of that period:

We have the inflation of the term and its erection into a veritable myth. To such an extent does everyone speak of serving—baptising the administrative, parish-pump or philanthropic activity with a word that has become banal—that Christian declarations in this style appear merely to be following in the wake of the spirit of the times without any expression being given to just where the service of the church is to be distinguished from various humanitarian projects unless this is by way of a vocabulary that is obscurely technical

---

55. My translation of the title: *Un lien si fort. Quand l'amour de Dieu se fait diaconie* (Paris: Editions de l'Atelier, 2009). Grieu is gracious in acknowledging that *Diakonia: Re-interpreting the Ancient Sources* has introduced "a broad revision of how the term is to be understood" (p. 15), but in the pages devoted to a critique of the revision (pp. 99–108) fails to take account of the basic semantic reality that the Greek term draws all its meaning from the context in which it occurs, and that outside of a context has no identifiable meaning at all. Further, he misconceives the relational element within the semantics: in the usage of *diakon-* terms, the relational orientation is exclusively to the mandating authority not the recipient of the mandated action.

56. See Déclarations des évêques de Belgique 29, *Envoyés pour servir. Année de la diaconie* [2003], http://www.catho.be/index.php?id=582.

57. http://diaconie.eklablog.com/alphonse-borras-diaconie-de-l-eglise-et-ministeres-ord onnes-a5932867

(ministry, *diakonia*) and of a pious phraseology which attempts to give substance to it.[58]

The committee which the French bishops established to make preparations for *Diaconia 2013* contributes—like its 2003 Belgian predecessor—to the misunderstanding of the ancient Greek word that began in the early nineteenth century when the EKD founded the first modern groups of deaconesses and deacons. The new coloring of the word and its entrapment within a narrow semantic spectrum focused on the notion of benevolent service continue to dominate institutional and professional discourse about diaconate and ministry within the EKD and associated traditions.[59] From that base, it has long permeated Roman Catholic discourse in those same areas,[60] a practice which recent usage at the highest levels of curial and even papal pronouncements would seem to have canonized.

Conclusion

The problem with this, however, is that over the course of the last twenty years, scholarly re-interpretations (Collins, Hentschel) disavow any semantic connection between ancient *diakonia* and benevolent activity. The German *Diakonie*, as an expression for loving service of another, is a misnomer. It might better be named the misconceived brainchild of an era now past. This fact raises a further and disturbing problem. If we continue to legitimize the German term and its derivatives in other languages, we raise the expectation in all who read the New Testament that

---

58. Collins, *Diakonia*, 45 (my translation), citing Claude Bridel, *Aux seuils de l'espérance: La diaconat en notre temps* (Neuchatel: Delachaux et Niestlé, 1971), 62.

59. See the recent collection of papers illustrating contemporary pastoral practice in the light of the nineteenth-century tradition of *Diakonie* in Michael Herbst and Ulrich Laepple, eds, *Das missionarische Mandat der Diakonie: Impulse Johann Hinrich Wicherns für eine evangelisch profilierte Diakonie im 21. Jahrhundert*, 2nd edn (Neukirchen-Vluyn: Neukirchener Verlag: 2010).

60. See my account of such developments prior to 1990 in *Diakonia*, 5–45. For the ongoing trend in contemporary Roman Catholic thinking in Germany, see the papers from a conference in Fulda in 2008 on the diaconate in Richard Hartmann, Franz Reger, and Stefan Sander, eds, *Ortsbestimmungen: Der Diakonat als kirklicher Dienst* (Frankfurt am Main: Verlag Josep Knecht, 2009). With one exception, the papers show no cognizance of any other than the conventional German perception. The exception is Bettina Eltrop's "Biblische Grundlagen zum Diakonat," 91–99; even so, her brief account of the Collins/Hentschel re-interpretation (91–93) makes room for overriding values based on the traditional Beyer/*TWNT* perceptions of lowly service.

when they encounter a *diakon-*/service word they are reading an encoded message about love. Such mass misreadings of the scriptures have no place in a church. Nor is it enough to concede the existence of a century of mistranslations and misreadings and attempt then to discount these misreadings as nonetheless "productive" because the nineteenth-century view of *diakonia* laid the foundation for a century and more of high-minded outreach to the neglected of our societies.[61] In so doing, we merely distract the churches from the tasks, first, of discerning the foundational ecclesial reality trumpeted by Paul in "the *diakonia* of reconciliation" (2 Cor. 5:18) and, second, of confronting the challenges of embodying that reality in their institutions.

---

61. This "productive" view of the errors of the past is presented by both Hentschel and H.-J. Benedict. The former, however, urges the priority of the real meaning of the biblical text ("Diakonie in der Bibel," 20), while the latter pragmatically resigns himself to seeing *Diakonie* maintaining its place in the church's vocabulary ("Diakonie als Dazwischengehen," 133). Eberhard Hauschildt addressed the implications of the hermeneutical "blunder" in "Was bedeuten exegetische Erkenntnisse über den Begriff der Diakonie für die Diakonie heute? Eine historische und hermeneutische Skizze," *Pastoraltheologie* 97.9 (2008), 307–14.

PART TWO

Diakonia in the Early Church

4

How Ancient Greeks Thought of Diakonia

WHY DID EARLY Christians use the name *ministry/diakonia* for the roles of preaching and of inter-church delegation and for a number of other functions within the community? To this question there is a widely accredited contemporary answer, and then there is the different answer that this chapter will provide. Both answers glow with the romance of language, the contemporary answer sparkling with an almost irresistible appeal. Let us first look briefly at that one. It is an answer with which many readers will be familiar.

The Servant Myth

Preceding papers show that people generally think of *diakonia* as being especially expressive of service to the needy and as originating in the ancient Greek vocabulary for slavery. Prior to the nineteenth century, however, virtually no one drew attention to such characteristics of this word or of its cognates. Perhaps the only thing about the words which attracted occasional comment was that while the words were almost always translated into English by words like *ministry* and *minister*, in two New Testament passages and in many other early Christian writings, the English words used are instead *diaconate* and *deacon*. Something similar happened in other European languages. We will not delay on this seeming inconsistency of translation, and only remark on it to indicate the level of interest these words attracted in previous periods of scholarship.

In modern times, interest in the words sharpened noticeably when a story began to emerge explaining why it was that the words came to prominence among the early Christians. How prominent this was we can infer from the way Luke named the basic churchly activity "ministry/*diakonia* of the word" (Acts 6:4). The story goes like this. Early disciples were particularly responsive to the fact that the Lord Jesus had lived, taught, and died in lowly and even degrading circumstances. In seeking to represent this leading characteristic of their master in their own code of behavior and in their way of association as a congregation or church, they looked around for a suitable set of words to adopt. They did not have to look far because the best words were already part of the language of their central rite. This rite, of course, was their eucharistic meal, at which they celebrated—among other things—the memory of the master who said he was among them "as one who serves/*diakonōn*" (Luke 22:27).

With this tradition about Jesus as a beginning, the story of the words soon developed along broader lines. If the master chose to be seen as a servant, the leaders of congregations had to follow. As a point of language within their organizations, this meant that they could not use the normal Greek terms for masters and rulers because these implied dignity and power. Hence their choice of the *diakonia* words. The background of these words, so the story is careful to explain, was where the story about Jesus at the supper put them. They were words for the slaves who waited at tables, and they were part of the everyday language of the Greek world, a world so full of slaves of various kinds. Gradually the words were used to apply to more and more of the life of the Christian community and were constantly signaling to Christians that whatever they did was to be done in the spirit of the Lord who served others (compare, as always, Mark 10:45).

When modern writers trace this story of the words, they often remark on how the meanings of the ordinary Greek word "developed" under the impact of this experience within early Christian communities. They may comment too on how innovative and, indeed, how creative the early Christians were in developing this part of their terminology. The story is represented in many influential books and encyclopedias published around the 1960s. Some are still in use as textbooks in theological colleges, like Eduard Schweizer's *Church Order in the New Testament* and Hans Kung's *The Church*.

The theological student—and today this student is as likely to be a mature adult seeking a renewed appreciation of his or her position in the church as to be the young man or woman studying for ordination—will be directed at some stage to the second of the twelve volumes of Kittel's *TDNT* for the purpose of reading the article about *diakonia* and its cognates by H. W. Beyer. This study appeared in German in 1935 and in English in 1964, and for our purposes can be considered the scholarly prop on which the contemporary view of ministry/*diakonia* leans. Beyer presents a lot of information on occurrences of the words in pre-Christian Greek literature before moving into an account of the words in the New Testament. The lines of development are as just sketched here, and one comes away with a view of *diakonia* as expressing "the full sense of active Christian love for the neighbour" and as a mark of true discipleship of Jesus.

An illustration of how far this view has traveled since 1935, and at what depth it is still working in the churches, is in the report that the general secretary of the Central Committee of the World Council of Churches made on the eve of the World Council's Eighth Assembly in Canberra in 1991. The second of the report's three sections is devoted to a vigorous discussion of the churches' responsibility for what is called diakonia—no italics, just another English word—and described as "a manifestation of practical love for human beings who are in need" as well as being held up as "constitutive of our identity as the church"[1] There is nothing new in this. The fashion was established in the World Council's policies in the 1950s, and it derives from the word studies of two or three scholars and the uncritical reception of their conclusions by writers on church and ministry.

What follows in this chapter is a sampling of what Classical and Hellenistic Greek literature evidences about *diakonia*. This will reveal part of the actual story of how early Christians came to designate their leading religious functions as *diakonia*. The story is not as romantic as the one just briefly told, but is true to the ways of language. We will begin with an incident from the life of one of the great storytellers of those times.

The Prophet Who Lived in an Emperor's House

Jotapata was one of half a dozen important towns of Galilee that a well-to-do thirty-year-old Jew known to us as the historian Flavius Josephus was commissioned to defend against the Roman army during the revolt of the Jews in 67. The Roman army was under the command of Vespasian, who, in an unsettled period in the succession of power in Rome, would be proclaimed emperor by the army in the Middle East in 69 and reign for ten years. The lives of these two men became intimately connected in almost unbelievable circumstances.

After a siege lasting forty-seven days, Vespasian subdued Jotapata—at the expense, Josephus records, of the lives of forty thousand

1. E. Castro, "Report of the General Secretary", *The Ecumenical Review* 42 (1990), 337–48, citing 340–41.

inhabitants—and two days later captured Josephus, who was hiding in
a cave. Imprisoned, Josephus was to be sent for display to Emperor Nero
but within two years had instead become an associate of Titus, Vespasian's
successor as Roman military commander in Judaea, during the long siege
of Jerusalem. When Jerusalem's demolition was complete, Josephus
accompanied the victorious Titus to Rome to spend the rest of his days
living in a villa that had been the home of Emperor Vespasian.

For an explanation of this remarkable change in the fortunes of
Josephus we have to rely on his own writings. While scholars discuss both
the reliability of his account and the motives inspiring his portrayal of
this critical period of Jewish history, there is no denying the drama of the
story or the literary skill of the narrator. For our purposes, the interest is in
how Josephus's fortunes changed as a direct result of him claiming to be
a minister/*diakonos* of God.

Josephus had not been hiding alone from the Romans in the cave
by Jotapata. With him were no less than forty other fugitives. They were
discovered, and Vespasian sent for Josephus to surrender. This his companions would not allow a Jewish general to do, and they instructed him
to either commit suicide or receive execution from them. Josephus coun-
tered by making a speech on the immorality of suicide, which so inflamed
the group that they attacked him. Surviving this, Josephus next proposed
that they draw lots to determine which one would kill another and thus
they might all escape the taint of suicide. As Josephus tells it, the fugitives
died one by one until he and one other were left alone, whom he then
persuaded—for the best of ethical reasons—not to proceed any further.
Josephus surrendered to the Romans and was taken to Vespasian.

Josephus emerges from this stratagem not quite the coward as at first
appears because built into the tense scene, but not mentioned in our summary, is an account of how at this moment he came to an awareness that
he had an as yet unfulfilled role to play before the Romans in the name of
the Jewish God. He was thus under an obligation to survive. This awareness
broke upon him during a parley with the Roman representative who had been
sent to press for his surrender and as the threatening shouts of the crowd outside filled the cave. His words are carefully chosen and, as we can sense even
from the English translation that follows, are rhetorically balanced to achieve
an imposing effect. The passage is from his *Jewish Wars* (3.351–354):

> Suddenly there came back into his mind those nightly dreams in
> which God had foretold to him the impending fate of the Jews and

the destinies of the Roman sovereigns. He was an interpreter of dreams and skilled in divining the meaning of ambiguous utterances of the Deity; a priest himself and of priestly descent, he was not ignorant of the prophecies in the sacred books. At that hour he was inspired to read their meaning, and, recalling the dreadful images of his recent dreams, he offered up a silent prayer to God. "Since it pleases thee, who didst create the Jewish nation, to break thy work, since fortune has wholly passed to the Romans, and since thou hast made choice of my spirit to announce the things that are to come, I willingly surrender to the Romans and consent to live; but I take thee to witness that I go, not as a traitor, but as thy minister [*diakonos*]."

The list of Josephus's credentials here is impressive. As well as being a priest from a line of priests, and thus in the eyes of his readers set apart to mediate between God and mortals, he was also skilled in divination and thus enjoyed access to God's "ambiguous utterances" in dreams. Beyond that, he was versed in the Jewish scriptures and, at that moment, had arrived at the perception of their ultimate prophetic import.

Compounded with this professional knowledge was the ominous realization born of communing with God in dreams about the hidden fortunes of Jews and the Empire. The most astonishing aspect of this apologia appears in the prayer where he expresses the belief that God's work with the people of the ancient covenant was at an end. In such a momentous context, choosing his words carefully, and leaving the word of his choice to the very end of his elaborate Greek period, Josephus nominates himself as the minister/*diakonos* of God who must not die before he has delivered God's message to the Romans.

Josephus takes his role as God's minister/*diakonos* more deeply still into his history of the times. On hearing that he is to be sent to Emperor Nero, he requests an audience with Vespasian, and in the presence of his son Titus and two of Titus's friends, addresses him boldly (3.400):

You imagine, Vespasian, that in the person of Josephus you have taken a mere captive; but I come to you as a messenger of greater destinies. Had I not been sent on this errand by God, I knew the law of the Jews and how it becomes a general to die.

For "messenger," Josephus here writes *aggelos* instead of *diakonos*, and in his address goes on to announce, while Nero is still emperor and while the complex historical events of his succession are yet to unfold,

> You will be Caesar, Vespasian, you will be emperor, you and your son here. Bind me then yet more securely in chains and keep me for yourself; for you, Caesar, are master not of me only, but of land and sea and the whole human race. For myself I ask to be punished by stricter custody, if I have dared to trifle with the words of God.

The immediate impact of this daring prophecy was not great. Vespasian tended to discount it as a piece of special pleading, but at least Josephus was not sent to Rome, and for two years was a prisoner of war in Caesarea under not particularly arduous conditions. He took a second wife, a fellow Jewish prisoner. When, however, the army in Caesarea proclaimed Vespasian emperor in 69, Josephus reports that Vespasian began to reflect on the providence that had brought him to this state and was reminded of the prophetic words of the Jewish general. On finding that Josephus was still in chains, Vespasian called a gathering of officers and friends to remind them also of "the divine prophecies" of this one-time military opponent, and he declared (4.626):

> It is disgraceful that the one who foretold my attainment of power and was the minister [*diakonos*] of God's voice should still rank as a prisoner of war or endure the lot of a bound criminal.

We have seen what Josephus's subsequent career and rewards were: he would be the favorite of emperors and the historian of the conflict between Rome and his own people. But while scholars continue to discuss the accuracy of this picture of himself—a comprehensive survey is by Per Bilde, *Flavius Josephus between Jerusalem and Rome*—we can be sure of the words he used and of the value he attached to them. In this almost melodramatic turnaround in his personal fortunes, the pivot is his realization that he is a spokesman for God. What God requires him to announce is a secret of the future and a mystery of greater proportion than any prior prophet of his race had comprehended. It was the end, as he wrote, of God's "work" for his chosen nation.

At the very moment he discovers his calling and accepts it in prayer before God and at the moment the emperor acknowledges the role of the prophet, Josephus writes the word *minister/diakonos*. As a writer, he could not be more emphatic in the attention he is drawing to the significance of this designation. Other terms were at hand; one of them he used in presenting himself to Vespasian at Jotapata (*messenger/aggelos*), but for the climactic moments in his dramatic account of the incident that changed his life Josephus selects *diakonos*. His choice speaks to us not only of the place the word held in his own literary thesaurus but also of the place he knew it held in the esteem of his readers.

The World's Greatest Storyteller

In the next pages we will draw on other passages from ancient literature that illustrate in a significant way the uses writers made of the word *diakonia* or its cognates for the purpose of expressing ideas about delivering messages, especially messages which came from another world. From these we will move to passages demonstrating the authority of the minister/*diakonos* and will conclude by examining what it meant to be a minister/*diakonos* at a banquet. In all of this we will take note of how ancient writers found these words suggestive of the religious connotations they wished to raise.

The first story speaks for itself. It is based on the life of Aesop, which itself lends the story a particular prestige. The life was written in the first century (*Vita G*) and was thus almost contemporary in its use of minister/*diakonos* with letters written by Paul and his colleagues in the early Christian churches.

One day Aesop was working in the fields. He was a simple and good man and knew more about the fields and about the animals that lived there and about the life of mortal beings than he was ever able to say. For Aesop had been dumb from birth.

As Aesop was working, a stranger came across the fields to ask him the way. Aesop could not speak but he had good eyes for seeing, and in the stranger he saw the goddess Isis. He bowed in reverence before her.

Aesop could only make signs to show the stranger the way. The sun was hot, and Aesop kindly offered the stranger his own food and water to help her on her way. In the heat of the afternoon, he went aside to the shade to rest and sleep.

The stranger did not forget the kindness of the man in the field. She was not really Isis. Isis was the precious bond of the universe, and this fair form was her herald on earth. And now she prayed that Isis would reward Aesop for his kindness.

Isis heard her prayer. While Aesop slept in the fields, Isis sent Aesop the power of speech, and she sent the Muses to give him the gift of noblest eloquence.

Isis did this because Aesop had shown the way to her straying messenger from heaven (*diakonos*).

Aesop woke up, his tongue was loosed, and he began to give names to what he saw around him: the hare, the lamb, the ants, and the lion.

Winged Feet

Hermes, known to many through the Latin mythology as Mercury, son of Zeus and Maia, and—as he boasts—grandson of Atlas, was mischievous and efficient. For him, efficiency meant speed. Among his several roles, being messenger of Zeus held priority. As often as not, Zeus's messages were assignations with mortal women, and because—as Maia observed—lovers tend to be hasty, Hermes had to be smart about his task. But he had other jobs to fit in. He was a cupbearer to the gods, most of whom had very little to do and could thus keep him busier than he would wish. He had also on occasion to convey the dead to Hades, which could involve him, as we shall see, in a tête-à-tête with Charon that he could do without. He liked to fit in a bit of thieving, too. One haul as a child, on Lucian's account at least, included Poseidon's trident, Ares's sword, Apollo's bow and arrow, and Hephaestus's smithing tongs. Mortals respected this naughtiness and made him the patron of thieves. One fed-up Athenian who had been robbed of a lambswool cloak left an impious prayer wishing hell on the thief and for Hermes the messenger/*diakonos* to take him there. Hermes was the patron of merchants, too, but whether this was because merchants were considered shifty and two-timers or because their trading took them on many laborious journeys it might not be polite to inquire.

For all his chattiness, Hermes had his serious moments; his presence at a banquet was esteemed as promoting good conversation. In the fifth book of Heliodorus's impossibly romantic novel, *Theagenes and Charicleia* (perhaps familiar to readers also as *The Ethiopians*), on the occasion of a sacrificial feast in honor of Hermes, the rogue merchant Nausicles is well pleased with himself for having traded the fair virgin Charicleia for a precious stone that he was more enamored with and settles down to relax in conversation over wine. His companion compliments him on the whole arrangement and cannot fail to see the connection with the god of discourse whom they had just honored in sacrifice.

> I am filled with admiration at the sumptuousness of your sacrifice, and I cannot think how anyone could render Hermes more propitious than by making a contribution to the feast of the thing which is appropriate to Hermes—discourse.

To the Hellenist Christian, Luke, Hermes was never far out of mind. In one story from the hinterland of Asia Minor, when Paul and Barnabas find themselves among the god-enthusiasts of those parts, they are wildly received as gods visiting earth. The priest of the temple of Zeus organized bullocks for the sacrifice and flowers for the sacred garlands of the banquet, while the mob recited their theology and made Barnabas their Zeus and Paul their Hermes. Luke explains that they identified Paul as Hermes because he was "pre-eminent in speech" (Acts 14:12). These people of Lystra were speaking the native Lycaonian language of the region, but had they spoken Greek, Paul and Barnabas would have heard through the hubbub much mention of "minister/*diakonos*."

Another Hellenist from the century before Luke, Diodorus Siculus, would have understood this scene as clearly as Luke because he too had written in appreciation of Hermes's "clarity in expounding everthing given into his charge" and had praised his "art of the precise and clear statement of a message" (5.75.2). A later writer knew that the reason Hermes was "pre-eminent in speech"—to re-use our translation of Luke's phrase, because the Greek here is almost identical—was because he was "the guardian of true knowledge of the gods" (Iamblichus, *De mysteriis*, 1).

Luke was aware of such popular perceptions and of the dangers to his gospel if men like Paul were to be taken for "gods in the likeness of men" (Acts 14:11). For this reason, I suspect, he was careful never to call any of his heroes of the mission *diakonoi*/ministers, even though he saw great value in calling the mission a *diakonia*. He wanted no confusion in the minds of his Greek readers and listeners about the kind of ministry/*diakonia* they were receiving or about the kind of messenger/*diakonos* who carried it out. These were men engaged in a ministry to deliver a message about God's deeds on earth; they were not men—much less godlike men—who were visiting this earth with news of their god from heaven.

Heaven was Hermes's home, and he begrudged the time he had to spend rushing down to Hades or about the Aegean islands and beyond on errands for Zeus—at least that is how the irreverent Lucian liked to present him (*Dialogues of the Gods*, 24):

Here I am only just back from Sidon, where he sent me to see after Europa, and before I am in breath again—off I must go to Argos, in quest of Danae, "and you can take Boeotia on your way," says father, "and see Antiope." I am half dead with it all.

Lucian, who wrote a century after the first Christians, depicts in one essay an encounter between Hermes and Charon, the boatman of the underworld who conveyed souls of the deceased across the river of the dead. On this occasion Charon called out to a passing Hermes to take him on a tour of the earth where all the souls come from. Hermes had to decline because he was on his way "to deliver something concerning mortal affairs for the God above." For "deliver" Lucian here writes the verb form of *diakonos* (*Contemplantes*, 1). In reply, Charon dug deep into his mythology to appeal to Hermes as "co-conductor" of the dead, that is, the one who shared with him the task of bringing the dead to the underworld. In this he returned to Hermes's title of honor in Homer, which is *diaktōr*, a poetic older cousin of the newer word *diakonos*. Sharers in the Greek culture were totally familiar with this linguistic connection. The great medieval dictionary of Byzantium explains that *diaktōr* means "conveyor of the dead" and gives *diakonos* as an alternative word (*Etymologicon magnum*, 268).

Getting to Heaven

In another essay, Lucian aims to poke fun at those who believe that the gods have all the answers. So he puts it into the head of someone who has got into a muddle in the schools of philosophy to fit himself out with a set of wings. His plan is simple. He will fly up to heaven and with some first hand advice up there will settle the unanswered questions once and for all. His name is Menippus, and all goes well. We need not bother with what he finds out in heaven but can take note of a few words between himself and the moon as she sees him passing by. The moon, Selene, is accustomed to seeing messengers passing that way and takes Menippus for another of them. She, too, is fed up with philosophers always wondering who or what she was up there in the sky, and wants Zeus to wipe the lot of them off the face of the earth. Her gentle voice coming out of the silence of the skies rather startles Menippus. "Get me a message to God," she called, and Menippus understands at once, because she uses the verb related to the word for the messenger/*diakonos* of the gods (*Icaromenippus*, 20).

Almost the same phrase occurs in a piece of religious literature that was probably contemporary with the first Christian literature. *The Testament of Abraham* recounts the blessings the patriarch wished to bequeath. As he neared death, Abraham expressed a desire for one last blessing: to be granted a vision of everything his God had made. God's commander-in-chief, Michael, visited him to hear what his last wish might be. Almost overcome with the honor of such a visit, Abraham managed to seize his opportunity to use Michael's high services to get his prayer to God. As one translator put this many years ago, Abraham said, "Be the medium of my word...unto the most High" (G. H. Box, 9.24).[2] The Greek word used by this ancient Jewish writer is again the verb related to the noun *messenger/diakonos* of the gods.

Josephus, the Jewish historian from this era, adopts the same expression when he wanted to retell in the kind of Greek that his non-Jewish readers would appreciate a story in the life of the prophet Jeremiah. The Babylonians had occupied Jerusalem, and the surviving Jewish leaders approached the prophet to know the mind of the Lord on what they should do. In our translation of Jeremiah's Hebrew text we read the reply of the prophet (Jer. 42.4 RSV):

> I have heard you; behold, I will *pray* to the Lord your God according
> to your request, and whatever the Lord *answers* you I will *tell* you.

Here I emphasize the words *pray, answer,* and *tell,* because these are indicating the process of intercession and communication that is to go on in this circumstance. The prophet is in the middle between the people and God; he will go to God in prayer and bring back a response to the people. There is of course no suggestion that the prophet is to visit God's abode, like Michael or Menippus in the preceding passages, but he is to mediate in a prophetic mode. For Josephus this is simply and effectively expressed in Greek through the *diakon-* verb. His Jeremiah has only to say that he

---

2. The Testament of Abraham (London: SPCK, 1927).

will "*diakon-*/approach God at their behest with their message" for his Greek readers to know that the prophet is about to engage himself in the religious business of getting messages to and from heaven (*Antiquities*, 10.177). Coincidentally, in the episode of Josephus's own prophetic role at the beginning of this chapter, Josephus casts himself as a *diakonos* and goes on, in recounting his role as an intermediary between the Roman commander Titus and the besieged Jews of Jerusalem, to cast himself in the role of Jeremiah.

In translating this passage of Jeremiah we notice that the Septuagint, the translation of the Hebrew Bible made for Greek-speaking Jews more than two hundred years before Josephus, simply uses an ordinary word for "praying" to God. And this was good translation, but the comparison with the smarter translation by Josephus reminds us that the Jews who produced the Septuagint seemed to hold the *diakon-* words in some disregard, hardly ever using them in their vast work. In all likelihood this was because the words were too suggestive to them and to Jews living in the Hellenistic Diaspora of the ways of the Greek gods with humans. Let us move a little closer to that world.

The In-between World

Plato shows us the intimate association between the *diakon-* words and the Greek way of thinking about the religious connection between this world and the world of the gods. The most immediate lines of communication— and the most public and official—between gods and mortals were through priests and diviners. Priests were the leaders of sacrifice and were usually identified with the kings in cities that had kings, or with public officials in times of republican rule. Sacrifices were often civic festivals, and the people who gathered at them to feast and sing or perform were conscious that their city was about its business with its gods. Likewise, divination or pronouncement of oracles enjoyed a high civic profile; the city fathers or prominent public officials down to the lowliest citizens would send to a speaker of oracles to know the fate allotted them by the gods.

Given that these parts of their religion were so public and so closely tied to priests and to diviners, we can understand why Plato turned his mind to priests and diviners when he was looking for candidates within society as he knew it who might qualify for the highest role within society as he would like society to be. To determine whether a diviner or a priest would best head the state, Plato analyzes the function of each and characterizes each function as "diaconic" (*diakonos*). He says that the diviners practice "a diaconic skill" because they are interpreters for the gods to humans, and that the priests practice "a diaconic skill" because they give gifts to the gods from mortals and by petition win gifts for mortals from the gods (*Politicus*, 290c–d).

The Jewish philosopher Philo, who was a contemporary of the early Christians, shares with Plato this way of talking about priests. Viewing life from God's perspective, he sees God as needing a "mediating agent" to reconcile humans to himself as well as extend his blessings to men and women. Philo's word here is *[hypo-]diakonos* (*De specialibus legibus*, 1.116). He uses the same word to depict the priests as "intermediaries bearing God's powers" (1.66). In Philo's world there is a whole intermediate range of activity between the great Creator and the merely finite and visible. Sharing responsibilities there are those souls that have not yet become embodied; they are God's agents (*diakonoi*) in governing mortals (*De gigantibus*, 12).

Other philosophers discussing the merely profane processes in which they perceived mediation to be at work similarly write of "diaconic" function. Alexander of Aphrodisias recognizes the "diaconic" process, for example, in the way color reaches us through an intervening body of water (*De mixtione*, 5): the water itself is not colored but transmits the colors of other objects. Similarly, one material (like a piece of glass) can, by transmitting the heat of the sun, cause something else to burst into flame without itself catching fire; by nature it *mediates/diakon-* (*In Aristotelis meteorologicorum libros*, 19). In analyzing the functions of our sense faculties, Themistius points out one basic difference between touch and other senses: in touch we are in direct contact with what we touch, whereas when we hear a sound we are some distance from the source of the noise and need— he says—an intervening body to carry the sound. He writes of "a body *mediating/diakon-* in between" (*In de anima*, 125). When Ammonius wants to explain how ideas come to human beings, he ascribes them to the process of communication through language by which the human voice "acts as a medium" between one soul and another. Again, he uses *diakon-* (*in Aristotelis categorias*, 15).

All these expressions from ancient literature and philosophy show us that in the *diakon-* words the Greeks possessed a subtle tool of language. The words could apply to a good range of activities and were especially useful when a writer needed to convey an idea to do with mediation. The

Greeks were not using these words all the time, however. Many writers never used them at all. But in such instances as we have seen we readily recognize that the words had some special usefulness and were well suited for talk of relations between gods and mortals. In this, of course, the words could add significant perspectives to the way we view what early Christians were trying to say to us in choosing them for what we call ministry.

One of the most striking passages from this point of view is from the Neoplatonist philosopher Iamblichus, who begins his tract *The Mysteries* by reflecting on the difference between the divine and the creaturely. What marks the divine, he concludes, is the power to rule and determine, to set the course of the universe. Apart from that, the divine does not have a role in the created sphere. To ensure that the course of the universe duly unfolds according to divine purposes, however, the Creator has supplied creaturely beings, daemons, superior to mere mortals, to conduct the sphere of things. To humans they may appear divine, but their role is only to do what the gods require; in short, they are "diaconic" or ministers of the divine (*De mysteriis*, 1.20).

Ministers of State

Ministerial activity, in the sense of fulfilling the responsibilities of one's office within governmental, political, and military spheres, is also expressed by the ancient Greeks as *diakonia*. Such usage closely corresponds with our modern-day sense of ministry within government except—and the exception is important—that the Greeks were not using the words in a technical sense. Thus their governments contained officers or used agents who may occasionally be recorded by a writer as having engaged in some ministry/*diakonia* or other, but minister/*diakonos* was not a designation or title of any officer, as the term "minister" can be with us. Demosthenes actually played part of his defense against attacks by Aeschines around the distinction between the designation of office/*archē* and *diakonia* as a general term for an undertaking under a mandate from the state; Aeschines conceded the distinction (Aeschines, 3.13–16; Demosthenes, 18.311).

For Plato, to minister/*diakon-* can apply in a general sense to carrying out duties within the republic (*Laws*, 955c). And here and there among other writers we encounter prominent men being thus designated as they go about their public engagements. Dio Cassius refers to a procuratorship of Gaul as a ministry/*diakonia* (54.21.4); Paenius records Vespasian, the future emperor, as the Roman general who held the mandate to bring war to the Jews (6.18.5); and Aristides, in defense of the high principles under which the Athenian generals Miltiades and Themistocles carried out war against the Persians, argues that they were not merely under a mandate from the state but one from the gods. Aristides adds that to minister/*diakon-* for one's superiors is man's noblest and greatest capacity (2.198–199).

The writings of Josephus contain numerous instances of the author designating mandates of different kinds in this way. In the bitter confrontation of the Jewish deputation with Petronius, legate of the Emperor Gaius (Caligula) to Syria who wanted his own statue erected in the Temple enclosure of Jerusalem, Petronius constantly tried to placate the Jews by stating that he was merely carrying out his mandate from a higher authority (*Antiquities*, 18.262–304, nine instances of *diakon-*). This familiar line of argument did not hold for the senior officers in Caligula's own bodyguard whose consciences could no longer cope with carrying out imperial mandates to torture and to kill (*Antiquities*, 19.41, 42), so they turned on the emperor and assassinated him. In retelling the fate of Haman in the tale of Esther, Josephus works a neat Greek phrase to represent the meaning of the biblical passage. The Bible relates that when the king asked Haman how best to reward a deserving person, Haman outlined a glorious array of honors, thinking he was in line for them himself. The king replied, "Make haste, take the robes and the horse, as you have said, and do so to Mordecai the Jew" (Esth. 6:10), whereas Josephus writes, "Be the minister/*diakonos* of what you have advised me so well about" (*Antiquities*, 11.255).

At Table with the Gods

Among the numerous forms of ministry/*diakonia* we have been encountering in these passages from Greek literature, we have not met any slaves. Nor has any form of the ministry/*diakonia* been of a slavish kind, although we recognize that in one instance of killing and torture it was of an unworthy kind. In that instance, the ministry remained nonetheless a mandate from the highest worldly authority, namely, the Roman emperor. Moreover, those performing other kinds of ministry/*diakonia* have also belonged to ranks of society—or of the gods and spiritual beings—with which we do not associate any derogatory connotation. On the contrary, they have belonged to esteemed levels of society. In such ways is the character of a usage built up. From the uses writers make of their words, from the associations the words gather from the kind of use they are put to, and from the level of language the words are put to work at, we come to know their meaning in particular applications.

In the section above called "The Servant Myth," we met an assessment of ministry/*diakonia* totally different from the kind we have been framing. The assessment began at the level of waiting at tables. Because waiting at tables was considered to be a slavish action, the *diakon-* words were allocated a place in translation of the New Testament and in theology within the terminology of the ancient Greek servile state and culture. From this level, the scholarly comment informed us that the early Christians selected the words for the purpose of matching the values at work in their communities with the values they perceived in a Son of Man who came "to serve" (*diakon-*, Mark 10:45).

Because our own perception of the Greek ministries is at odds with this modern view, a good step for us now will be to test our perception in the same literary environment of waiting at tables that gave rise to the modern view. By considering passages that report servants and slaves waiting on tables, we should encounter instances of the *diakon-* words which will enable us to characterize the usage in this connection. We need to be reminded, however, that most ancient writers refer only incidentally to this aspect of eating and drinking. To build up an adequate picture of waiting at table on the basis of these literary fragments would require many minute references and become tediously academic. (The material is discussed in my *Diakonia*, 154–68.) One way to dodge that academic effect and yet achieve our purpose will be to work through a few of the passages where an ancient author has spent a little time elaborating on his scene. Before sampling that material we will look at one precious source put together by Athenaeus under the Greek title *Deipnosophistae*, a title we might translate as *Philosophers of the Dining Table*.

Philosophers of the Dining Table is a long book from around the end of the second century. Reference books tend to list its author as a linguist, but Athenaeus would be disappointed to be pigeonholed like that. In this book he at least tried to develop a format that might have an appeal for his reader. Today we still enjoy eavesdropping at dinner tables by way of published diaries and the gossip of newspaper columnists. We get inklings about the character of individuals we have heard of but are never likely to meet; we hear what they ate and how much they drank; we pick up ideas for menus and for arranging parties. Athenaeus worked up a format along these lines, allowing his philosophers to do the talking, but he was less intent on gossip and personalities than on registering information and opinions across as broad a tract of life as he could swing the table conversation to.

Among the large array of topics the book discusses are those which occasion a reference to servants and slaves. Naturally, the topic of slavery is itself one of these. Another topic is religious festivals, because these required attendants to apportion shares of the sacrificial meat and wine to the devotees. Related to festivals is the role of the cook, a poor word in English for the man responsible for the ritual slaughter and preparation of the meat; he also required assistants. Dinner parties in grand houses and reports of the eating customs of foreigners or barbarians are likewise occasions for talk about servants. On each of these topics we have not only reports of what the learned gentlemen of this book thought but also a wide range of views gathered from ancient and contemporary literature on the subject. In fact, the philosophers try to outdo each other in the parade of their learning. For today's scholars, this aspect of Athenaeus's book is probably its most significant. In its pages are preserved fragments of many works otherwise lost to the world. For our purposes, however, the book's advantage is that on the topic of servants and waiting at tables we get the view of the author himself and then the views in the literary passages his characters refer to.

We are calling the setting of the book a dinner, but the ancient Greek arrangements for a dinner were more complex than ours. The guests—and the occasion was for men only—were not seated around a table but were reclining or sitting on cushions while low tables were brought to them, each with a course laid out on it. As the courses passed, servants took some tables away and brought in others. This was for the main courses, which together formed the dinner proper or *deipnon*. At its conclusion, a second stage of the gathering began, so separate that other guests might be invited for it. This was for the drinking of wine and eating of desserts, and could be the occasion of musical performances, dancing, and even games. The wine gave its name to this part of the gathering, a *symposion* or "drinking together." This was an occasion not just to indulge in but also to celebrate wine, the gift of the gods. In fact, the first wine of the night was poured out in tribute to the gods. The wine was always mixed with water, the mix being at the discretion of the host. The *symposion* had a ritual air to it and was very ancient. Naturally it required servants, who might be given the formal name of "cupbearers."

Such is the setting in which Athenaeus writes of different kinds of servants. If we look at those moments in his *deipnon* and *symposion* when servants bring in new courses or attend to cupbearing duties, we find that Athenaeus uses several words from the group that the ancient Greeks used for servants and slaves (*pais, oiketēs*, and others), but never *diakonos*. Nor, significantly, is this word or its cognates among terms used by his characters in the discussion of the orders of slavery. The only uses of *diakon-* terms by his characters are in the citations from poets and historians that embellish the discourse, and these all bear reference to the rituals of dining. Because almost all of the cited literature is known to us only in these fragmentary references, we will not attempt to present the details here.

The *diakon-* words would thus seem to be used differently from other words for servants. When we look at Athenaeus's own practice, we see why this is so. Not having used the words to designate the ordinary servicing of the guests at his banquet, Athenaeus turns to them when he is reflecting on the significance of the *symposion* within Greek culture. In this context Athenaeus reveals some of the deeper motivation underlying his decision to compile his book on dining. From at least Homeric times, for the Greeks to gather over food and drink required the presence of their god, to whom the first offering of food and drink was made. The presence of the god enjoined respect on the part of all. The gathering became an acknowledgment of a common Greek heritage, of a historic protection under the gods, and of a commitment to shared values. Highest among these was their identity as Greeks, to whom the greatest indignity would be subjection to barbarian rule or the loss of individual freedom. With this in mind, we appreciate the force of the following statement by Athenaeus (192b):

> With the Greeks of old the only reason for gathering to drink wine was religion, and any garlands, hymns or songs they used were in keeping with this, and the one who was to do the waiting [*diakon-*] was never a slave; rather young sons of free men would pour the wine...just as we read in fair Sappho of Hermes pouring wine for the gods.

Here we notice the emphasis on freedom, the essence of the Greek ideal, and how the ideal must not be compromised by association with something less worthy through the services of a slave. Other writers witness to customs of waiting at tables that enshrine the same ideal. We shall read one of these shortly. Next, from the beginning of these few lines, we notice how a sense of religion encompasses all, giving meaning to the flowers, the songs, and the formalities attending the drinking of the wine. The mention of Hermes is not coincidence. What is good for the gods is a privilege for mortals to share, and in the rituals of the cupbearing-god, mortals have the rationale and model for their own *symposion*. From such an idealistic presentation of the meaning of the Greek banquet does the ministry/*diakonia* of attending to tables take its color and religious value.

A Ritual for Kings and Worshipers

In 1890, scholars published an inscription first discovered in 1883 in a remote and mountainous corner of Asia Minor. The inscription had been cut at the command of King Antiochus I of Commagene in the first century BCE. Unlike many other royal inscriptions, this was not a celebration of a military campaign but was a proclamation or, indeed, revelation that the king was God. In celebration of the divine presence, the inscription lays down the rituals to be observed at the annual sacrifice and banquet commemorating the divine epiphany (the king's birth) and the royal coronation. Regulations for the vesting of the priest and rubrics for the presentation of gifts and execution of the sacrifice are all a prelude to the culmination of the solemn ritual when the god-king decrees that all—both native and foreign—are to participate in the communal feast. They are to enter the holy precinct and be ministered to (*diakon-*) from vessels that the god has consecrated.

The historian Bato of the second century BCE tells of a ritual in Thessaly that is cast on a more human scale but is of no less religious import. King Pelasgus was confronted one day by a stranger who reported the marvel of a lake giving way to the surfacing of new plains. The king responded to the news as to a message from God and set about honoring the bearer of the message. The stranger was to be the center of a festive meal. The king's other guests were instructed to join him in attending on the new guest, but the king himself was the only one who carried out the ministry (*diakon-*). According to Bato, as reported by Athenaeus (640a), the mysterious occasion was the origin of the Thessalonian festival of "kindly fellowship," during which prisoners were freed and strangers and slaves were received as guests, while the masters of households performed the ministry (*diakon-*).

In such ways does the ministry/*diakonia* of tables appear in Greek literature. As noted, basic to its character as religious ritual is the quality this ministry/*diakonia* attains through the nobility of the freedom of its ministers. Nothing servile or slavish attaches to providing either the food which has been given to the gods or the wine which has been the gift of the gods to mortals.

The Jewish philosopher and apologist, Philo, a contemporary of early Christians, was conscious of the Greek claims for the high religious significance of their *symposion* and drew a rather forced comparison between it and a religious ritual of the Jewish sect known as the Therapeutae, whose name means "worshipers" and whom Philo is intent on presenting as the only true worshipers. His purpose was to illustrate how their Jewish ritual meal enshrined a much nobler religious ideal than the Greek, which he portrayed as merely sensuous and degrading. As a feature of either ritual he identifies the service of the attendants as ministry/*diakon-*, ensuring only that in the case of the Greeks the ministry/*diakon-* is defiled by the presence of slaves. while among the Therapeutae, in a truly "holy *symposion*," only free men perform "the ministerial/*diakon-* duties" (*De vita contemplativa*, 70–71).

Special Words

In both Philo and Athenaeus, we surely detect propagandists of Jewish and Greek rituals. To sort out the rights of either claim is not our business. We are simply observing what ancient writers made of the table ritual of ministry/*diakonia*. This designation would seem to be especially marked by them for use in reference to religious ritual. As such, the usage reflects characteristics which we have been observing also in other areas: thus, the *diakon-* words provide a title for a god (Hermes), designations for messages to and from heaven, operations of the powers/*daemons* under God, and the processes of prophecy and intercession. These are all uses within the sphere of religion. Applied to the profane sphere, the words designate undertakings of high moment by persons of some distinction. Were we to provide a full coverage of usage, we would encounter instances of the words referring also to the functions of menial attendants. What we would be drawing attention to in the usage would be the quality of the language and the character of the literature, finding that we were on the high literary levels inhabited by orators, barristers, philosophers, and writers of satire and romance.

Having seen as much as we have, however, we are in a good position to return to some early Christian statements about ministry/*diakonia* that have proved critical in the development of contemporary views about ministry in Christian communities.

5

Diakonia in the Teaching of Jesus

ONE OF THE striking characteristics of the gospels is that they abound with stories of Jesus freeing those who are victims of powerful forces. Jesus restores sight to those who cannot see; Jesus accepts those who are socially marginalized; and Jesus displays in his strong deeds God's good will at work in the world. According to the scene Luke presents at the prophetic beginning of Jesus's ministry in Galilee (Luke 4:18–19), this is also the primary emphasis in what Luke was proposing to teach about Jesus to his community of Christians. The program pulses with the Spirit Jesus claimed for himself on that occasion: "The Spirit of the Lord is upon me...to let the oppressed go free."

In what we read elsewhere about Jesus's ministry, such activity is often presented as the *diakonia* of Jesus. This is particularly evident in books and other materials prepared for deacons. As all deacons know, their very title in the church is *diakonos*, a title clearly connected with *diakonia*. Thus, deacons easily come to see their role as participating in the *diakonia* of Jesus by acting as a *diakonos* or servant of those in need. Of course no gospel writer could have had church deacons in mind because these officers appeared somewhat later in early Christian communities. Lessons to be taken from these gospel narratives are for all those who would follow Jesus.

Occasionally in the narratives—but only occasionally—we actually encounter in the Greek text these *diakon-* words. The following selection of such passages we will read in the light of perceptions about *diakonia* that are possible now that preceding reflections have provided us with more detailed information about what *diakonia* stood for in the ancient Greek-speaking world.

The Diakonia of the Son of Man

The Son of Man came to carry out his mission and give his life as a ran-som for many. (Mark 10:45)

One of the most powerful influences in establishing a servant model of Christian discipleship is a group of teachings in the gospels that appears to establish tight connections between servanthood and discipleship. The most striking piece of teaching in this group occurs in Mark's Gospel and is actually about Jesus himself, but at this point of the narrative the teaching about Jesus is prompted by what Jesus has just been teaching the disciples. Deacons in particular have probably reflected on this pas-sage of the scriptures more than on any other, just as they have heard bishops, theologians, and fellow deacons deliver homilies, lectures, and exhortations on this passage more than on any other. The passage is the one presenting Jesus as "the Son of Man" who "has come not to be served but to serve, and to give his life as a ransom for many" (Mark 10:45). This is the statement that the Second Vatican Council chose for the purpose of giving definitive shape to the role of the church in the modern world. In December 1965, the Council opened its final Constitution with the declar-ation: "The Church is not motivated by an earthly ambition but is inter-ested in one thing only—to carry on the work of Christ...to serve and not to be served."

Breaking the Sentence in Two

In developing teaching for disciples on the basis of this saying, most teach-ers and preachers will use the first part only to form the basis of what they want to say. They will declare, "The Son of Man came not to be served but to serve," and will make it sound as if this is a statement that stands on its own. (The punctuation in the NRSV translation cited above encourages this practice.) In doing this, however, they are leaving off the rest of Mark's statement: "...and to give his life as a ransom for many."

Dividing Mark's whole statement into two parts at the point of the comma after "to serve" certainly makes that first part a convenient tool with which to shape a servant model of the church, of discipleship, and of diaconate. It is Jesus himself who speaks, he appears to be casting him-self in a servant role, and the statement is ultimately directed at disciples because it forms the climax of teaching to the disciples that began at verse

38. In particular, by means of Greek *diakon-* words that our bibles translate these days in terms of service, Jesus is linking the standard by which he has lived with the standard required of disciples.

By contrast with this almost universally accepted understanding of Mark 10:45, the first thing that a close examination of the statement makes us realize is that the saying must be treated not as two halves but as one whole. There is no independent part A, "The Son of Man came not to be served but to serve." There are two reasons for stating this. One arises from what we have come to understand about the way this particular Greek word for "serving" works in sentences, and the other relates to the structure of this particular sentence.

Keeping the Sentence Whole

We will consider the structure of the sentence first. Even before interpreters became fully aware of the meanings this serving/*diakon-* term can carry, they realized that the so-called part A was to be understood only in relation to the second half or part B of the statement. That is, we are not in a position to understand what kind of service Jesus is referring to until we read part B: "and to give his life as a ransom for many." Thus we are to understand that the service of Jesus consists in giving his life as a ransom. It is not service of any other kind.

Preachers—at times even translators and commentators—commonly tell us that in this statement Jesus is saying that he came to serve people. One English bible actually reads "to help people," and in 1989 the prominent lexicographers Louw and Nida recommended this approach to translation of *diakon-* here. On such an understanding, Mark's statement invites us to envisage those nameless suffering and distressed people who crowd around Jesus in so many Gospel stories and receive health and solace. And on the basis of this kind of service, all Christians—in particular the church ministers named deacons—are urged to commit themselves to a similar involvement with the suffering and distressed people of their societies. In such ways are we to associate ourselves with the service or *diakonia* of Jesus.

Further reflection upon the sentence at Mark 10:45, however, leads us to the realization that we are not permitted to read the statement in this way at all. An understanding of standard patterns of language explains why. It also shows that at the end of what we are calling part A, it is not people who are the recipients of the service. Parts A and B are linked by "and" in a way that enables the second part to clarify what kind of service the speaker had in mind in the first part. This is a common pattern of speech in situations where the first part of a statement expresses itself through a word that lacks a referent or that is indeterminate in meaning. We all make such statements frequently.

An illustration of the pattern in English would be the following: "She was determined to serve again and make the company profitable." On reading that sentence it is not until we pick up clues from the words *company* and *profitable* that we are in a position to know the type of service which the individual is determined to undertake. From those clues we perceive that she was a strong-minded businesswoman and that the type of service she intended to provide would consist in business management. Change a word or two and we arrive at another kind of service. Reading "comfortable" instead of *profitable*, for instance, we enter a different situation: "She was determined to serve and make the company comfortable." We are now in a dining room or a restaurant, and we are encountering an embarrassed host or waitress who is determined to repair a delay caused by a guest's faux pas or by an accident with the soup.

Manufacturing a Theology of Service

We can learn a little more about this common pattern of language by contrasting it with a different pattern formed around "and." In this second pattern, the significant word in the first part of a statement does have a referent, that is, it does identify a specific situation. Thus, "She was determined to serve out her term and begin a new venture." Here "and" is simply coupling two discrete actions whose only relationship to one another is that they are to be performed in sequence. We clearly perceive each action for what it is.

This is the way many people are reading Jesus's saying in Mark 10:45. Consequently, they think Mark was writing of two separate activities of Jesus, one referring to his work of service among people and the other referring to the offering of his life, one in the course of his public ministry and the other on the cross.

Given the broad acceptance of such an understanding of Mark 10:45, some are drawn to speculate theologically on the connection between two such aspects of Jesus's ministry. In fact, some of this speculation colors reflections on the theological character of the ministry of deacons. It does so in the following way: in extending selfless and loving service to those in need, deacons would be extending across time the *diakonia* of Jesus by which he brought redemption to the world.

Getting Back to the Meaning of a Word

Readers may be interested to know that some such theological connection between these so-called parts of Mark 10:45 was what attracted me to the study of *diakonia* in the first place. Mark's verse appeared to me at the time to offer rich possibilities for deepening an appreciation of the nature of ordained ministry, opening up its Jesus-power.

Attractive as such a hypothesis may have been, however, its window of opportunity closed once a study of how ancient Greeks used the *diakon-* words revealed that the service Jesus was speaking of was indeterminate. In other words, Jesus's statement in the so-called part A about coming to serve cannot be understood until we read part B, where we discover that his service is to give his life as a ransom for many. The pattern of this statement is, then, the same as the pattern we considered above about the business woman "determined to serve *and* make the company profitable," where "and" introduces the few words explaining the kind of service she is offering. In such cases, we need clues from the rest of the sentence before we know what the service consists of.

Identifying the Diakonia of Jesus

This leads to another observation about the structure of this saying attributed to Jesus in Mark. We have been referring to part A and understanding it to contain, "The Son of Man came not to be served but to serve." Since the meaning of such a statement is incomplete or at least obscure, we would be better advised to restructure the sentence. This restructuring makes the following words part 1: "The Son of Man came not to be served." We will look at this new part 1 in the following section. For now, part 2 of the sentence becomes: "but to serve and give his life as a ransom for many." With the sentence restructured in this way, part 2 is self-contained and conveys a full and free-standing idea: "The Son of Man came to serve by giving his life as a ransom for many." (Grammarians have a word for this kind of "and" in a sentence; they call it *epexegetical*, and by that they mean that "and" introduces the part of the sentence which explains or clarifies the part preceding "and.")

The other thing in Mark's famous sentence requiring further clarification is the question about who it is that the Son of Man is serving. The answer is not far away. The whole of Mark's narrative is about the answer to that question. At Jesus's death, the centurion said, "Truly, this man was God's son." At his baptism at the beginning of the narrative, a voice from heaven proclaimed about that same Son, "You are my son, my loved son: I take my delight in you." The Gospel that Mark then proceeds to write follows the Son's path from one proclamation of his identity to another because that was the path of the Son's calling. It was also the path that the disciples and the Markan community were called to follow. The *diakonia* of Jesus, as dramatically contextualized by Mark in chapter 10, at the end of the Galilean mission and on the road to Jerusalem, was to serve the One whose voice called to him at his baptism, and the Son of Man would perform this service by carrying out the mission to which that voice had consecrated him.

This picture of the *diakonia* of Jesus is what Mark thought we would make of his carefully constructed scene. That is how he understood the service of Jesus. No ancient Greek would have had a problem arriving at this understanding. Certainly Mark had no worries about the statement not being clear. In fact, he would be very surprised to find us getting confused about it.

Realities of Life Among Disciples

The Son of Man did not come to have attendants waiting on him. (Mark 10:45)

If what we have been discussing provides us with the gist of what Mark meant to say in part 2 of this pivotal statement about the mission of the Son of Man, what are we to make of part 1, "The Son of Man came not to be served"? Here again there would have been no problem for the ancient Greek and, indeed, the context eases even the reader of a modern translation into its meaning. The writing is in fact very effective.

The immediate context is an argument among the disciples as they followed Jesus along the road from Galilee to Jerusalem. After James and

John have sought high places beside Jesus in his glory, the other ten complain of the arrogance and self-seeking of these two. Jesus's response is forceful and sets the tone and imagery for what issues at verse 45 in his statement about service. Let us look into the first part of his response.

To disciples under an illusion of impending grandeur, as James and John have just been portrayed—"one at your right and one at your left" (Mark 10:37)—the teacher gives a sharp reminder of the realities of life.

In the mention by Jesus of the government (verse 42: "their rulers"— let us think of grasping Roman representatives of an absolute despot in the Emperor Tiberius and most of his successors in the first century), of "great men" (let us envisage grossly conspicuous consumers and rapacious exploiters), of how they "lord it over people" (disdaining what we call individual rights), and lastly—the most terrible of all—of "authority" (read an easy disregard for life and property when it comes to an issue of who rules the day), we glimpse a Mediterranean world where wealth of an enormous scale resided in an elite comprising little more than 1 percent of the population. Among the masses, 30 percent were slaves, while the rest were either unemployed (in metropolitan centers like Alexandria and Antioch) or were being ground down under imperial imposts and by labor in the fields from dawn to dusk to try and keep ahead of debt to landlords and religious authorities.

A small middle class of civil servants and merchants experienced some sense of security, but their interest and social obligation lay in aping the style of the impossibly rich in the pursuit, at any cost, of the most precious possession the ancient Mediterranean world had to offer. This was honor. Honor was the public perception that one owned cash, property, and slaves, and could entertain expectations of recognition within the great empire of the divine Caesar of the hour. With honor came the correlating obligation to despise the general populace.

A Different Kind of Honor

Jesus said:

> You know how those supposed to govern the Gentiles lord it over them,
> and their great men exert authority over them;
> but this is not your way.
> Instead, whoever wants to be great among you will be your servant,
> and whoever wants to be first among you will be every one's slave.

Let us recall that Jesus is speaking to two men who think he is taking them on the road to what they call "glory." By "glory" we are to understand "honor," at a level unparalleled even by the legendary honor of emperors.

Jesus's opening comment—"this is not your way"—brusquely disillusions anyone living in hope of honor. A new kind of society opens before those who have been harboring visions of a share in imperial greatness. In terms of social reward and personal satisfaction, the panorama is bleak. It is empty of the timeless symbols of upward mobility, dignity, and success. The contrast between the political and social realities of the first century and the conditions of being within a discipleship of the Son of Man is absolute. So absolute in fact that there is no point of contact between them.

In contrasting the lordship of the great men with conditions of discipleship the sayings are not presenting a sociological spectrum, with the emperor at one end of a continuum and slaves at the other. Rather, the sayings present an alternative way of looking at life. Instead of passing from one glorious end of the social spectrum to another that is extremely less comfortable and privileged, the sayings make a switch from the Roman Empire to a totally different realm, to a kingdom not of this world, where awful power and glowing honor are not factors at work. In contrast to the war, taxes, trade, exploitation, and wealth of Rome stands a realm of discipleship. Within the realm of discipleship operate forces unknown to emperors and military champions. These are the life forces within parables that tell of a young man reaching a solitary decision to leave a messy life behind (Luke 15:17–18), the tumultuous inner revolutions within the woman embracing Jesus (Luke 7:38), and the courage to drink the cup he would drink (Mark 10:38).

Empire and Discipleship

The clue to the meaning of these sayings about the nature of discipleship is in such sets of contrasts. The sayings, of course, put the contrasts in a condensed form, and are the more effective for that. And it would be a mistake on our part to take just one word out of this context, which is both complex and dense, and allow its supposed values to dictate the message of the teacher. Rather, the teaching is to emerge from the context of the passage and from the alternative values that the teacher dangles before obtuse followers.

After the descriptive allusions to the ways of this world, the teacher deftly contrasts the dominant values of the two realms of Empire and of discipleship within the kingdom of God:

Empires of the World	Discipleship of Jesus
great	servant
first	slave

The simple diagram, read with the text of Mark 10:43–44 and within the context we have just set, shows that the words *servant* and *slave* are introduced into the sayings for the purpose of identifying the extreme contrast between two social groups. These two words stand opposed to *great* and *first*. The imperial group pursues values that are immediately recognizable and have been part of our historical understanding and folklore from time immemorial. But Jesus insists that discipleship does not operate by the principles that make one "great" or "first." Instead, discipleship operates by principles that no social organization has ever known; rather, the sayings propose that discipleship is not a sociological function at all. The contrast with empire indicates that discipleship functions at a level where power does not exist. The situation is not only that power is inappropriate within discipleship, but that discipleship is an environment which is not receptive of power.

The two words *servant* and *slave* indicate that discipleship—the preferred term in the gospel tradition is "kingdom of God"—opens up a different plane of existence where the style and interplay of social forces have no relevance. One term is of no more significance than the other. The fact that one of them is the Greek word *diakonos* ("servant") does not give it greater significance than the other (*doulos*, "slave"). *diakonos* has no reference to later honorable functions within a settled ecclesiastical establishment. Moreover, it is wholly unlikely that anyone in Mark's audience knew what such a *diakonos*/deacon was. These sayings were circulating in Christian circles well before Mark composed his gospel in a period certainly predating the existence of people we call deacons. The term *servant/diakonos* in this saying is just a complementary expression to the term *slave/doulos*, just one word beside another to illustrate that the kingdom of God is not a political playground and is not to be defiled by ambition, greed, and oppressive surges of power.

A String of Sayings

This understanding of the sayings in one of Mark's most significant passages is confirmed by a consideration of similar sayings that occur elsewhere in the gospel tradition. One of these occurs in a situation not unlike that relating the ambitions of James and John. The disciples "had argued with one another who was the greatest" (Mark 9:34), and Jesus "summoned the Twelve"—a sign that Mark is considering issues of discipleship as they affect leaders in the community—and told them (9:35):

> If anyone wants to be *first*, let him be last of all and *servant/diakonos* of all.

At Matthew 23:11 we read:

> He who is *greatest* among you will be your servant/diakonos.

At Luke 9:48:

> The *lowliest* among you all, he is truly *great*.

This string of similar sayings reveals how deeply the teaching they contained permeated the tradition. These sayings are linked not only with one another but also with teaching that uses children as points of reference to the nature of the kingdom of God. At Mark 9:36 (similarly at Luke 9:47), Jesus moves on from rebuking the Twelve to "set a little child in the center of their circle," and "taking him in his arms," said to the Twelve:

> Whoever receives one of such children in my name receives me.

The introduction of the little child into the equation tells us much about the teaching expressed in the sayings about the lowliest, the last, the slave, and the servant. The little child does not participate in decisions which affect the shape of the adult world and yet, powerless, flourishes in the relationship of love and dependence with its parents. Incapable of deploying

power, the child enjoys the fullness of life and becomes another illustration of the paradox of the kingdom.

The Richest Experience

All the sayings are teaching disciples that in accepting a place in the
kingdom, members of the community are to abandon processes by which
societies operate. Instead they are to stand in relationships with God and
with one another in a community of discipleship. The sayings are not a
call to abstain from the management of affairs or to eschew the responsibility of authority. They are a call, however, to recognize that the management of affairs and the deployment of authority are activities of this
world, whereas the kingdom of God establishes itself in a community of
relationships. The community will no longer provide communion when
power distorts the dynamism of relationships.

In giving expression to this teaching the sayings have occasion to draw
on the word *diakonos*. There is nothing special in this choice. The term
does not contribute anything more specific to the discussion than what is
already conveyed about qualities required in disciples by the other terms
last, lowliest, and *slave*. The expression *servant/diakonos* is just another in
the series of analogies on which the sayings build. As the child is the most
immature of the human community, so within the great house the servant
is the most powerless. And as the child has the richest experience of love
and security, so the kingdom reveals its wealth and power where there is
the recognition of the least claim to it. We will see further reaches of this
teaching in Luke's presentation of the Lord as the community's enduring
friend.

The Community's Enduring Friend

I am in your midst as one who waits on you. (Luke 22:7)

Anyone reflecting on the mission of the Son of Man as expressed at
Mark 10:45 will eventually be led to reflect on the scene of the Last Supper
in which Luke also presents Jesus speaking of himself as a servant by
using a *diakon-* word. Although fifty years ago there was much scholarly
discussion on the relationship between these two passages, in my view
there can be no doubt at all that the character of Luke's passage is a result
of Luke's decision to recontextualize Mark's passage about the Son of Man

which we have just been considering. Luke was thoroughly familiar with this passage in Mark and recognized its importance.

Reworking Mark

In speaking like this, I am taking for granted that Luke used Mark as a source. In doing so I am aware that in recent years some scholars have been arguing against the standard working hypothesis of relationships between the Synoptic Gospels of Matthew, Mark, and Luke. The case of the literary relationship between Luke and Mark which we are about to touch on has long led me to feel at ease working within the standard hypothesis.

As I hope readers will discover, ancient texts like these speak more authentically and reveal surprising layers of meaning the closer we are able to analyze them. After all, their authors were not just writing stories or memoirs. The short works we call gospels—Mark is only about eleven thousand words—were closely considered in their composition, and the compositions are best considered as narrative theology. The expression is not to be misunderstood. *Theology* is the key word.

As noted above, the passage about the Son of Man occurs in Mark as Jesus moves along the road to Jerusalem with his followers. In Luke, by contrast, the passage occurs when Jesus and the disciples have been in Jerusalem for about a week and are reclining at the Passover meal on the night Jesus is to be betrayed. Luke has set this scene with care. After precise instructions on preparations for the Passover, Jesus declares the value to him of having them all gathered at the Passover table: "I have longingly desired to eat this Passover with you before I suffer." The sharing of the bread and wine follows. Then, unlike in Mark and Matthew, Luke's narrative does not move directly to the events leading to the arrest of Jesus but pauses while Jesus delivers a discourse to the disciples.

The discourse consists of pieces of teaching which have each had a place somewhere else in other gospel narratives. The dispute about greatness at the Passover table in Luke 22:24–27 clearly must stand in some kind of relationship to the dispute recorded by Mark prior to Jesus's arrival in Jerusalem (Mark 10:35–45). We will consider that. Following the dispute we have Jesus endorsing the status of the apostles within the kingdom—a title carefully nurtured by Luke (6:13; 22:14; Acts 1:2) to ensure that his own community strove to remain faithful to what he later calls "the apostles' teaching and fellowship" (Acts 2:42). In this part of the short discourse, however, Luke has constructed his teaching (22:29–30) on the basis of some teachings which he held in common with Matthew (Q, a collection of Jesus' sayings common to Matthew and Luke) and which Matthew used prior to Jesus's arrival in Jerusalem (Matt. 19:28). Next in Luke, Jesus—still at the table—addresses both a warning and a reassurance to Simon Peter; by contrast, Mark's prediction of Peter's denial occurs on the walk from the Passover room to the Mount of Olives (Mark 14:29–31). After addressing Simon Peter, Jesus delivers instructions to the apostles about preparedness for flight. These echo earlier instructions about the urgency of the mission, as at Luke 9:3. In other words, throughout Jesus's discourse after the Passover we encounter little original material, and I believe Luke has put the discourse together from a variety of sources for the reason that he wanted to present a discourse from the master at a meal with his disciples before the master was snatched from his intimate circle.

A Hellenistic Artist

Luke was a thoroughly Hellenized literary artist, although the material he was dealing with in the gospel tradition did not provide him with many opportunities to display the skills and tastes he had developed within his Greek culture. Nonetheless, in several ways Luke indicates that he was aware he was addressing people of his own kind. In the eyes of this Hellenistic audience Luke's scene of the final—if temporary!—separation of master and disciples at the end of a special meal would not be complete without a farewell address from the master teacher. In addition, the scene had to suggest the convention of the Greek dinner followed by its *symposion.*

Technically the *symposion* was a function distinct from the dinner, although it was only a prolongation of the dinner gathering and was conducted in the same room. Interestingly, an additional guest list might operate at this point, with people invited to share in the wine while the more stimulating and probably more learned participants displayed their skills and wisdom to the admiration and for the betterment of all. On particular occasions, a significant individual would be expected to hold the attention of the rest of the gathering. And this is the effect Luke creates here.

So it is that Jesus discourses on the nature of the kingdom, a theme in Luke's entire narrative. Luke has presented Jesus as born to sit on the throne of his ancestor David (1:32) and, on his entry to the city where David had reigned, has the crowd shouting, "Blessed is the king who comes in the name of the Lord" (19:38). Each of the other gospels also includes an acclamation of Jesus as he enters Jerusalem, but these do not insert the word *king* into this line from one of the pilgrim songs in the Book of Psalms (Psalm 118:26, "Blessed is *the one*..."). Luke builds Jesus's kingly status into the discourse after he has presented his version of the dispute about greatness. Jesus acknowledges the fidelity of the disciples and assures them of their place in the kingdom that his Father has assigned to him (22:28–30). Even in the report of the dispute, the emphasis is less on the nature of the conflict between the disciples than on the lordly manner in which Jesus resolves it. This is the true mark of the wise leader.

With other touches of detail, Luke Hellenizes Mark's address. Mark's phrase about those who were "supposed to govern the Gentiles" becomes "the kings of the Gentiles," to suit his readers' familiarity with a Hellenistic flowering of kingdoms, while the executors of royal decrees become "benefactors." These men were wealthy governors and other senior appointees from whom their Hellenistic clientele expected grandiose public works and civic amenities. Such a Lukan world generated honor for the benefactors of whom Luke's readers were vividly aware and of whom they stood in awe.

Next, moving to the resolution of the dispute, and closely following the lines of teaching in Mark's roadside scene, Luke changes Mark's images to suit the setting of his Hellenistic dinner and *symposion*. Instead of having Jesus overturn the Hellenistic value system of royal honors and public esteem via Mark's contrasts between rulers and slaves, Luke shifts to contrasts between the esteemed dinner host and those attending on him and his guests.

> The most senior among you must become like the junior,
> and the presider must become like the one attending at the table...
> Who is greater, the one reclining in the main place
> or the one attending on him?...
> Nonetheless, I am here in your midst like one who is attending
> at the tables.

Appropriate Words for a Symposion

Here "the one attending at the tables" is expressed in the Greek not by the noun *diakonos* in the sense of "the waiter" but by the present participle *diakonōn* (hence the English participle "attending" in the translation). The use of the participle is another detail of Hellenistic literary style. In reporting waiters at work, Greek writers preferred the participle to the noun because it gave a more immediate sense of the waiter in action. That stylistic detail is another small reminder that Luke's priority in this scene, for the purposes of developing its teaching, is to thoroughly Hellenize it. Hence also his use of the *diakon-* words. We need to take note of the significance of the presence of these terms in this scene. Their presence is to be explained on the basis of Greek literary convention.

Throughout the twentieth century, commentators regularly claimed that the *diakon-* words were—to use the often-repeated description—ordinary everyday words. Given their prominent place in the language early Christians chose to designate activities and roles in the early church—the title "deacon" is itself one illustration—commentators have gone on to propose that the very ordinariness of the words underlay the choice. In this, early Christians would have been flagging a rejection of the high language of temples and public office, pompous and even intimidating as these could be in the flamboyant world of Hellenistic religions. Commentators have even traced the early Christian preference for *diakon-* words to the ordinariness of Jesus's own everyday contact with people of a very ordinary station in life—and of no station at all. At such a level, we have been told, the language of the streets was more appropriate. Accordingly, if later Christian leaders were to be servants of their congregations in the way that Jesus said he was a servant among his own, then what better titles for leaders and for roles within the community than terms like the *diakon-* words taken from slavish language.

Luke knew better than this, however. He knew what has only become apparent again through a few linguistic studies over recent decades. Luke knew that Greek writers used *diakon-* words for waiters at table almost only in formal language and in composing accounts of formal meals. To this we need to add that for the Greek, any meal—particularly the formal meal—was a religious act, as it so often has been in other cultures. The style of the formal Greek meal and the expectations attending it are not to be confused with the laxities and extravagances of Roman feasts. Among the Greeks the first action of a gathering was to invoke the presence of the gods and then honor their presence with a ritual libation of wine. The occasion was ideally of such dignity and religiosity that Athenaeus, an apologist of conventions applying to these occasions, observed that the table attendants could not be slaves. The presence of such unworthy functionaries would be abhorrent to the gods and would drive away the divine presences. Thus, in Luke's simple narrative of the Lord's Supper, values abound in the code words he introduces and in the sensitivities to the occasion that he evidences.

On Another Level

Luke is advising his audience that this meal, with which they were thoroughly familiar from their own community practice of remembering the Lord in the breaking of bread, is a moment of sacred encounter. Luke has carefully modified the account he has inherited from Mark in order to help his Hellenistic audience recognize something more than a loving meal and a sad farewell. In the account of this last meeting between disciples and the Lord before he suffers, Luke has elevated to another level the simple, if challenging, ethic inculcated by Mark's story about the dispute among the disciples along the road.

In Luke's treatment, similarly to Mark's, the kingdom—even the king—does not function according to the protocols and pretences of the self-promoting seekers of power in public life. But Luke goes beyond Mark in having his Hellenistic audience read the signs that the kingdom functions only by reason of the constant presence of the community before the Lord. Luke's intention is to cultivate the community's awareness of the Lord's presence in it. "I am in your midst like one who is attending at the tables." This is the point of the resolution of the dispute in Jesus's discourse. Disputes must end because the Lord is "in the midst."

With the resolution of the dispute, the discourse immediately opens upon the promise of kingdom. As beneficiaries of that promise, they shall eat and drink "at my table in my kingdom" (22:30). Until then, however, the community table is the place of encounter. To create the conviction of that possibility among his readers, Luke has shaped his narrative, even to the point of the *diakon-* word. Luke's choice of this word is not the result of casual usage. Nor is its presence in the narrative for the purpose of inculcating lessons about lowly service by one member of a community to another. The only reason Luke uses the word is to contribute to the dignity of the occasion. As a minor stylistic feature, *diakon-* is recognizable to Luke's readers as marking the formal and religious nature of the occasion.

All Days

Something else about a master who waits on his dependants at table would also have been recognizable to Luke's readers. In the slave-based economy of the Roman Empire—and of the earlier Greek economy—all were familiar with annual festivals in which wealthy heads of households organized peers to assist them in providing a feast for the slave-born members of their often vast establishments. A major instance was the Roman Saturnalia, but smaller regional versions also took place. Such is the tone of Luke's presentation of the Lord's Supper, however, that one is justified in suspecting that Luke is playing off one institution against another: the public festivals against the intimacy of the Lord's table. To the advantage of the latter, of course.

We have emphasized how a close consideration of the discourse of Jesus after the meal leads to a realization that Luke is speaking of the presence of the Lord at all Christian ritual. But this kind of teaching is not confined to the account of the Lord's Supper. Throughout his gospel, Luke has immersed readers in teaching about the ongoing presence of the Lord in gatherings at table, as well as about the dangers attendant upon neglecting the opportunities such gatherings provide (4:39; 5:30; 5:34; 7:36–48; 9:12–17; 10:38–42; 12:35–40; 14:7–14; 14:15–24; 15:19–23; 19:1–10). Luke also evokes a dynamism in the Lord's presence. When it is the Lord who gathers a people in a household, one could indeed say, "Salvation has come to this household today" (19:9).

In the gatherings of Luke's community, its members were to understand that the saving and healing activity of Jesus was extending to their day—and then beyond, into the future of the church. Luke signals this conviction in the way he brings a definitive close to the Gospel as a whole on the basis of the meal between two doubting disciples and the risen Lord at Emmaus. He proceeds to project the theme into the story of the church (Acts 2:42; 3:43–47). His aim is to remind the church that thus it will always be. The superiority over the Saturnalia of such persistent teaching about a confirming and ongoing presence of the Lord is clear. The Saturnalia was a day off for slaves. Luke's Christian community has the Lord in its midst all days.

Feed the Hungry

Lord, when did you see you hungry and not serve you? (Matt. 25:44)

The New Testament provides strong indications that supporting the needy gives meaning to life within Christian communities—both for the community that gives and the one that receives. We will see this principle operating in accounts of relations between communities in Antioch and Jerusalem in Acts and again between the needy community of Jerusalem and the communities founded by Paul in Asia and Greece. These communal responses to need may be of particular interest to church deacons today, but support of the needy is also a responsibility of the individual Christian, and the call of the Gospel is heard most clearly from that perspective. Thus we will look at one story in the gospel which lays a claim on every Christian. The story is about the king judging the nations in Matthew 25.

Frustrations

Pursuing our lives within a culture that exalts the individual, we too easily lose sight of communal connections. Perhaps it would be fairer to say that we have connections with so many subcommunities that we draw more resolutely on our individual resources to hold the threads of life in tension and give it a necessary sense of purpose. The multi-directional focuses in our lives tend to deprive us of a sense of the communal dimension of the works of charity. This is not to say that corporate works of charity by institutions like the Red Cross and Amnesty International leave us unaware of the importance of our own involvement in strategic action. The situation for the member of a Christian congregation today is rather that the individual feels Christian charity is more than support of corporate projects. The individual retains a strong personal feeling of the burden of need, and of frustration (or even guilt) about how little an individual can do to meet need or create situations that prevent need.

These feelings are intensified for many because of the constant impact made on them by fleeting daily experiences like an unexpected encounter in a shopping center with someone affected by drugs, by regular front-page stories of loss and grief, or by a phone call at the end of a day's work soliciting financial support just as the television reports from a disaster area with distressing images. In addition are the regular mail drops, the advertisements and inserts for appeals in newspapers and journals, and finally the call from a priest at the end of a Sunday liturgy for a special collection. Strangely, this last can appear somehow far removed from the real needs of the world. It can also appear to have only a tenuous or at least artificial link with what the liturgical gathering has been about.

The Persistent Call

Such experiences do not make it any easier for Christians to know what to make of probably the most familiar saying of the Gospel—although it is really a word of the Torah—"Love your neighbor as yourself" (Lev.19:18; Luke 10:27). Their hesitations and confusion arise not only because they might not be sure what love means in regard to a neighbor—let alone in regard to an enemy, to whom Jesus also extends love (Matt. 5:44)—but also because the call for response to need today is put mostly in money terms. Most Christians—and most non-Christians—are themselves living below or on the borderline of financial security and manage their affairs with difficulty. But the sense of individual personal responsibility is all the more persistent because of the sheer success of two stories that the gospels attribute to Jesus.

Both of these stories are parables, and one of them challenges the story of the two lost sons in Luke 15 as the most famous of the stories in Jesus's teachings. It is the story of the Good Samaritan in Luke 10. Its impact is all the stronger because Jesus tells it for the specific purpose of answering the lawyer's question, "Who is my neighbor?" Today's audience ends up being confronted with images of an individual person performing a range of challenging, expensive, and time-consuming tasks almost certainly beyond the means and competence of individuals in our kind of society.

The call of the Gospel is nonetheless unmistakable, and its tone is nowhere more dramatic and its message nowhere more peremptory than in a third story that forms the end to all Jesus's public teaching in the Gospel of Matthew. Such a context says much for the story's place on the ethical scale in Matthew's estimation. The story is about the king judging the peoples of all nations (Matt. 25:31–46), and the decisive issue is who has and who has not attended to the needs of the hungry, the thirsty, the immigrants, the people dressed in rags, the sick, and those in chains.

When the story arrives at judgment upon the king's own palace staff, a small but striking shift occurs in the language used. All the staff are found guilty of not having fed, welcomed, clothed, and solaced those in need. Immediately they protest:

> Lord, when did we see you hungry or thirsty or a stranger or naked or ill or in prison and did not serve (*diakon-*) you?

They are devastated to hear the king explain:

> Truly...just as you did not do it to one of the least of these, you did not do it to me.

Why does the king not turn his staff's terms of appeal back on them by saying, "Just as you did not *serve* (*diakon-*) one of the least of these, you did not *serve* (*diakon-*) me"?

Two Clues

There are two clues to understanding how the story is working at this moment in the lives of one tragic group of its characters. One clue is in the structure of the story to this point, and the other is in understanding why the narrator draws on the service/*diakon-* word at the same point. Taking the *diakon-* word first, we recall that in the Son of Man's teaching about discipleship in Mark 10:42–45, Jesus developed the teaching on the basis of comparing life within the discipleship with life in the grand houses. In the grand houses of those governing the nations—that is, within the official establishments of Roman Prefects like Pontius Pilate in Caesarea—the persons who had absolutely no share in the exercise of the power by which the Prefect maintained the Emperor Tiberius's absolute control of the Jewish people were the many "attendants" (*diakonoi*) and "slaves" (*douloi*) who made life comfortable for the Prefect and his retinue of family, friends, officials, and hangers-on.

Now while the "attendants" may well have been slaves, they are called *diakonoi* because of their particular responsibility for the personal needs of the leading figures in such establishments, as well as for seeing that everything was in order for the efficient running of daily affairs there. One could compare status differences between mere household slaves and such attendants with the differences in the grander households of nineteenth-century London between the butler or valet and a kitchenhand. Ancient accounts of affairs in great houses and royal palaces present a similar picture of such *diakonoi*.

The setting of this story is in a royal court of the most awful grandeur because it opens with an image of the powerful figure from the vision in the Book of Daniel coming "in glory" and sitting on "his glorious throne" (Matt. 25:31). This figure is Daniel's "one like a son of man" (Dan. 7:13).

In that vision, when the Ancient of Days sat in judgment upon all the empires of the world, he gave dominion and judgment over all of them to "one like a son of man" whose honors ranked above anything known upon earth. Such is "the glory" that the opening of the story refers to. As the story develops, the storyteller keeps the audience keenly aware of the status of this dominant figure, henceforth identified as "the king." And the high reward for those in whose favor he judges is nothing less than to "inherit the kingdom that has been prepared" for them.

A Kingdom of People

The king's judgment of the group assembled at his right hand itemizes the deeds these people have performed, all of them deeds of assistance to someone in need: "You gave me something to eat...you gave me a drink...you took me in...you clothed me...you looked after me...you visited me." The striking thing about this judgment is that the king assesses as having been done to himself those actions which these people have performed to strangers and others in need. Clearly the king's kingdom is his people, not just a territory, and all people are to recognize the royal bond uniting them to one another and, together, to the king.

The way the storyteller makes it emphatically clear that the unifying bond within the kingdom is made up of the myriad threads of helping actions is by repeating the list of helping actions two more times. Thus, in response to the king's favorable judgment of them, the people on the king's right hand also put a series of questions to him: "When...did we feed you or give you a drink? When...did we take you in or clothe you? When...did we come to you?" The list appears for a third time when the king passes unfavorable judgment on the people on his left: "You did not give me anything to eat...you did not give me a drink...you did not take me in...you did not clothe me...you did not visit me." The impact of such charges is devastating. These people have already known before hearing the detailed list that they are to be consigned to "the everlasting fire prepared for the devil and his messengers."

In a Summary Fashion

Just as the story contains three detailed lists of the works the king requires of his people, so there are also three summary references to the list of the works. The first is the king's reply to the astonished query from the people on his right hand as to when they had acted so helpfully to the person of the king: "Whenever *you did these things to* one of these most marginalized of my family members *you did it to me.*" Similarly, to the condemned group on the king's left, he says: "As often as *you did not do these things to* one of these most marginalized people, *you did not do them to me.*" In other words, on two occasions, the king sums up the whole list of helpful actions of feeding, giving a drink, offering shelter, providing clothes, and visiting in the plain words *did* or *did not do* (*epoiēsate*).

In the third statement, however, this summary word suddenly changes. In their desperate appeal, the condemned people put the following question to the king: "Lord, when did we see you hungry or thirsty or a stranger or naked or sick or in gaol and not *serve* you?" The summary word changes from *doing things for you* to *serving you*, and the Greek word here is the *diakon-* verb for "serving a royal person." As such, the word has a significant role in the unfolding of this stage of the narrative.

At this point, by force of the detailed repetitions, the audience is thoroughly aware of what the teacher is teaching. Helping people in their specific needs is what gives a person entrée as a member of the king's household. The people who were favorably judged had been as unaware of this as the people who were condemned. They had to have explained to them how the king required his subjects to live in relation to each other. Those who have been condemned, however, are not open to any such explanation because the terms of their question to the king show that their lives are focused exclusively on the royal person and that they are totally unaware that other people matter. The clear indication that they think the only value in life is to attend to the royal person without regard to his "family members" is their appeal to their royal service or *diakonia.*

Grounds for Condemnation

Far from being a word relating to helping people in need, the *diakon-* word used in this story by the condemned people expresses their deafness to the call of the kingdom. The word is not a Christian code word for lowly and loving help, but rather a sign that the condemned have not yet begun to think of the nature of their place and responsibilities in the king's household. It is a sign that they are locked into a self-contained world. Inside their world they think only of the master and of rewards that may come to them from ignoring all other people in anticipation of the master's own indulgent inclinations.

6

The Mediatorial Role of Paul as Minister/Diakonos

IN PAUL'S SECOND letter to the Corinthians, the word *diakonos* and its cognates occur eight times in chapters 3–6 and three times in chapters 10–13. Two things can be said about this. One is that over the last twenty-five years, the term *diakonos* has at last been recognized as singularly important in these contexts, and the other thing is that commentators are still not confident about why Paul used the word or even what he meant by it. In stating what the term did mean for Paul, the following discussion will also show why the term was important to him.

Writers may accurately register the impact this word makes in Paul's discourse. Of one main occurrence, in the phrase *diakonoi christou* at 11:23, Ralph Martin has said that Paul is pointing to "the fundamental matter of the debate between himself and the antagonists at Corinth," that this title is "*the* hallmark of his life and work," and that it is "the capstone" of his rivals' claims.[1] Powerful commendation, surely, of this Pauline turn of phrase.

On the other hand, when we turn to hear what the word means—and we must say that, with the word so fundamental to the argument, we really need to know what it means—we can experience quite a letdown. Martin's contemporary commentator Victor Furnish, for example, surmised that Paul's rivals attached to the term "some kind of special meaning," but he does not venture beyond that to suggest what the special meaning might be.[2] And if we look for a lead to our modern bibles, we are not going to be further enlightened. Nothing "special" is apparent about the meaning of the phrase "servants of Christ," which is the translation we read in the NRSV, New English Bible (NEB), New International Version (NIV), and New Jerusalem Bible (NJB). The word *servants* here is a thoroughly modern

---

1. R. P. Martin, *2 Corinthians, WBC 40* (Waco, TX: Word Books, 1986), 374–75.

2. V. P. Furnish, *II Corinthians, AB 32A* (Garden City, NY: Doubleday, 1984), 197.

finessing of the earlier standard, nobler, but not much more helpful word *ministers*. We inherit that term from the Vulgate.

I have drawn attention to the last twenty-five years of scholarship because it was in 1964 that Dieter Georgi published his study of Paul's opponents, which has been available in English since 1986 with an extensive epilogue as *The Opponents of Paul in Second Corinthians*.[3] In this broad-fronted venture into the language and systems of religious propaganda within the Hellenistic world, Georgi's point of departure is to be found in some pages where he examined the titles that he said Paul's rivals claimed. The first of these, described as one of the opponents' self-designations for the task of being a religious propagandist, was the expression *diakonos christou*.[4] With this title, the opponents were presenting themselves, in Georgi's view, not in any general sense as "servants of Christ" but specifically as "envoys of Christ," as his "personal representatives."[5] The title resonates with "the sense of responsible, fateful representation and manifestation."[6] This is quite a leap: from the mundane *servants* to the arcane *envoys* [of a heavenly being]. Georgi made the move on indications to be found in the treatment of the *diakon-* words in the sixteenth-century *Thesaurus* of Stephanus and, in particular, after a consideration of usage in Epictetus.

Not all have been persuaded that in writing *envoys* (*Gesandte*) Georgi got his non-Pauline sources right. In his English epilogue of 1986 Georgi himself notes that he took more from two of his sources, Pollux and Thucydides, than the passages warranted.[7] This was in response to my comments on these passages in an article in the *Journal of Biblical Literature* in 1974.[8] Against this, however, in the epilogue Georgi insists that his main source, the Stoic Epictetus, supports his view. Accordingly, while I make a few points in these pages, I mainly refer to my study *Diakonia: Re-interpreting the Ancient Sources*,[9] where in chapter 8, "A

---

3. D. Georgi, *The Opponents of Paul in Second Corinthians* (Philadelphia: Fortress Press, 1986).

4. Ibid., 27–32, and see the later observations in the Epilogue, p. 352.

5. Ibid., 32.

6. Ibid., 29.

7. Ibid., 352.

8. J. N. Collins, "Georgi's 'envoys' in 2 Cor 11:23," *JBL* 93 (1974), 88–96.

9. New York: Oxford University Press, 1990. The interpretation of these instances, like all other instances of the *diakon-* terms mentioned below, is established through discussion of context in this volume.

Question of Diplomacy," I examine this part of the usage again to conclude even more strongly than in my article of 1974 that Epictetus uses *diakonos* only for the purpose of designating the Stoic or the Cynic as an obedient servant of the will of God; further, in this, the term is depicting the moral disposition of the Stoic or Cynic and never has any reference to the Cynic's mission to the world. This reading of what Epictetus intended by the common noun *diakonos*—supported as it is by the interplay of that word in these discourses with another word *hypēretēs* used to similar effect—is not affected by the fact that in his one use of the cognate abstract noun Epictetus names the Cynic's mission a *diakonia* (3.22.69). As a final comment on this, I note that if the Cynic teachers thus did not present themselves as *diakonoi*, we know of no sectarian preachers who did—apart from Paul and his school and, by imputation from them, possibly his rivals.

That *diakonos* ordinarily means "messenger"—although never in Epictetus—is one thing ("messenger" is one of two meanings, the other being "servant," provided in Liddell and Scott, who instance the tragic poets Aeschylus and Sophocles.), but another intriguing question is why Paul would have so keenly debated the right to call himself *diakonos* of Christ if *diakonos* meant only "messenger." In proceeding to show how it means more than "messenger" but less than "envoy," we will look first at some literature illustrating usage in the sphere of message. Then we will go further to see how the usage invites us to deeper levels of meaning in relation to how Paul envisaged the transference of the Word of God.

When we read of Paul and Apollos as *diakonoi* through whom the Corinthians believed (1 Cor. 3:5), we can be certain we have engaged authentic Greek usage relating to messengers of the divine. And comments suggesting that Paul is here using a word from ordinary everyday speech, that his term properly belongs to waiting on tables, or that he is launching a new term peculiar to practice within early Christian communities are wide of the mark and misleading. Such views are widespread in the handbooks and lexicons dealing with early Christian language and institutions, especially as these relate to ministry, and they take their rise from H. W. Beyer's article on the *diakon-* words in Kittel's *Theological Dictionary of the New Testament* (in the German, 1935). Beyer himself bases his views on Wilhelm Brandt's slightly earlier monograph *Dienst und Dienen im Neuen Testament*.[10] We leave all such views aside as we look at some characteristics of the usage.

---

10. Gütersloh: Bertelsmann, 1931.

The first and obvious characteristic of the usage is its comparative rarity. A search of the bookstacks in London's Classical Institute provided me with a list of only ninety-four ancient authors in whose works I could find instances of this word or its cognates. These authors ranged from Herodotus in the fifth century BCE to the Christian poet Synesios, seven hundred years later. (In addition, I collected instances in some forty-three papyri and from twenty-five inscriptions, the latter being mainly lists of dignitaries and officials at festivals.) In most of these works, the words occur only once or twice. For example, Thucydides provides two instances in the same passage, quoting from one of his sources. Herodotus provides three. Only ten authors provide more than ten instances: Josephus leading with some seventy, Plato next with thirty-three, then down to twenty-three in Lucian, seventeen in Aristides, sixteen in Philo and Plutarch, and so on. Often the instances tend to come together in a particular context. The three instances in Plato's *Politicus* fall close together and are interrelated; similarly, six in his *Republic*. Of the seventy occurrences in Josephus's large set of writings, twenty-two fall in two consecutive sections of the *Antiquities*.

Mention of Josephus brings to mind that other great collection of Jewish Greek, the Septuagint. Curiously, here the words are virtually eschewed, occurring only in one proverb peculiar to the Septuagint (Prov. 10:4a), five times in Esther to designate various officials of the royal court, and one in each of 1 and 4 Maccabees.

Let us observe Josephus using Esther as a source. When Esther was using her eunuch Hathach in her interchanges with Mordecai, the Septuagint has the following wordy sentence to depict Hathach's role (4:15): "Esther sent back to Mordecai the same one who had come to her." This is the Greek version of some straightforward Hebrew: "Esther told [him] to reply to Mordecai." Josephus too went for succinctness; in place of the Septuagint's phrase "the same one who had come to her," he wrote one word: "Esther sent the same *diakonon*" (AJ, 11.228). We see Josephus doing the same thing later in the story when the king dispatches Haman to convey to Mordecai notice of the honors he will receive that Haman had sought for himself. In the Septuagint, the king says to Haman (6:10): "Do for Mordecai the Jew what you have said." Again Josephus is succinct; the king says, "*isthi diakonos*," which the Marcus translation in the Loeb edition relates as: "*You shall be the one to carry out* those things about which you have given good counsel" (11.255). The phrase *the one to carry out* has the character of an agent who is dispatched to complete a task. These two uses, "messenger" and "agent," account for nine of fourteen instances of the common noun in Josephus. Other messengers include Jonathan and Ahimaaz whom David engaged to bring him news of developments in Jerusalem during his flight from Absalom: they are *pistoi diakonoi* (7.201, 224). Another is Solymius, whom a young man named Joseph begged to act as his go-between (*diakonos*) when he was enamored of the dancing girl at Ptolemy's feast (12.187).

In this connection we note that one of the more specific applications of the *diakon-* words is to this role of the go-between in love affairs. We meet it in the romances of Heliodorus and Xenophon of Ephesus, in an anecdote of Aristaenetus (2.7), and in the Hellenistic Jewish *Asenath* (15.7) and *Testament of Juda* (14.2). It is also found in the following prayer, one of two such to have survived among papyri. The prayer is addressed to a magic lamp (and we notice that the prayer is cast as a formula with gaps for the names of lover and beloved, a telling sign of how widely familiar this usage was.) The devotee says to the lamp: "You acted as a go-between [*diakonēsas*] for him [the god Osornophoris] when he was in love with his sister...so now be a go-between [*diakonēson*] for me, so and so, in regard to so and so" (*P. Warren*, 21).

Of seemingly greater moment than these lovers' go-betweens are those who operate between mortals and the gods—only seemingly, however, because the bringing of lovers together was itself a work of the gods. The public link between heaven and earth for the ancients was, of course, the priesthood, and closely associated with that, divination. In analyzing both functions in the *Politicus*, Plato draws on *diakon-* words, just as he does in analyzing the roles of merchants and other intermediary functionaries in the make-up of his republic (*Republic*, 370e and elsewhere). Thus, diviners are "interpreters for the gods to men," and the priests "know how to give to the gods...gifts from us by means of sacrifices, and to win for us from them by means of petition the bestowal of good things" (*Politicus*, 290c–d). On this analysis of roles we see clearly that both diviners and priests are at the point of interchange between the two worlds. Plato defines their functions as part of what he calls a "diaconic" skill: "*epistēmē diakonos*" (290c, d; see further, 299d).

We see the same intimate linguistic connection between things of heaven and things of earth in one of the more carefully elaborated narratives of Josephus. In the *Jewish Wars* we read how Josephus came to prophesy that Vespasian would be emperor. At two critical moments in this dramatic, if improbable, autobiographical reconstruction, Josephus writes of himself as *diakonos*, even "the *diakonos* of the voice of God" (*BJ*, 3.354; 4.626). The first of the two moments is when Josephus perceives with piercing clarity his calling to the prophetic role, and the second— a whole book of the *Wars* later—when the emperor publicly acknowl- edges that role. These passages, which are intriguing even from a literary point of view, merit very close attention by students of Paul's ministry at Corinth, and yet—despite long-felt ambiguities in regard to the character of Paul's usage in that context—the passages are only fleetingly noticed, if noticed at all. Thus, on the one hand, in his 1959 German study—still widely consulted—*Church Order in the New Testament*,[11] Eduard Schweizer noted in passing that Josephus designated himself as "the mediator of divine prophecy." By contrast, in 1976, Bultmann left the question of Paul's usage at 2 Cor. 3:6—"ministers of the new covenant"—just hanging in the air: "Is the usage terminological?" he asked.[12] And yet in these pas- sages of Josephus we have as near contemporary usage to Paul's as we need, and the context created by this skillful writer is powerfully redo- lent of interchange between the Jewish God and a Jew of the priestly line who was learned in sacred prophecies. Wholly pertinent to the weight we ought to give to these passages is what this latter-day prophet perceived. This was none other than the end of the covenanted nation of the Jews and the beginnings of a new fortune, under the Jewish God's pleasure, for the Romans.

The studied choice of the word *diakonos* by Josephus in this account of his transition from defeated general to seer honored by his conqueror, suggests that Paul too would have been no less studied in his use of the word in his grave controversy about apostolic status. Today's commenta- tors, prompted mainly, it would seem, by the notoriety attaching to the word as a consequence of Georgi's work, have belatedly recognized this much. But we need to go further and assess the character of the usage much more sensitively. With Paul's usage we are in fact in touch with a long Greek tradition of designating functions that relate earth to heaven as "diaconic." Centuries after Paul the tradition continued. The Neoplatonist Iamblichus divided the powers of heaven into two orders of deity and dae- mons, saying of the orders, "That which is divine is of a ruling nature

---

11. Eng. trans. (London: SCM, 1961), 174, 21c.

12. *Der zweite Brief an die Korinther, KEK Sonderband* (Göttingen: Vandenhoeck & Ruprecht, 1976), 79.

[*hēgemonikon*]...but that which is daemoniacal is *diakonikon."* And he explained, "The daemoniacal order receives whatever the gods may announce, and promptly goes to work, as it were, in things which the gods perceive, wish and command" (*De mysteriis*, 1.20).

There are numerous moments in literature, rich in context, where we encounter this side of ancient usage. In this paper we are not able to enter closely into context, but I present the following for their obvious relevance to the way Paul has chosen terms like *diakonos* in speaking of his role as a purveyor of revelation.

In the *Testament of Abraham*, the patriarch asks God's chief captain, Michael, to be—using G. H. Box's 1927 translation of the verb *diakonēsai* (9.24)—"the medium of [his] word...unto the most High."[13]

In Lucian's *Icaromenippus*, a syntactically identical phrase occurs as Menippus flies past the moon on his way to heaven and hears Selene, the moon, call out—here we can draw on H. W. Fowler's translation of the same verb *diakonēsai* (20)—"do me an errand to Zeus."[14]

In Lucian's *Contemplantes*, Charon asks Hermes to drop by, and the busy messenger of Zeus declines, explaining—and this translation of the participle *diakonēsomenos* (1) is by F. G. Fowler—"I am on certain errands of the Upper Zeus."[15]

A curse inscription of the third century BCE consigns thieves to—among other gods—Hermes *diakonos*, a title translated by the editor, G. W. Elderkin, "Hermes messenger."[16]

Hermes is, of course, the same messenger of Zeus whom Prometheus calls *diakonos* in Aeschylus (*Pr.*, 942); the other messenger, Iris, is also so named by Aristophanes (*Av.*, 1253). We might note that this title of Hermes goes to the roots of the Greek tradition. The philologist P. C. Buttmann proposed in the nineteenth century that the words *diakonos* and the Homeric epithet for Hermes *diaktoros* were etymologically the same.[17] We might also note that, as a consequence, we have no real cause for surprise to find *diakonos* and its cognates occurring in passages of high religious moment. We will run through some.

---

13. G. H. Box, *The Testament of Abraham* (London: SPCK, 1927), 14.

14. H. W. Fowler and F. G. Fowler, *The Works of Lucian of Samosata*, vol. 3 (Oxford: Clarendon, 1905), 137.

15. Fowler and Fowler, *Lucian*, vol. 1, 168.

16. "Two Curse Inscriptions," *Hesperia* 6 (1937), 389.

17. *Lexilogus*, trans. (London: Murray, 1861), 230–33.

In the year 324, Emperor Constantine issued a proclamation concerning the Christian religion. The text is preserved in Eusebius's life.
The emperor writes of his commission under God to spread the enlightenment of God's holy law from the distant west to the east, and acknowledges this "most excellent *diakonia*" (*Vita*, 2.29).[18]

This is in the language of an imperial notary. A more personal and
genuine awareness of acting on a commission from God is expressed by
Epictetus in his description of the call of the wandering Cynic preacher
(3.22.69): "Not tied down by the private duties of men, nor involved in
relationships" but "wholly devoted to the commission (*diakonia*) from
God...free to go about among men" as "messenger (*aggelos*), scout, and
herald of the gods."

A mission of a lesser (but no less religious) kind is acknowledged
by Clitophon in the novel by Achilles Tatius. When Clitiphon's lover
Leucippe is dangerously drugged, Clitophon receives news of a remedy
from a young man called "a savior...sent by God," and Clitophon thanks
him piously for his *diakonia* (4.15.6).

In an earlier dramatic scene, when Clitophon thought Leucippe had
been cruelly eviscerated, Clitophon was relieved of his anxiety by some
sleight of hand by Menelaus, to whom Clitophon then turns in awe as to a
"*diakonos* of the gods" (3.18.5).

Finally, in more reverent mode, and in a truly touching scene from the
first-century *Life of Aesop*, we learn that the fabled and sainted storyteller
received the gift of speech from Isis, supreme god and "precious bond of
the universe," as a reward for kindnesses to a herald of hers, her *diakonos*
(*Vita G*, 7), who had lost her way.

We could go further into such literature and considerably extend the
perspective it offers on the background of Paul's usage. This would be by
way of one set of material illustrating roles in the deliverance of a message
in a more or less profane setting and by way of another set illustrating how
the same words give expression to notions of agency. (In the process we
would come to understand why Paul uses these words also in connection
with the collection for the saints in Jerusalem.) We might just pause over
Paul's image of the letter in 2 Cor. 3:3. In translation and commentary
we still find a lot of unsureness here. For example, when the RSV broke
away from the traditional "epistle of Christ ministered by us" and wrote

18. See the intriguing story of the confusion surrounding the translation of this passage in
mid-twentieth-century scholarship in Collins, *Diakonia*, 105–07.

"delivered," not all translations followed suit. The NJB abandoned its own predecessor's "written by us" (JB) and, in an unusual move (a touch of desperation?) went back to a version of R. F. Weymouth (originally of 1902, no less) that said "entrusted to our care."[19] Greek usage, however, demands "delivered"; in the light of the kinds of uses we have been touching on, "delivered" for *diakonētheisa* will be entirely appropriate for a letter written from heaven but delivered on earth. From the novel by Chariton, we can usefully provide an instance of a person being designated as the deliverer of a letter through the participial form of this verb (*diakonoumenos*, 8.8.5).

The rest of this paper will first refine the notion of the message-bearer as a medium and then savor Paul's writing in this light.

A close consideration of contexts in which *diakon-* words occur reveals that the underlying conceptualization has to do with the go-between. This is more frequent and clear in passages dealing with message and agency than in those dealing with waiting at tables, although in the latter the connotation is by no means always missing. We can say that the words never entirely cut loose from their etymological moorings in *diōkō*, "to pursue, chase, urge on"; this makes of *diakonos*, in Buttmann's phrase taken up by Trench in the nineteenth century, " 'a runner' still."[20] The *diakonos*-waiter, as much as the *diakonos*-messenger, is a runner, an in-between person or a go-between. A striking reminder of the capacity of contexts to project this connotation is provided in the list of meanings prepared by B. Justus for Rengstorf's concordance of Josephus; these include "middleman, go-between, messenger."[21] Also recall, from earlier in this paper, Schweizer's word, "mediator."[22]

An instructive source for this dimension of the words is the usage of some early commentators on Aristotle. These were writings dealing in abstractions and tangling with the intricacies of cause and effect in areas like reflections of light. An illuminating example is Alexander of Aphrodisias's (c. 200) explanation of translucence. He makes the following simple observation about air and water: air and water are of themselves colorless, but each can take on the color of other things while yet

19. *The New Testament in Modern Speech*, 3rd edn (London: Clarke, 1910).

20. R. C. Trench, *Synonyms in the New Testament*, 9th edn (London: 1880, reprinted Grand Rapids: Eerdmans, 1953), 32.

21. K. H. Rengstorf and others, *A Complete Concordance of Flavius Josephus*, vol. 1 (Leiden: Brill, 1973), 456.

22. See note 11 above.

letting the color of other things pass through them. In sum, they are thus receptive (*dektikos*) and conductive. His word for conductive is *diakonos* (*De Mixtione*, 5.14). He then writes: "The translucent body will transmit (*diakonēsomenon*) the colours of other things."

Writing on the *Meteorologica* of Aristotle, Alexander enunciates the principle that any object which passes on an effect from a first body without being itself affected is a "conductive" body; again his word is *diakonos* (*In mete*, 18.25). Thus the moon passes on the light of the sun without itself being on fire: the word for "passes on" is the verb *diakoneisthai* (*In mete*, 19.6).

On Aristotle's *De anima*, and in connection with sense faculties, Themistius, writing in the fourth century, points to a basic difference between the faculty of touch and those of sight, hearing, and smell. Touching puts one in immediate contact with the object; not so, however, when we see, hear, or smell, for then there is something between us and what we sense. This in-between body is "acting as a medium in between" (125.9 *heterou sōmatos metaxu diakonountos*).

Ammonius, writing in the fifth century, observes that when souls are first united to bodies they are vacant of ideas; souls come by ideas only by hearing of them from others. The human voice is thus the medium of ideas for souls (*In cat.*, 15.9: *diakonousēs autais tēs phōnēs*).

We could adduce more of such usage to show writers drawing out the connotation of mediation. This connotation, however, is never far from the broader usage in less technical writing, and once we are aware of it we are often able to resolve apparent problems of interpretation or clarify or enrich perception of what an ancient author was intending.

In bringing our familiarity with such usage to the writings of the Christian Paul, we can immediately recognize that in using *diakon*-words he was not taking up language off the streets, indulging in neologisms, drawing on some in-house jargon, or borrowing the sectarian argot of rival propagandists; rather, he was dipping into a rich tradition of language and selecting terms appropriate for what he had to say. These words were indeed from the store of the literate, the learned, the rhetoricians, the poets. They were words of acknowledged quality and character, capable of expressing subtleties of the kind his mysterious encounter with revelation evoked. At the same time, they breathed a nobility engendered from a long association with language about gods and their messengers to earth. We can be sure that Paul chose his words well.

We do not need to question the *diakon-* provenance. Whether he was urging the Corinthian believers to acknowledge the authenticity and dignity of preachers—"What then is Apollos? What is Paul?" (1 Cor. 3:5)—or whether he was taking the fight to the Corinthians and demanding that they confront the question he put to his opponents (2 Cor. 11:23), do we need to ask why he should use these distinguished entitlements: Apollos and Paul are *diakonoi*, he is demonstrably more genuinely *diakonos* than the opponents have shown themselves to be. Paul's demonstration of his own authenticity as *diakonos*, we may note in passing, is the catalogue of his labors, for these show to what extent he has gone to get his message through. A faithful *diakonos* always gets through.

Finally, we should reflect ever so briefly on an earlier passage, 2 Cor. 2:14–6:13, where Paul's use of these words is more nuanced under the demands of his talk of revelation. That Paul speaks with great sensitivity of the process whereby he and believers are caught up into revelation has often been expounded. Throughout these letters, Paul's appeal is to the experience of revelation that the Corinthians have enjoyed: if they will look into their own hearts they will know that God is revealed there and that the only way this revelation came was through his *diakonia*. The writing here is full of sensual imagery: aroma and brightness. While the brightness is the end result of revelation possessed by the believer, the aroma says something of the process. God's Word, held and proclaimed by the *diakonos*, is pervasive. It is not the word of argument but convinces by the presence of the Spirit as the Word carries into the heart. The role of the *diakonos* in this is to be the Word's purveyor, its passage or medium. Thus, Christ's letter is not a message Paul had brought from a community of believers in Jerusalem or Antioch and delivered to Corinth: this would be peddling the Word. Rather, Paul is trying to make the Corinthians aware that the letter is from on high to the heart. Because he is speaking *ek theou* (from God), he is only God's *diakonos*, and the Word he has spoken becomes a Word of revelation between the believer and God. Ultimately the *diakonos* is expendable, but not until he knows that the Word is possessed and known by those to whom he has been called to declare it.

The *diakonia* of the Spirit, the *diakonia* of righteousness, the *diakonia* of reconciliation (2 Cor. 3:8, 9; 5:18) has not operated unless the people have the Spirit, become God's righteousness (5:21), and rejoice in their reconciliation. Making revelation a real experience in this way is the role of the *diakonos*: God makes the appeal through the *diakonos* (5:20), and the *diakonos* puts no obstacle in the way (6:3). Then is his an unimpeded ministry, a pure *diakonia*, a mediation without fault (6:3), and he commends himself in the way that *diakonoi* of God should, for these are known by their fidelity to their task, by their labors, kindness, truth, and in the power of God revealed (6:4–10).

It was much more important for Paul to be known as a *diakonos* of God than as an apostle. As an apostle, one needs credentials, and credentials can be challenged. The authenticity of God's *diakonos*, on the other hand, speaks for itself: it is the Lord who speaks.

7

Ministry as Office

READERS WHO HAVE spent time on other books about ministry in the early church will have noticed that here we have not become involved in identifying and differentiating among the roles of those who performed various functions within the first Christian communities. Who were *elders* or *presbyters* and what did they do? Or *bishops*—perhaps we should call them *overseers*? And then there were *deacons*. Is the coupling of *overseers* and *deacons* as we first meet the words in Phil. 1:1 just a composite Greek expression for what the Jewish Christians called *presbyters*? And what about *teachers* and the popular but problematic *prophets*? This exercise has been done again and again in the more than fifty years since Eduard Schweizer's book on *Church Order in the New Testament* and, while it yields a lot of information about what the various titles seem to mean, the exercise has clearly not provided enough new insights into what churches basically think they are doing in ministry. Otherwise there would not be so much talk about a crisis in ministry, nor would the ecumenical impasse in ministry look so redoubtable.

Of course, in times prior to our own—one might say from 1950 back to the period of the Reformation—inquiries along these lines were intense and often bitter affairs. A book usually set out to defend a particular style of church organization, often allowing itself generous space to denigrate attempts to defend or promote some other style. Anything to do with bishops, for example, was argued with a huge amount of scholarship and not a little invective because some churches had bishops—indeed, considered them to be the authentic sign that a group of believers was a church—while other churches got along quite nicely without them and even considered them an aberration. This debate was not just between Protestants and Roman Catholics but was actually more minutely argued among churches coming from the reform like the Anglican and Presbyterian. As for the more intransigent debate between Protestants and Roman Catholics, the sticking points here were the role of the bishop of Rome as Pope and the kind of priesthood claimed among the Roman Catholics for their ordained. Our daily language still shows signs of these ecclesiological contests, being littered with words like *priest, pastor, minister, parson, presbytery, manse, vicarage*, and so on, which people who have been brought up in the various denominational traditions use with impeccable propriety.

When early in the twentieth century churches began to come together in ecumenical consultations, decades passed before they introduced the question of their different styles and systems of ministry to the agenda, and then such were the difficulties and tensions that delegates to the consultations counted themselves fortunate to be able to leave agreeing to differ. Conferences at Lausanne (1927), Edinburgh (1937), and Lund (1952) produced nothing on which to build for the future; in fact, at Lund the question was left aside entirely. Great was the satisfaction, accordingly, at the Fourth World Conference on Faith and Order at Montreal in 1963 when a working principle for a shared theology of ministry emerged—not without a tussle—in the proposition that ministry is not the exclusive prerogative of the ordained but is the responsibility of all the baptized.

This principle (see discussion of its provenance and implications in chapter 11) has transformed approaches to the problem that for centuries presented itelf any time one church spoke to another of an ecumenical accommodation in the practice and reception of ministry. The general acceptance of the principle has also occasioned this book (*Are All Christians Ministers?*), which repeats from various viewpoints what *Diakonia: Re-interpreting the Ancient Sources* aimed to demonstrate, namely, that if under *ministry* we mean to embrace what the early Christians included under their word *diakonia*, the principle is wrong. At no earlier point in Christian history have advocates of mainstream churches attempted to claim that Christians are endowed with *diakonia*/ministry by virtue of their name or baptism.

Ministers of Gospel and Mystery

This reminder of where the thinking now stands on churchwide ministry is the appropriate point for us to turn to what is widely recognized as a normative passage in the letter to the Ephesians (4:11–12). For the last forty years there has been an almost universal consensus that in chapter 4 verse 12 we are to understand that the role of the teachers is to equip the baptized for ministry. Across preceding centuries, by contrast, the widely—although never universally—agreed position was that ministry was the work whereby the teachers equipped the saints and nurtured them to maturity in knowledge and love. What we will do now is make clear that, in view of what ministry/*diakonia* was for ancient Greeks, Christian or not, the writer of this letter could not possibly have entertained the idea of all the saints being called into the restricted activity that they designated *diakonia/ministry*.

In demonstrating this, however, we will not be engaging in a set piece of academic exegesis or interpretation. Rather, what we propose to do is to provide in a nontechnical form the results of what close exegesis might come up with. After all, we have already worked our way through a large amount of material and built up our appreciation of what the term *ministry/diakonia* can contribute to a piece of ancient writing about church. We might remind ourselves that our concentration on this one term has been prompted by the nature of the debate that theologians and ecumenists have been carrying on. As just noted, in the modern discussions about ministry, the focus has shifted away from individual offices like that of bishops or elders to what is considered to be the more fruitful area of ministry in general. The reason for this shift is simple. The word *diakonia* is the word that occasioned the entry of the word *ministry* into discourse about church in the English language. This is not meant in an etymological sense; only very few English words—and these are of the *deacon* kind—can claim an etymological connection with *diakonia*. What happened is that the Latin or Vulgate New Testament translated *diakon*-terms by means of the Latin *minister* terms, and since the Vulgate New Testament became the New Testament of Western Europe, the Latin *minister* terms established themselves in the languages of people who became absorbed into the Roman Empire. Thus French, Italian, and similar languages used to represent *diakon*- words in "ministerial" terms, whereas Germanic languages, including the Nordic, could not; they generally represented functions of a churchly kind by words denoting "office"(*Amt* in German): thus Martin Luther in his final version (1545) of Ephesians 4:12,"[das] werck des Ampts."[1] The 1997 *Gute Nachricht Bibel*, by contrast, invokes the word, *Dienst*/service ("die Glaubenden zum Dienst bereitzumachen": NRSV, "to make believers ready for service"), which is now conventional throughout related languages and across the New Testament.

---

1. See http://lutherbibel.net/.

In the same way, modern English translations have shifted from *ministry* words to *service* words.

In drawing up a profile of ministry as practiced by Paul (in the preceding chapter) we found its most prominent feature to be an involvement in and responsibility for the ministry of the Word. We found that this ministry commonly intimated the process of purveying to believers the mystery of God's saving intention for men and women. Through this process, that is, on the occasion of the ministry and through its efficacy, believers are presented as actually experiencing an encounter with the mystery at some level or in some aspect relative to the openness of the minister to the divine word and of the believer to its power of enlightenment. We might refer once more in illustration of this to Paul's exposition of the process of ministry in 2 Cor. 3:2–18, drawing attention in particular to the outcome of the process so boldly stated in verse 18 that believers, both minister and those who have received God's Word through him or her, "are being changed into [the Lord's] likeness from one degree of glory to another."

From a later period—either of Paul's life or of the churches associated with him—we encounter in Col. 1:13–23 another powerful evocation of this association of ministry with the mystery God has in store for believers. In this passage, being the purveyor of the mystery is what constitutes Paul the minister. We shall see (Chapter 10) that Luke's profile of ministry in Acts adds to Paul's concept of purveying mystery the exclusive prerogative to ministry of those whom the Lord or the church commissions, if indeed this characteristic is not already clearly implied in the altogether special role Paul ascribes to the minister. To recognize that this is in fact the case, we need only recall the vigorous way Paul dismissed claims to ministry of those whom he considered uncommissioned.

Accordingly, as we move into the exposition on the nature and calling of the church as laid out in the letter to the Ephesians, we are alerted to the fact that ministry is of this same kind as soon as we find the writer engaging with mystery and revelation at the beginning of chapter 3. More exactly, this is where the writer spells out those words, although the letter has actually been celebrating and expounding the mystery from the beginning. We notice that at the end of chapter 2, the writer has also tied the experience of the mystery in faith to the teaching of the apostles and prophets of the past, which makes of Paul and contemporary apostles and prophets an extension among the Gentiles of those predecessors (2:5). Only by reason of his election by God, in a liberal divine gift that worked powerfully in him, does the letter identify Paul as a minister/*diakonos*

(2:7). As such a minister, he is to make known "the plan of the mystery" (2:9). And as a result of the work of this minister, Christ can dwell by faith in the hearts of men and women (2:17).

The Ephesian Principle

The common experience of life "in the unity of the Spirit" (4:3) makes of the group of believers "one body" (4:4); at the same time believers experience the mystery at different levels or in different degrees (verse 4:7). Accordingly, the writer wishes to put before the believers a vision of what the common experience can lead to. A condition of organic unity and growth among them, however, is that all realize they are under the grace or gifting of Christ. He is the source of all life and enlightenment. That comprehended (4:7–10), the writer moves on to outline both the process by which the unity and growth is achieved (4:11–14) and the profile of the fully developed body of believers (4:15–16).

Throughout these phases of growth—always under the Spirit and in the gift of Christ—the controlling principle of life is the enlightenment shared by the believers. Unity of faith and knowledge (4:13) and freedom from confusion (4:14) allow the body of believers to mature and fill out to the stature of Christ himself. The enlightenment does not just arrive from on high for a number of lucky individuals, nor does it remain and increase within the body of believers by its inherent energy or through an instinctive interplay of faith and knowledge among the believers. It is not self-sustaining and does not originate in the gifting of individuals, as if Christ gathered believers to himself by random selection among the Gentiles.

On the contrary, according to the writer, Christ ensured that a body of believers would form by giving first a group of suppliers or practitioners of enlightenment. These are the apostles, prophets, evangelists, pastors, and teachers (4:11). Although we are no longer able to determine exactly the roles of these people or to discriminate closely between them, what is clear is a common responsibility in the provision and maintainance of enlightenment among the body of believers. To the recipients of the letter, on the other hand, the character and the differentiation of roles among these were well known because the writer has simply had to list the functionaries, some of whom—in particular, apostles and prophets—may have been remembered from an earlier stage in the development of the churches.

If these functionaries of verse 11 have the general responsibility of sustaining the church in unity of faith, we have only to follow the writer one step further to know how they are to carry out their responsibility. This step takes us into verse 12, whose fate under the judgment of modern translators we regularly observe throughout these pages. Here we will review the verse from the first edition of the RSV, reading that Christ has given as gifts these sets of teachers "for the equipment of the saints, for the work of ministry/*diakonia*, for building up the body of Christ." Again we come to our question: whose ministry is this? This time our answer is confident and well founded. Without needing to look for meaning through subtle considerations of the grammatical structure and interrelationship of the phrases here, we can be certain that the ministry/*diakonia* belongs to the teachers. The context requires it, and the Greek word itself demands it. Let us remind ourselves why.

The writer has prepared us to consider this ministerial arrangement for the church through his reflections on the role of the minister/*diakonos* within the purveying of mystery (3:7). This was just a few hundred words earlier, and the general context has not changed. Rather the context has grown richer with the marvels of heaven's mystery as it has narrowed to a vision of the church as the precinct of heaven's gifts. Further, conscious of the weight and character of both the term *minister/diakonos* and the term *ministry/diakonia* in any context of revelation or of message from heaven—we can think back to how effective these words were in the stories presented in chapter 4 about Josephus as a prophet, about Aesop recognizing the messenger of Isis, about Hermes, and in passages about the sphere in between heaven and earth, as well as in the powerful antecedents in the Christian prose of Paul himself, especially 2 Cor. 3:3–18. We recognize what the author is signaling, namely, that through the process of ministry/*diakonia* the enlightenment by which the church lives is transferred from Christ in the heavenly sphere to the body of believers in the earthly. The transference is what "the work" (4:12) is. The transference is that process called *ministry* which we have seen illustrated in the work of one *minister*, Paul, and the special character of the Greek term is itself the signal that such a *minister* has been appointed to the task either by heaven or by an authoritative source on earth.

To appreciate the import of this statement in Eph. 4:11–12 we must recognize the significance of the words in the passage before we begin to juggle the sentence around to find its intent. The writer has contributed the key word *ministry/diakonia* to the sentence precisely to emphasize the sacred and exclusive character of the teachers' responsibility. No ancient reader of his Greek phrase could mistake his meaning. When late-twentieth-century Christians turned his word into a nondescript service within the capacity of any believer, they gravely distorted his meaning.

The ministry of the early church, then, in the view of the author of this letter, was the work and responsibility of a select number of preachers and teachers. Such work supposed a profoundly religious engagement with the Christian mystery and was named *ministry* by virtue of this engagement. Implied in the writer's insistence on the need for unity of faith and knowledge is the coherence of the ministry across various functions which the various titles point to, as well as the continuity of the ministry from one generation to another. This in turn would seem to require the integration of all the works of ministry through a process or within a framework of something like a synod—not as an elite source of coercive power but as a function of the whole local church. Its role would be to evaluate the church's life in the face of the mystery it harbors.

The contribution of the believers to such a process or system is likely to be substantial but is not constitutive of the ministry. The ministry is established by the mandate of the heavenly Christ and maintained and issued by the holders of the mandate to others whom they bring under it. What believers might contribute here we leave to the imagination, to hope, to the shared experience of faith, and to freedom under grace. No doubt we should envisage believers advocating the causes of those among themselves whom they recognize as worthy candidates for ministry. This would be after the scriptural precedent enshrined in Luke's account of the institution of the Seven (see chapter 10).

Perhaps only one other comment on the Ephesian principle of ministry is necessary. Today's majority is likely to find any suggestion of an exclusive or hierarchical style of ministry repugnant. It flies against the democratic instinct of the age, runs counter to the strongly charismatic quality attributed to ministry in current thinking, and seems only to endorse the style of the incumbents of the traditional Christian hierarchies. What we need to recognize, however, is that the hierarchies many of today's Christians find repugnant are not so much structured on the Ephesian model as borrowed from the political hegemonies of the ancient world. Such hierarchies early became hegemonies for the exercise of political and coercive power within the realm of the people's new religious experiences of Christian faith, and only in later times misguidedly appropriated for this jurisdiction within the religious sphere the designation "sacred rule" or "hierarchy."

The author of Ephesians, however, is speaking of another sphere altogether, one unconnected with worldly power and rule and imbued with the authenticity of an exclusively religious kind. The sphere is that of powerless faith and knowledge. Within this sphere everything is enlightening and heartening, but nothing can be effected by power, politics, or law. Within it everyone receives from the same source (4:13) and there are no grades of station. All grow into love (4:16). That some have the requirement put upon them to ensure the vigor and continuity of faith and knowledge gives them no power but lays them directly under the mandate of Christ. As Calvin put it (*Commentaries*, 122), theirs is "the ministry by which God reigns among us."

A *Loss of Principle*

Calvin wrote that phrase in the introduction to his commentary on Ephesians. In his treatment of chapter 4:11–14, he emphasizes again and again the official and exclusive character of this ministry: by "the will of God and the appointment of Christ" the church possesses an "order" in what he calls "the external ministry of the Word," namely, the group of men—and for him they could only be men—who are the pastors and teachers (*Commentaries*, 177–184). While insistent, he does seem a little taken aback that God should arrange the church so, when men and women could have been brought directly into salvation "without human assistance." Here he is conscious of the claims of those in his day whom he calls "the fanatics, who invent secret revelations of the Spirit for themselves" and then of "the proud, who think that for them the private reading of the Scriptures is enough." They demonstrate to him the waywardness of the human spirit and how right it is for the church that Christ should "prescribe the way in which it shall be built," namely, through the "offices" of "the outward preaching."

I return to Calvin not for his authority, which is by no means obvious in all aspects of his reading of these passages, but because, writing out of a time which was given over to controversy about the functioning of church, he was so overpoweringly convinced of the intent of the author of Ephesians at this point of ministry. Such an understanding fits exactly the understanding a contemporary Greek would have taken from the author's use of *ministry/diakonia* in this passage.

In our day, by contrast, as we discuss especially in chapter 11, the ministerial order constructed by the author of Ephesians has been dismantled, and all the believers, by virtue of their baptism into Christ from which they all share in his priesthood, are now said to share in his ministry. We will not comment further on how awkward this has made all talk and thought of the ordained ministries in the churches today, but a reminder of the scale of the change is useful. It was precisely the possibility of such a change, for example, that Calvin was anticipating and resisting. He knew, and could observe, that with the dismantling of the ecclesiastical offices of the Roman church, the body of believers was exposed to any number of enthusiasms that might claim to be the inspiration of the Spirit of God. While the enthusiasm within the reformed tradition he established was contained by the clarity and efficiency of official ministerial structures, the same effect was not so securely achieved in all reformed churches. In particular, within the Lutheran tradition, the question of ministry was never satisfactorily resolved. A tension has remained from the beginning, and has expressed itself within different churches at different periods, as to whether ministry is an office as such or whether it is a function confided to some in the church for the purposes of good order. If it is the latter, all in the church can conceivably possess a ministerial capacity, although only a few are called upon to use it. Of itself—and apart from the fact that the scheme is not compatible with how the early Christians thought of ministry—one might think this could work. In fact, however, it leaves the function of ministry open to a powerful influence. This is the enthusiasm to which Calvin disparagingly referred.

Being enthused, whether enjoying a spiritual conviction or being on a spiritual high, is one of the perennial attractions, rewards, and dangers of religious experience. In all periods of their history, Christians have been enthused in either way. Much good has come of their experiences, as with John Wesley, and much brutality and tragedy, as in the suppression of the Cathars and the mass suicides of Jim Jones's disciples in Jonestown, Guyana, in 1978. And in theology there is strong undergirding of enthusiasm in the talk of gifts of the Spirit or, in the Greek form, *charismata* or charisms. Conceived of as a capacity with which the baptized person is endowed, ministry could claim to be called forth in an individual's response to the Spirit. Ministry would thus be essentially charismatic. One would say—as many do say—that if the church chooses to speak of office, the office must be understood as coming through the gift of ministry. On the contrary, says the author of the Ephesians, ministry is by definition an office, and those called to it are the gift of Christ to the church. The fact that they possess gifts apt for ministry does not make them ministers; they become ministers when they are installed in the office of ministry.

8

Ministry Among Gifts

PAUL IS OFTEN presented as the champion of a charismatic ministry, and a great amount of exegesis, theology, and history has been written to support this viewpoint. The cause is misconceived, however, and its underlying proposition is seriously misleading.[1] In chapter 12 of 1 Corinthians, from where the discussion mainly takes its rise, Paul is proposing that the teaching roles of the church provide its cohesion. Through his image of the church as a body, he is acknowledging the variety of capacities within a church and endorsing their exercise. In doing so, he is making the point that each capacity is proportionate to the needs of the body and is to be exercised within that scope. No one function is to encroach upon or to impede other functions. And the first functionaries within the body of believers, appointed by God, are apostles; the second are prophets; and the third are teachers (1 Cor. 12:28).

Keeping Enthusiasm in Check

Within the context of the diversity of the body's functions Paul could hardly have brought greater emphasis to bear than he has here on the priority in the church of the teaching functions. These are the functions that guide, direct, inspire, curtail, develop, and train. The body will perform only as well as it is educated. Its many other gifts—its powers of healing, tongues, administration, and so on—show that it is alive and well, but it remains a body, that is, an organic union of many people, by virtue of

---

1. My reading of ministry as gift here (being chapter 9 of *Are All Christians Ministers?*, 1992) takes my assessment of 1 Cor. 12:4–6 one significant step further from the "broad" understanding of authoritative activity identified in my *Diakonia: Re-interpreting the Ancient Sources*, 233; 255–56, to a recognition of the "varieties of ministries" as the specific apostolic ministerial mandates of Paul and his colleagues. See, similarly, *Deacons and the Church* (Leominster: Gracewing, 2002), 82–84, and the section "Re-reading Gifts and Ministry" in Chapter 12 pp. 205–09 below, with further reference there.

having been fashioned through the work of the founding preachers and then nourished by prophets and teachers. As we know from Paul's mind in this letter, this founding work was a collaboration with God (3:9), and in that connection we cannot escape the implication of Paul's conceptualization of himself and of the other collaborators as ministers (3:5). Theirs is the responsibility and prerogative of making the believers into a church. In chapter 3, one image of this work is farmers preparing a crop, and another is builders raising a temple. In chapter 12, the image is of a living body, the leading function of which is its consciousness activated at different stages by apostles, prophets, and teachers. Of interest to us in the following sections is the relationship between the first two of these. (Of teachers Paul says no more.)

An apostle and a teacher we assume to be such by appointment, but a prophet? A prophet arises, and prophets were a main source of enlightenment and growth for the early communities (Rom. 12:6; Eph. 4:11), and they carry authority because they are placed by God (1 Cor. 12:28). In the Corinthian church, the activity of prophets is more clearly observable than elsewhere, especially in chapter 14. Prophecy is the gift to be desired (14:1) because prophecy builds up the community, encourages, and consoles (14:3), and is thus superior to the esoteric experience of speaking in tongues (14:5). Prophecy is intelligent and penetrating and can reveal the presence of God even to the unbeliever (14:24–25). Accordingly, it is to be cherished and dwelt on, and all are free to seek some expression of it, subject always to good order and growth (14:29–32; 37–40). Thus the utterances of the prophet do not share the exuberant or mysterious quality of what is spoken in tongues (14:23) but are a measured reflection, subject to the critique of companions in the gathering, on the mystery that the believers have gathered to share.

These prophetic statements are a teaching device, deeply affirmative of the shared faith, and they seek also to be illuminating. From what is shared at this level the community gathers greater cohesion and direction. Clearly, from Paul's indications in chapter 14 and from our own perceptions of such a process, not all in a mixed community are equipped for prophecy; some are inhibited by inadequate instruction, others by lack of experience or by spiritual immaturity. The community itself, when it honors good order, knows its prophets, and nothing in 1 Cor. 12:1–7 implies that a prophet's role is any less orderly or any more enthusiastic than that of an apostle or teacher. Like apostle and teacher, the prophet is bound by the harmonies of the body. The prophet's authenticity is known in part from the effectiveness with which he preserves and promotes the harmonious growth of the body.

In 1 Cor. 12:1–11, Paul places these upbuilding functions of prophecy among a number of others as gifts of the Spirit. In doing this Paul is not drawing up a constitution for a church, that is, implying that a church functions only when it has all the gifts he lists operating effectively. He is being much more realistic than that. He is cutting his coat to suit his cloth. The Corinthian church operates through prophecy and other gifts, they are making inquiries of him about relative values or priorities, and Paul casts his response in their terms and in the light of what he knows of that community. With another community the emphasis would be different. What matters for Paul is that the community draws life from its experience of faith, maintains its unity, and sustains growth.

Splitting up Gifts

The Corinthians are finding their most intractable problem in the use and disposition of their newfound spiritual skills at worship. How newfound these are may perhaps be open to question. Some scholars suggest that one of the problems among the Corinthians may have been that in their Christian worship they were introducing too much of the ecstatic style of their pre-Christian cults. What is clear is that Paul addresses himself with great deliberation to things of the Spirit, beginning here at chapter 12 and concluding only at the end of chapter 14. And his opening observations, for all the warning signals they contain, are very affirming of the convictions which the Corinthians held about the place of the Spirit in their lives. In 12:1–3 he assures them that everything done in faith and in worship is done by the power of the Spirit. With remarkable rhetorical emphasis he develops and reinforces this teaching down to verse 7, and then illustrates it in a rich medley of spiritual activities down to verse 10, concluding in verse 11 with the same Spirit he began with.

Unfortunately and unavoidably, our English translations cannot represent the rhetoric with its balances and wordplays. Thus Paul begins in verses 4–6 with the idea of a wide distribution of heavenly gifts; once distributed across the church, these gifts appear as different kinds of spiritual activities so that the end result is a variety of gifts in the church, and this is what the translations generally concentrate on in speaking of *varieties* or *different kinds*. In concentrating on the result, however, such translations miss the process which the writer evidently had in mind because his Greek word suggests the act of dividing or splitting something up. First, he uses the word as a noun in verses 4–6 (*diaireseis*), giving it first place (apart from simple conjunctions) in each of the three sentences and then, after he has illustrated the kinds of gifts he wants to talk about, he returns to his idea in verse 11, this time expressing it by the cognate verb (*diairoun*). Here some of the translations, especially the traditional ones, pick up his idea by printing *dividing*. This began with the 1535 Tyndale translation and mostly remained so until the 1881 RV; the RSV writes in a similar vein that the Spirit "apportions to each one." Thus the idea of dividing, which emerges clearly in the English verse 11, is actually only echoing and reemphasizing the idea already expressed and emphasized in the Greek verses 4–6. This invites us, surely, to look closely at what Paul had in mind with his division of gifts.

What is being divided up and distributed are *charismata* (translated "gifts," but the Greek word is often now used in English as well), *ministries/diakoniai*, and *operations*. For this last I use Tyndale's good word, which went through all English translations until the RV switched slightly to the sharper *workings*. The Greek is *energēmata*, and while the RSV writes "varieties of working, but it is the same God who inspires [*energoun*] them all," I prefer to reflect the interplay of the two Greek *energ-* words by writing "*activities* but the same God *activates* them." (NRSV also made this change.) Each of these three divisions or distributions is aligned with a distinct divine principle—namely, Spirit, Lord, and God—so that we have the following pattern (see figure 8.1):

What to us is reminiscent of a trinitarian formula should not distract us from the writer's overriding thought, which is concerned with the divine origin of all the powers at work in the church. Paul is not specifying the origin of the gifts, the ministries, and the activities in three distinct sources; after all, in one place he writes that "God activates them all" (12:6) and in another that "the Spirit activates them all" (12:11).

This perhaps leads us to ask what Paul was actually intending to convey through the threefold division. It remains a notable rhetorical device,

---

gifts—	Spirit
ministries/*diakoniai*—	Lord
activities—	God

FIGURE 8.1 Alignment of gifts

especially with the repetition of the leading word *diaireseis/divisions/varieties*, and we might wonder whether Paul has constructed it with the simple intent of saying that what is distributed from heaven can be called by different names, or whether he intends something totally different, namely, that what is distributed from heaven is to be divided up in a number of ways. If his three words are simply a matter of three names for one and the same reality, then we can draw up the following formula:

gifts = ministries = activities

In fact, this would be by far the commonest understanding of the relationship between the three words among those who have written on this section in modern times. Assisting this view is the nearly common understanding of the middle term *ministries/diakoniai* as a term meaning "services to the community," and commentators are further encouraged in this view by the fact that in Paul's own following statement the heavenly distribution is for the good of the whole community (verse 7: "to proffit the congregacion," as Tyndale boldly translated); anything anyone does has to be for the better functioning of the body (verse 25) and for the upbuilding of the church (14.12: "the edifyinge of the congregacion," Tyndale). If we are to read verses 4–6 like this, with the three words as just a string of names each of which applies equally appropriately to activities in the community, we are left with a simple but inspiring passage about God's liberality toward the church. In that case, however, Paul's strong rhetoric would seem to be overplayed and, what is more telling, we would be reading the passage without taking into consideration what was possible and what was not possible for Paul to intend by his term *ministries/diakoniai*.

Paul's preference for *ministry/diakonia* to say something specific about roles in the church is basic. In 1 Thess. 3:2, Paul has already used *minister/diakonos* in his pastoral career to lend authority to Timothy's mission among the Thessalonians (if we keep to the reading argued in *Diakonia: Re-interpreting the Ancient Sources* [223–24]). Now, within this letter to the Corinthians he has already used the same term at 3:5 to claim the same authority for himself and Apollos and thus cut off at the source a threatening challenge to the unity of the community. And in his next letter to the Corinthians, he returns to this terminology to stake his strongest claims among them (see 2 Cor. 11:23 and the discussion in chapter 6 on Paul as minister above). Outside of evangelizing roles, he applies the terminology equally effectively to delegations (chapter 9) to other churches, as in his collection for Jerusalem (e.g. Rom. 15:26), in the case of Phoebe

(Rom. 16:1), and in the case of Stephanas (1 Cor. 16:15). That is just about the ambit of his uses, and they are not uses peculiar to him but exemplify usage of other Christian and non-Christian Hellenistic and earlier Greek writers.

To look again at the possibilities in our passage, we would have to say that neither Paul nor any other ancient writer could have used the term *ministries/diakoniai* to mean what an eminent German commentator here began calling, over a century ago, "strictly service to the brethren."[2]. Here, with the mention of the "Lord," the term can only mean "servicesministries at the Lord's command." The Lord's command, in other words, is what constitutes them as *ministries*. Our next question, accordingly, is to ask who in this case is considered under the Lord's command. And for that we need to return to the structure of Paul's paragraph.

1 Corinthians 12:4–6

In verses 4–6, as we have already emphasized, we are to think of Paul writing about the distribution of heaven's gifts. In being divided up, different parts of heaven's gift necessarily go to different individuals; this phase of the process is exemplified very clearly in the way Paul writes verses 7–11, and is the foundation of the image of the body with members functioning in many different ways. Now, how is this concept of the division of heaven's gifts reflected in the sentence structure? In Paul's arrangement of the Greek there may be subtleties which are not easily translated, but if we construct a chart (see figure 8.2) with a word-for-word rendering in one central column, the RSV's translation in a left-hand column, and a new translation in a right-hand column, we may be able to illustrate more effectively and economically the subtleties we are confronted with.

The main differences introduced in the new translation are three: (1) the word *divisions* instead of *varieties*, and the reason for this change has been discussed; (2) the word *ministries* instead of *service*, also for reasons already largely provided; and (3) the use of *both/and* instead of *and/and*. The second and third points are connected, and we will look into them together.

Probably the least appreciated aspect of Paul's rhetoric in this passage is his reference to *ministries/diakoniai*. The meaning of "services to the community" has already been rejected. Should we be equally confident that "the word here has nothing to do with 'ministry' in the technical

2. J. Weiss, *Der erste Korintherbrief* (Göttingen: Vandenhoeck and Ruprecht, 1910).

RSV	Word for Word	New Translation
Now there are varieties of gifts, but the same Spirit;	divisions however of gifts exist, but the same Spirit	Divisions exist among gifts, although the Spirit is one and the same
and there are varieties of service, but the same Lord;	*and* divisions of ministries/*diakoniai* exist and the same Lord	*both* divisions of ministries, the Lord too remaining the same
and there are varieties of working, but it is the same God who inspires them all in every one.	*and* divisions of activities exist, but the same God the one activating all things in all	*and* then divisions of activities, with God of course remaining the same, the one who activates all these things among us all.

FIGURE 8.2 Translating I Cor. 12:4–6

sense," as influential commentators insist?[3] On the contrary, as indicated by our brief review of Paul's use of this word and in light of our discussion about general usage, we have no reason to think that Paul would be using the word in any other sense than what we might best call a technical sense of ministry. By this we mean a ministry that consists in carrying out the mandate to reveal God's hidden purposes in Christ, namely, the ministry carried out by Paul and others like Apollos. In fact, we can say that no other meaning than this is available for this context. Paul's ancient readers—they were actually hearers—were not going to be mistaken in this. This word said to them at once "sacred missions," and they were totally aware of what these had been among them: had not Paul in the early chapters of this letter (1:10–12; 3:3–6) pointed to the different *ministers* they had received?

Charismata and Pneumatika

If this was the import of the word for the Corinthians, we have to adjust the way we think of verses 4–6, because the introduction of *ministry* in the sense of "sacred mission" immediately wrecks the three-way equation we set out above: gifts = ministries = activities. This equation can no longer stand because the activities are activated in everybody (verses 6 and 11), whereas the ministries are reserved for the few to whom the Lord has committed them. Instead of a church replete with gifts, ministries,

---

3. C. K. Barrett, *A Commentary on the First Epistle to the Corinthians*, (New York: Harper and Row, 1968), 284; H. Conzelmann, *I Corinthians*, Eng. trans. (Philadelphia: Fortress Press, 1975), 208.

gifts/*charismata*	{	ministries/*diakoniai*
		activities/*energēmata*

FIGURE 8.3 Gifts of Two Kinds

and activities churchwide, Paul presents a church replete with gifts of two main kinds, ministries and activities. We can put that in the following diagram (see figure 8.3):

Several perspectives of church open up once this diagram is applied. But before commenting on those, it is helpful to note that the division of gifts represented by the diagram, if not quite our understanding of the gifts themselves, has also been advocated by E. Earle Ellis in *Pauline Theology: Ministry and Society*.[4] Similarly, a much earlier but notable scholar, Willem van Est, wrote simply in his commentary on this chapter in 1709 that *gifts* were a genus and *ministries* were a species within that.[5] In regard to the meaning of *diakoniai* in this passage as designating distinctive ministries rather than general ones within the charge of all, Joseph Fitzmyer has endorsed the view presented here largely on the basis of the linguistic factors advocated in *Diakonia: Re-interpreting the Ancient Sources* and in my other published comment.[6] Of particular interest is Fitzmyer's rejection on these grounds of the long-standing and hugely influential view of Ernst Käsemann supporting an understanding at 1 Corinthians 12 of community-wide ministries.[7]

For newer perspectives of church to emerge clearly from the divisions of gifts outlined above, we need also to remind ourselves that the word *charismata* is to be understood just as we have it here as "gifts," a notion that is not to be obscured or elaborated by the addition of what we have come to include in the modern English word *charisma,* (e.g. as applied for

---

4. Grand Rapids: Eerdmans; (Exeter: Paternoster Row, 1990), 35–36.

5. *Commentarius in Cap. XII Epistolae I. ad Corinthios* (Amsterdam 1709), 326.

6. Joseph Fitzmyer, *First Corinthians: A New Translation and Commentary* (New Haven, CT: Yale University Press, 2008, 465, in reference to my 'Ministry as a Distinct Category among Charismata (1 Corinthians 12:4–7)', *Neotestamentica* 27 (1993) 79–91.

7. 'Ministry and Community in the New Testament' in id., *Essays on New Testament Themes*, Eng. trans. (London: SCM Press, 1964), 63–94. See extensive discussion arising from Kasemann in Chapter 12 below.

example to a a politician whose character or public image has an almost irresistible appeal in the electorate), nor with what we associate with the word *charismatic* (i.e. gatherings of Christians who give voluble expression to their joy and confidence in the Lord in song and praise, perhaps also in tongues and healings). To associate *gifts/charismata* in such ways with the contemporary sense of *charismatic* is to confuse Paul's idea of *charismata* with Paul's other important word here *pneumatika/spiritual*. Indeed, one may say that the so-called charismatic churches and charismatic movements within churches of today have made it difficult for us to think of *charismata* not being the same as *pneumatika/spiritual*. But it is important, if we are to appreciate how Paul envisages the functioning of church in this passage, that we distinguish two realities here.

Paul has begun this long section of his letter (chapters 12–14) announcing abruptly, "Now concerning spiritual *things*," and our discussion is not helped by the fact that translations from as far back as the Great Bible of 1539 very often insert the word *gifts* here in place of *things*: the Greek has neither of these nouns and uses the plural adjective *pneumatika/spiritual* by itself as a noun. In verse 1, Paul is not announcing a discussion about gifts at all but a discussion about the types of religious experience that the Corinthians have found exciting; they have asked Paul about them, and Paul gives us a fairly clear impression of them in 12:8–10 and throughout chapter 14. These are spiritual or pneumatic experiences and activities, and that is what he calls them again as he introduces chapter 14 (the adjective alone *pneumatika*, without the addition of the word *gifts*; English translation of this verse goes back to Tyndale).

In handling this subject for the Corinthians, Paul sets himself a very clear objective, as we can see from the overall effect of the chapters. Presented with a community giving preference in some of its gatherings to a spiritual or pneumatic experience called speaking in tongues, Paul—who spoke in tongues himself (14:18) and does not want to discourage the practice among the Corinthians (14:5, 39)—develops a firm instruction on how to moderate the potentially disruptive effect on the gathering of this pneumatic phenomenon and directs the Corinthians to develop their skills in and give preference to another pneumatic activity called prophecy. As he says (14:19), he would rather teach something in five intelligible words than utter ten thousand words of praise that no one understands.

With the moderation of tongues and the nurture of prophecy his objective, Paul pays little attention to other pneumatic activities apart from acknowledging their presence and value in the community (12:8–10;

14:28–30). (In our discussion here we have no occasion to comment on Paul's treatment of the pre-eminence of love in this context, chapter 13.) What he does give close attention to in the introduction to chapter 12, however, is the place of these spiritual things/pneumatika in the way a church is constituted. Only in this context does he speak of them as *gifts/charismata*, but he makes it clear that gifts/charismata include more than pneumatika. As we have seen in the last diagram, gifts include both ministries, which are not pneumatika, and activities, which are. In other words, everything that a church does faithfully or is capable of doing in faith is charismatic in the sense of being the implementation of heavenly gift. The Pauline church we see at Corinth is at the same time, within itself, spiritual or pneumatic, because it lives and develops from the exercise of the pneumatic activities Paul alludes to. But the sum of its pneumatic energies does not constitute the whole of what God gives to the church. Over it and moderating it is the work of the ministry, represented in this case so clearly by Paul. It happens that in this case Paul the minister is absent from his charge, because his role is to exercise ministry in other churches as well.

Ministry and Prophecy

The perspective of church which this understanding of 12:4–6 provides is thus of a group of believers who have been brought together in Christ through the minister's proclamation of the Word, who then reflect on this Word in the power of the Spirit's illumination and build one another up through the prophetic teaching which emerges from this experience—no less than five times in chapter 14 does Paul urge the community's responsibility for upbuilding—and who remain within the tutelage and guidance of the ministry.

Interestingly, ministry holds the same place in the perspective of church held by the writer of the letter to the Ephesians (4:12). There too it is a gift of Christ, just as in 1 Cor. 12:5 it is associated with the name of the Lord. One difference is that the later writer's larger historical perspective allows him to look back on the whole known development of the churches and to see all those who have relayed the revealed mystery as workers in ministry, whether they be the apostles or prophets of old or the teachers of his own day. The perspective Paul is asking the Corinthians to keep in view is different. He too puts apostles, prophets, and teachers in the first rank of God's appointment for the church (12:28). His purpose is not to identify what is the ministerial function within the church. This he has no need to do because the Corinthians had already been reminded in chapters 1 and 3 of who the ministers were. Rather Paul was making a statement about what functions in the church are more important. This issued in the advice that the intelligent encounter with the Spirit in prophecy was of more value in building up a house of the Spirit in Corinth than encounters that could not be articulated intelligibly and thus shared with others. Accordingly, Paul concludes, teaching—along with the intelligent critique of teaching (14:29, 32)—is where the communal upbuilding will begin, and this function in the community belongs to "first apostles, second prophets, third teachers." In Paul's language, and the Corinthians understood this instinctively, the only ministry/diakonia in this list was that of the apostles, although a later writer was also correct from the point of view of usage to include within his concept of ministry/diakonia a wider range of teaching functions.

In everything Paul taught about church in these chapters he was governed principally by the needs of the Corinthian church. In other words, he was teaching what the church in Corinth was or should be, not what every church was or could be. Because the Corinthians were becoming confused amid the richness and vitality of experiences that they identified as the work of the Spirit, Paul's objective was to bring them back to the gospel he had preached to them and to the means whereby knowledge of that gospel would become sounder among them and express itself more surely in their lives and relationships. In the proper understanding of God's ways with the church, made clear in the measured reflections of the prophets among them, their best spiritual experiences would take their rise. The whole church would then be healthily spiritual or *pneumatic*. Thus Paul was not putting together a systematic statement on church, nor do we have a prescription for other churches in this picture of the spiritual wonders at play in Corinth.

From Paul's correspondence with other churches and from later writings we get glimpses of how the several congregations ordered their experiences. These are the details that Eduard Schweizer brings to our attention in *Church Order in the New Testament*. Because we are concentrating on the notion and place of ministry in the early churches rather than descending to such detail, however, we will simply point to what is still today the most instructive complement to Schweizer in the way that it isolates the unity and purpose of ministry amid the diversity of the earliest

congregations. This is André Lemaire's *Ministry in the Church*,[8] a translation of his French book of 1974 (itself developed from his scholarly 1971 *Les
ministères aux origines de l'église*).[9]

Moving on from those more obscure expressions of church life
and Paul's presentation of the priority and authority of ministry to the
Corinthians, we turn to see him on one other occasion acknowledging
the complementarity of ministry and prophecy in his words about gifts
to the church in Rome. Paul's thinking in Romans is what he put together in the course of his work and experience among the Corinthians.
Not surprisingly, some ideas that came to expression in his correspondence with the Corinthians find a more developed treatment in the letter
to the Romans, while some of the themes elaborated for the Corinthians
are expressed more succinctly to the Romans. We see the latter exemplified in the question of gifts at Rom. 12:3–8.

Here we meet again the concept of the congregation as one body,
of the members having different roles, of individuals receiving
gifts/charismata, of the gifts being different from one person to another
according to the measure of faith, plus a list of the leading and some
of the auxiliary gifts. These are, in order, prophecy, ministry/*diakonia*,
teaching, exhortation, and other gifts relating to liberality. What is notable for our purposes is the conjunction once again, at the head of the
list, of prophecy, ministry, and teaching. Clearly for Paul these are the
gifts a church needs—if one prefers, the gifts that God first provides
so that a church may be. The interesting factor in this situation between Paul and the Roman church, however, is that Paul has not yet
been to Rome: this circumstance affected Paul's introduction to Rome
of Phoebe as a delegate of the church in Cenchreae (Rom. 16:1).Paul's
lack of contact with the Roman community likely explains the odd ordering of the leading gifts, with prophecy first and ministry second. The
ministry/*diakonia* (12: 7) certainly includes the ministry of Paul, whose
reputation as a minister to the far-flung churches of the east has pre-
ceded his letter to Rome. In placing ministry second to prophecy, Paul is
acknowledging that the Roman church owes nothing of its formation to
his ministry—and yet his ministry is a prime agent of God's saving power
among the Gentiles, as he had proclaimed earlier (11:13)—but in the first

---

8. London, SPCK, 1977.

9. Paris: Cerf, 1971.

place he is acknowledging that the Roman church has grown to its maturity through the workings of prophecy in its midst. No mention here of possible obscuring of the prophetic message through an exuberance of pneumatic energy. Paul simply places the normal processes of church growth as he knew it within the framework of gifts/*charismata* that he had elaborated in his instructions to the Corinthians. Of the status he expected the Roman church to accord to his own ministry/*diakonia* we have no need to inquire; the letter itself speaks for that.

Similarly, in the three chapters of 1 Cor. 12–14, —we have a demonstration of the power and authority of Paul's ministry, a ministry which he acknowledges in 12:5 to be as much a gift of God as the least consequential revelation of a Corinthian prophet.

We would also seem to have an exhibition of one of the constitutive principles of church, namely, that although ministry is a gift—and a charismatic one by implication of language—it is by nature an office among whose responsibilities is the good ordering of other gifts (spiritual and pneumatic) in the church. Whereas the Corinthians had led themselves to think that the church was essentially pneumatic—meaning, by their understanding of that term, a group of individuals exposed to variegated divine inspirations—Paul was advising them that the church was essentially charismatic and that ministries took precedence over the spiritual experiences and activities which they called the *pneumatika*. Accordingly, to the extent that we neglect to take account of the authority inherent in the concept of ministry/*diakonia*, contributions to the debate concerning the relative authority of gift and office—which is a debate initiated in 1892 by Rudolf Sohm—are made under a grave handicap. One might even suspect that the debate should never have begun.

Ministry and Authority

Paul was to hear worse news out of Corinth than confusion about how Christians should run their gatherings. Other visiting missionaries were soon to be questioning the way he conducted his ministry, questioning even his right to claim a place in ministry. We saw what response this elicited from Paul and what profound insights into ministry his response revealed (See chapter 6). At the end of his first letter to the Corinthians, however, problems with ministry were not what he was anticipating. He had received the delegation from Corinth composed of Stephanas and his colleagues, and undoubtedly discussed with them the nature and extent of the problems he had given advice on in chapters 12–14 of his letter. In sending the letter to the church with these returning delegates, he recommended them as leaders. Whether the Corinthians took that advice, we have no way of knowing. If they did, the leaders were in for a rough passage: the community was to split once again.

From these subsequent developments during Paul's ministry at Corinth perhaps all we can add to a profiling of early Christian ministry is a perception of how far its authority stretched. And really that was not far at all. If Paul succeeded in having good order established in the meetings of the Corinthian Christians, we would say the authority of his ministry had been vindicated; if the Corinthians acknowledged in Stephanas and his colleagues the same level of authority that Paul recognized, again Paul's ministry showed its authority. But Paul had no control over the reception of his ministry or the measure of authority the Corinthians might attach to it. And he knew that the authority carried by ministry was not a coercive, political, or legal authority but one arising from the power of the gospel made available to believers via ministry. The ministry had a capacity to effect change in the lives of individuals and in their organizations only insofar as it opened believers to the summons of the gospel. One might say that of itself ministry did not possess authority, but that it transferred authority to those being ministered to. Theirs were the decisions, and the decisions became authoritative in so far as they conformed with the gospel.

In this process, as we saw in Paul's handling of the conflict about the authenticity of his ministry, an authoritative exercise of ministry challenges members of a community to work their way to a response on the deepest levels of their experience as Christians. If we wish to think of this as a consultative process, we need to understand that the consultation is not between the minister and the Corinthians but among the Corinthians themselves as they bring to bear upon the problem the wisdom that has accrued from their experience of life in a Christian congregation. In chapter 14 of his first letter, Paul encouraged them to recognize how resourceful prophets can be—or so it would seem—to "weigh what is said" (verse 29); certainly, anyone with the prophetic spirit is to contribute to the community's need at such a time. In *The Spirit and the Congregation: Studies in 1 Corinthians 12–15*, Ralph P. Martin has written helpfully on this aspect of the prophet's responsibility in the community, showing clearly that Christian order is not the result of "an imperious call to obedience" but of discerning "the mind of Christ" (1 Cor. 2:16).[10] In this sense, the consult-ation that takes place is as much with Christ in the Spirit as it is with one another, and in its resolution the authority of ministry finds its expression. (Even the extreme case of the incestuous man in chapter 5 of this letter conforms to this pattern. See verse 4: "When you are assembled, and my spirit is present, with the power of our Lord Jesus, you are to...")

Historical experience of Christian ministries and ministers has not left many of today's Christians with the impression that the authority of min-istry ultimately rests with those who are not ministers. How many congre-gations live by the conviction of giving living expression to the authority of the gospel and realize that unless the authority of the gospel does reach expression among them the ministry has been ineffective? Rather, is it not the case that when we encounter ministerial titles we too easily assume that the title confers an authority on its holder that he or she is entitled—as we say—to wield within his or her designated field of ministry? That is to say, we assume that ministry confers authority over people. In what we see here, however, this is not the case.

Within the historically constituted churches, of course, authority over people does exist in matters outside the sphere of ministry. Local churches have real estate, employees, programs of social welfare, and much else. Each of these has to be appropriately managed. Yet the living body of the faithful can easily be harmed and its functioning as a community ser-iously damaged when the processes of managerial authority are mis-takenly thought of as exercises of ministerial authority.

Interestingly, in our time, large sectors of the educated lay members of churches, especially hierarchical churches, would heartily concur with this evaluation of the authority of ministry and would gladly accept the respon-sibilities it requires of congregations. It would appear to correspond with their calls for a church that has a more consultative style, abdicates ab-solutist claims inherited from a dubiously Christian participation in the kingdoms of this world, and at last might open itself to power from below. But in this they would be working on grounds very different from the ground we are working on. For many of these contemporary Christians, ministry must not attempt to display the signs of worldly and coercive power because the meaning of the *diakon-* words requires Christians to make their ministry a service of one another. The instinct leading them to advocate their approach to Christian authority is no doubt sound, and

---

10. Grand Rapids, MI, 1984, 80, and see 60–68.

their desire to live in a church where they actually participate in shaping the congregation is authentically Christian, but their linguistic argument cannot support them, for, as we have seen, *ministry/diakonia* is not that sort of word at all.

A church will develop a consultative style or display the democratic aspect of the people of God in so far as the ministry reaching it issues in attitudes and actions the congregation has arrived at in the process of discovering the mind of the Lord; therein the church will also be manifesting the authority of its ministry. We can say this by virtue of what ministry meant for the ancient people who gave us the word. Clearly, if we wish to institute this early Christian perception of an authoritative ministry in our churches, we have much to learn and we have risks to take. The title *minister* does indeed indicate that a person has been charged with a responsibility, but because the responsibilities of Christian ministry are coextensive with—that is, do not exceed—the limits of the gospel, the titled minister has also to learn the limits of ministry's authority.

9

Paul, Delegate to Jerusalem

MINISTRY IN THE church is of heaven. The evidence for this in the language of the first Christians is so strong that one has to be surprised at the ease with which most churches began to lose touch with this legacy in the middle of the twentieth century. In considering ministry as an office within the church (Chapter 7), we observed how the modern phenomenon found special expression in the virtually universal accord that one seemingly normative biblical passage—Eph. 4:12—means the opposite of what churches had previously taken it to mean. To propose the traditional understanding now in ecumenical circles is to invite bemusement, and the proposal is likely to be disregarded as reactionary.

Switching Ministry

The ease with which this switch of principles has been made, whereby all Christians are ministers, is to be attributed in a significant measure to a new way of understanding the language of ministry/*diakonia*. The term now designates a service that just about anybody can do. From what we have seen so far, however, Paul reserves the use of ministry/*diakonia* for those in the church who carry an apostolic mandate. We will encounter the same usage in Luke's writings (see chapter 10). In Paul's letters we observe powerful claims that what gives him his role among the churches is his heavenly mandate for ministry/*diakonia*. What we want to move on to observe now is how this heavenly ministry embodied itself in the activities of the churches at their beginnings.

The churches we will be looking at are those Paul founded, because those are the ones we mainly have the information about. In Paul's dealings with a number of them, he speaks of himself and of the churches being involved in a ministry/*diakonia* very different from the one by which he had been mandated to found churches. And at this point, I think we can say, we begin to see how the modern switch in the understanding of ministry/*diakonia* became possible. Because the ministry Paul writes about here involves going to the help of the poor, people began to think that servicing people's needs was what made up ministry as *diakonia*. The thinking became that since some of our needs are spiritual and some are material, and since ministry is the action of servicing needs, ministry has to be within the capacity of every sincere Christian. This line of thinking was forcefully endorsed by scholarly linguistic views proposing that early Christians had chosen the *diakonia* words to express what they did in their churches precisely because these were words from the world of slaves and service.

Again, our impression of the words in the language of Paul is different from that. These were words that Paul favored when he needed to express his views on the rights and duties of people who had been mandated by God to proclaim a heavenly mystery. In naming an operation for the relief of the poor a ministry/*diakonia*, Paul would not be saying that *diakonia* is service of the needy but that service of the needy comes within the mandate of a particular other kind of *diakonia*—same word, different reference. The heavenly ministry by which believers are brought under the gift of God invests them with the earthly responsibility of sharing that gift with others. How this works out in the use of the language of ministry, and what the words actually mean in this connection, can be observed in the story of the collection for Jerusalem.

The Delegation to Jerusalem

In several passages of his letters, Paul has a lot to say about a delegation to Jerusalem that he was instrumental in planning but of which he wanted the churches themselves to take the leading part. These were the churches he founded in Asia Minor and in northern and central Greece (Macedonia and Achaia, the latter including Corinth and Cenchreae). His idea was a splendid gift of money from these churches to the church in Jerusalem as a public attestation of a sense of fellowship with strangers who were yet brothers and sisters in the Lord. Mounted as a delegation, the presentation of the gift would be a powerful statement by these remote churches of the vigor of the new life in the Spirit that had been opened to them through the ministry of Paul. It would assure the leaders in Jerusalem that, different as the Greeks were from the Jewish followers of Jesus in their response to the new faith—not adopting the Jewish foodlaws, for example—they were true followers.

Getting the delegation together, however, presented some problems, although these did not surface immediately. The churches in Macedonia, where Paul initiated the project, were well organized. Though poor, they had "a wealth of liberality" ready for despatch (2 Cor.8:2), and they appointed two delegates to accompany Paul. These are called "apostles of the churches, the glory of Christ" (8:23), which is an indication of how highly Paul esteemed their role and at what level he was pitching the delegation.

In Corinth, things did not run so smoothly. The church was given instructions to make weekly savings for the gift so that there would be no last minute bottleneck (1 Cor.16:2). They were also instructed to have their delegates selected and furnished with letters of appointment (16:3). In regard to this part of Paul's instruction, readers will notice that some translators want us to understand that these letters of introduction are to be written by Paul, but our discussion aims to show that Paul's concept of the ministry of the churches in this undertaking is such that writing letters of introduction himself for the delegates from Corinth is precisely what he does not want to be doing. About this side of the arrangements Paul was especially careful. He wanted each section of the delegation to appear clearly in Jerusalem as a representation from a particular Asian church; at the same time, the delegation as a whole would represent one fellowship of churches.

In trying to get the Corinthians to see things this way, Paul knew he had to avoid appearing to be intrusive, for while the idea of the delegation may have been his own, he wants it to take on the authentic character of a work of the churches themselves. Accordingly he indicates that he will join the delegation only"if it seems advisable" (16:4). In spite of his having shown this kind of consideration in his approaches to the Corinthians, we notice a year later he is still urging—cajoling, really—them to at least finish the collection of money. To this end, Paul sent Titus and the two Asian delegates to give the Corinthians a lead (2 Cor.8:6,23).

For what is perhaps a third time, he writes to them betraying his con-tinued anxiety about their readiness. Perhaps a comment on how many letters Paul wrote on this matter could be helpful. Views among scholars are divided on the number of letters Paul wrote to the Corinthians, on which ones were lost, and on how many fragments were put together to form what we call 2 Corinthians, if indeed this document contains any fragments at all. For our purposes, however, these unresolved questions are not of basic importance—even though I write as if letters were being written one after another—because what we are mainly looking for in any text that has survived is indications of why Paul estimates as "ministry" the churches' involvement in a delegation with an aid package for the poor in the church in Jerusalem.

At this point in the text (2 Cor.9:2),we read more coaxing: "I know your keenness and I boast about it," but Paul goes on to say that he is still going to send some organizers to hustle the Corinthians along, revealing the true level of his anxiety. Unashamedly he tells them how embarrassing it would be for all, not least for the church in Corinth, if the delegates from the northern churches should stop by to receive hospitality in Corinth before proceeding in the company of the Corinthian delegates only to find the Corinthians in a state of confusion and not ready to take part (9:3–5).

This being a possibility too distressing to contemplate, Paul seizes the rhetorical moment for a short but intense homily on the virtue of generosity. Here we find what became our English saying, first formulated in William Tyndale's translation, "God loves a cheerful giver"(9:7). But Paul does not indulge in mere platitudes—and this saying was already one in Paul's day—because he proceeds to press the Corinthians to weigh up just what it means for a local group to send a substantial gift by the hand of their own accredited delegates to a distant group of unknown foreigners on the grounds only that they share a common faith in the generosity of God.

Paul works toward his most persuasive idea only gradually. He moves from the "cheerful giver" to some assurances that a generous God will make up for anything should generosity run the Corinthians short (9:8–10). Even this, one is tempted to surmise, could have sounded pious and hollow when read aloud to an assembly of people whose daily lives depended on the hard-nosed commercial bustle of Corinth. Paul's concluding reflection, however, would have been a challenge to all believers because it homed in on what such people experience in belief.

Believers then, like believers now, knew themselves most surely to be Christians in experiencing gratitude for "the unsurpassing grace of God" which gives them fellowship in Christ and the Spirit (9:14). An awareness of God's graciousness is what kept them in the communion both with God and with one another. Paul's own sense of gratitude was, of course, vibrant, and he seeks to evoke a response by striking this chord in those to whom he is writing. He puts it to them that if they enter fully into this charitable project there will be a remarkable effect in distant places. The believers in Jerusalem will not merely be grateful for the gift but will be moved to thank God for the generosity of the givers. He asks the Corinthians to consider that these distant strangers will be enlarged in heart at the realization that foreigners have been moved to such generosity and to the exquisite niceties of a delegation as their confession of the gospel (9:13). On hearing this, the Corinthians could only turn within themselves to see how real the gospel was for them. Was blessing such a part of their new life and experience that they should give material expression to it in favor of those unknown people who, they were told, shared with them the same blessing?

Subtle and intimate as this appeal by Paul clearly was, it was marked also by a poignancy that is easily lost to the modern reader. Today's readers are never going to know the exact history of Paul's dealings with this community of Christians founded by him in Corinth, and they may need to be reminded that long passages of Paul's correspondence with the community evidence aspects or perhaps phases of an intense conflict between the founder and the believers. We alluded to this conflict in chapter 6 when discussing Paul's address to the Corinthian church as a minister.

Whatever of the details of his relationship—and it was all compacted into a period of four or five years—and at whatever stage of the conflict Paul wrote 2 Corinthians 9, in his appeal there for wholehearted support of a demanding and complex community undertaking, Paul had to cope with both the feelings the conflict provoked in him and the feelings that were either building up or were residual among the Corinthians. One can imagine Paul determining to use the challenge of a composite Asian deputation to Jerusalem as a means of repairing the damage that this purely local conflict had caused in the relationship with him, but more especially in relationships among the Corinthians themselves.

A Right and a Wrong Way

If the obscurity of the historical circumstances is one obstacle in the way of today's reader coming to appreciate what it meant for Paul to undertake a collection for the church in Jerusalem, a more awkward hindrance is the obscurity of some of the language used in our translations at certain critical points of Paul's references to it. More critical than anything else is the way the translations handle Paul's references to the collection as a ministry. The approach of the translations has repercussions in the translation of other elements of language in the context. Mainly, and most unfortunately, the translations fail to represent Paul's basic conception of the whole operation as a ministry.

We encounter the same problem in Luke's brief references to the delegation that the Christians of Antioch sent to Jerusalem. In each reference (Acts 11:29; 12:25) the term *diakonia* occurs, and we find translators confusingly translating this term in one passage a "mission" and in another "aid" or "contribution." Our own reading made it a "sacred mission" in both passages,[1] and indeed this mission was itself a ministry. To appreciate how Paul is using the term, we can probably best compare two translations of the relevant passages (see figure 9.1). This will help limit discussion, and should also clearly show what a difference it makes to our perception of what Paul is saying when we understand his ministerial terms as referring to a commission or a mission. In one column are phrases taken from the RSV and in the other is my translation set within Paul's understanding of ministry. Translations of the same Greek phrases are parallel to one another in italics; translations of the Greek term for what we call "ministry" are in bold italics.

In comparing these translations the reader is likely to be surprised at the degree of the variations, and not just the variations between the two columns but those also within the left-hand column alone. After all, the words highlighted there are all intending to represent in English what Paul meant by his one Greek term for "ministry" or "ministering" (*diakonia*, the noun, and *diakonein*, the verb).Yet in the left column, in regard to the noun, we are presented with an idea of "service in general," of "service for people," then of providing "relief," of making an "offering"of a gift, and lastly of "rendering" a service; for the verb we are given "aiding" people, "carrying on" a task, and "administering" a gift. We know that a foreign word may often have to be put into English in different ways to meet the foreign word's meaning in different contexts, but in such various translations we would normally discern an underlying linking notion, whereas in the RSV passages from Paul above we cannot discern in English any semantic connection between ideas like "administering"a responsibility and "aiding" someone. In the right-hand column, we can discern a consistency in all Paul's references to the collection as a "ministry"or as a task needing to be "ministered," even though we have needed to represent

1. Collins, *Diakonia*, 217–221; see also A. Hentschel, *Diakonia im Neuen Testament* (Tübingen: Mohr Siebeck, 2007), 346–50; *Gemeinde, Ämter, Dienste* (Neukirchen – Vluyn: Neukirchener Verlag, 2013), 87.

Conventional	Revised
2 Cor.8:4 (RSV)	
the churches of Macedonia	
gave according to their means...	
and behond their means,	
of their own free will,	
begging us earnestly	
for the favour	
of taking part in the **relief**	*of taking part with us*
of the saints	*in the* **sacred mission**
	to the blessed people
2 Cor.8:19–20	
he has been appointed	*he has been appointed*
by the churches	*by the churches*
to travel with us	*as our fellow traveller to foreign parts*
in this gracious work	
which we are carrying on,	**in bearing** *this gift*
fior the glory of the Lord'and to show	**under mandate**
our good will.	
We intend that no one should blame us	
about this liberal gift	*in this generous undertaking*
which we are administering	**that we have been commissioned to**
	carry out
2 Cor.9:1	
Now it is superfluous for me	
to write to you	
about **the offering**	*about* **the sacred mission**
for the saints	*to the blessed people*
2 Cor.9:12–13	
the **rendering**	**carrying out the sacred mandate**
of this service	*of this community undertaking*
not only supplies	
the wants of the saints	
but also overflows	
in many thanksgivings to God.	
Under the test	*In the public reception*
of **this service**	*accorded to* **this sacred mission**
you [they*] will glorify God	*they will praise God*
by your obedience	*for your commitment*
in acknowledging the gospel	*to giving expression to the gospel.*
**Alternativre translation in RSV*	

FIGURE 9.1 Translations of *diakon-* in Collection Texts

Rom.15:25
At present, however,
I am going to Jerusalem
with aid   **on a mission**
for *the saints*   **from** *the blessed people*
Rom.15:31
[pray]
that **my service**   *that* **my sacred mission**
for *Jerusalem*   **to** *Jerusalem*
may be acceptable to the saints

FIGURE 9.1 (CONTINUED)

these in English by expressions like "sacred mission" and "carrying out a sacred mandate." A quick recall of English usage relating to government ministers and their ministerial responsibilities might be helpful to those readers to whom the concept of ministry within a Christian community has come to mean service to people instead of its pre-twentieth-century meaning of service under the mandate of the church through appointment or through the ritual of ordination.

Restoring Ministry

This is not the place to explain why the approach taken above to translating the words is correct. As noted earlier, the detailed explanation has been presented in earlier studies by Collins and Hentschel. One or two points, however, are worth repeating here. The first is a curious item of no great moment from a scholarly point of view. It is helpful in that it perhaps illustrates how the ancients could think of ministry/*diakonia* as a mission. In some manuscripts of Paul's letters to the Romans, including the prestigious *Codex Vaticanus*, at 15:31, instead of *ministry/diakonia* (translated as "my sacred mission"), we read the Greek word *dōrophoria*, which means "carrying of gifts" and thus makes excellent sense at this point where Paul expresses the hope that the gift of the collection will be well received in Jerusalem. In whatever way this variant word entered the tradition of the manuscripts—it entered into the Latin Vulgate (in the odd phrase *obsequii mei oblatio*) and from there was represented in the early English translation of Rheims as "oblation of my service"—the idea of "carrying of gifts" corresponds closely with the idea of a "mission," especially as Paul's word *diakonia* implies in this context that his mission is one of getting something from one place to another.

A second point of language is rather more important. And it is this: to the eye of anyone who reads Paul's Greek, the traditional translations are obviously struggling to come to grips with how he expresses himself, and here and there the translators have left signs that they have just not been able to cope. Three times Paul uses the word *eis*, which we most often find ourselves understanding as "into" or "toward"; one of its common functions is to accompany words indicating movement toward a destination. In the right-hand column above, we see this *eis* represented as a mission *to* the people in Jerusalem; in the left-hand column, however, there is no trace of this *to*. An old-fashioned schoolmaster would not be pleased to see the little word not only ignored but replaced by the word *for*, as in "service for" Jerusalem, "offering for" the saints, and by *of* as in "relief of" the saints. Interestingly, even the latest Vatican edition of the Vulgate has replaced the age-old *obsequii mei oblatio* ("the oblation of my service") of Rom. 15:31 with *ministerium meum pro Jerusalem* ("my ministry for Jerusalem"), committing the same solecism.

A last point concerns the modern habit of seeing in these ministry/*diakonia* words a sign that Paul was thinking along the lines of helping the believers in Jerusalem. Helping was certainly one clear objective of the collection. But writers and translators frequently evidence a conviction that helping was what these particular words signified here. Thus at 2 Cor.8:4 we read in the Good News translation that the Macedonians are "having a part in helping God's people in Judea." The same idea is discernible in its translation of Rom.15:25, "I am going to Jerusalem in the service of God's people there," and in the RSV above, "I am going to Jerusalem with aid for the saints." Such translations cause us to completely lose touch of a basic notion of Paul's in regard to the collection.

We have been emphasizing that what Paul organized was a mission or delegation. Now of its nature a delegation has a delegating authority behind it. In this case, the authorities are several because each group of churches in Macedonia and Achaia has given a written mandate to its representatives on the journey. When we understand Paul as speaking of going to Jerusalem with aid for the saints—notice how the Good News translation emphasizes just which saints are in question with its phrase "God's people there," namely, in Jerusalem—we miss the idea of representation altogether. The saints Paul is talking about at this juncture are

not the saints in Jerusalem at all—he mentions those in the next verse—
but are the saints in the churches who have commissioned Paul and his
companions to undertake the journey to Jerusalem. They are the saints
in the churches of Macedonia and Achaia. The explanation of why this
must be so is very simple. It is a point of standard Greek grammar[2] that
in a phrase like "ministering for the saints,"the saints have got to be the
persons who give the mandate for the ministry.[3] The reader of English
translations needs to be aware that "for the saints"in Rom.15:31 translates a
different Greek phrasing from that translated "for the saints" at 2 Cor.9:1.
In the latter instance, the Greek phrase begins with the preposition *eis*
referred to in the preceding paragraph, while at Rom.15:31, the Greek word
for "saints" stands without any preposition because it is simply the in-
direct object of the verb.

Delegation as Ministry

This has been a long discussion of grammatical, historical, and literary
aspects of Paul's writing in connection with the collection for Jerusalem.
We were led into it by the fact that Paul refers to the collection in terms of
diakonia. Further, because his references to the collection as *diakonia* are
second in frequency only to his uses of this and its related Greek words
in reference to his preaching ministry, and match the pointedness and
nuances of those instances, we surely have something to learn from the
phenomenon of the collection if we are seeking to appreciate the dimension and import of ministry for early Christians. Outside of these two major
fields of ministry/*diakonia*, namely his own and that of these churches of
Macedonia and Achaia, Paul's only other references to ministry/*diakonia*
are made in passing or without the depth of context which allows us to see
the measure and weight of what he had in mind.

From his own experience as a minister/*diakonos* of the gospel, Paul
knew that he was under a powerful call from God. A singular aspect of
this call, as is evident in everything he wrote, was that it not only gave
direction to all his activities but also ushered him into a new phase of
existence, which was his life in Christ. One is almost tempted to think of

---

2. Collins, *Diakonia* 327, note 9.

3. A. Hentschel makes the same grammatical point in relation to this passage in *Gemeinde*, 130, note 361.

him experiencing the transition as an entry into a new world rather than into a heightened religious awareness. Certainly his whole philosophic outlook was irrevocably altered, and this extended to his new view of the structure, power, and purpose of the universe, as well as to the dislocation of the previous religious framework of his personal life. In other words, his role as minister/*diakonos* placed him in an immediate connection with the sphere of the divine and required him to extend the influence of that sphere among as many as might be open to the grace of its illumination. Those who believed had entered into it. His task thereafter, and the believers' own task within this new phase of existence, was to maintain the vital connection and to nurture the new vitality arising out of it.

Another dimension in his perception of the new world is that women and men are constituted as a society—one might say *at last* constituted as a society because, finally in Christ, the Creator's purpose was now realizable. One of his expressions of this social dimension was in the "communion"of all believers with the Son (1 Cor.1:9), in the Spirit (2 Cor.13:13), by the grace and illumination of faith (Philem.6), from the common reception of the good news (Phil.1:5). Within this communion, life necessarily expressed itself in love and mutual accord (Phil.2:1–2). This was the life within the sphere of God. Paul's most powerful literary representation of the communion of believers was, of course, in the living body of Christ that the churches are (1 Cor.12:12–27). His most forceful representation of it in his capacity as a pastor, however, was his orchestration of the Asian churches in the collection for the poor in the church of Jerusalem.

We underestimate the significance of this complex undertaking, which absorbed a great deal of Paul's time and energies, if we look on it merely as an act of charity, heroic in scale but a collection nonetheless. In addition to being a collection with a practical objective we can easily appreciate, the project also had what might be called a political objective in that the Jewish church in Jerusalem would be encouraged to trust the orthodoxy or authenticity of these foreign groups of Christians who had been inspired to offer them generous material assistance. Beyond this objective is another and more important one: in extending practical charity in the demanding circumstances of travel over such distances and terrain in that area of the ancient world, all those contributing in any way to the undertaking would be actively engaged in giving expression to the reality of their communion with one another, which is to say, the interdependence of all within the body of Christ. Paul even says that the Asians will "make communion" in the interests of the poor. The Bishops' Bible of 1568 translates "make a certaine common gathering for the poore saints" (Rom.15:26) and proceeds to include this idea in going on to provide the rationale: if the Gentiles are "in spiritual communion" with the Jews or "hold the things of the spirit in common"with them, they ought at least attend to their material needs (15:27).

For this sense of communion to find expression in any one church, a certain number of things had to happen. For a household to put together a contribution, for example, a special savings program had to be introduced. Paul recommended a program of weekly savings. In whatever way a program was initiated, consideration had to be given to the means and the affordability, especially in communities that were not well off (1 Cor.16:2; 2 Cor.8:2–3). This required each household to closely consider not only how much they could afford but why they were entering into this difficult financial commitment from which they would receive nothing practical in return. Once the couriers set off with the money, that was the end of it.

We also notice that Paul mentions putting the savings aside on the first day of the week, and are reminded that when the Christians came together "in assembly" or as a church (1 Cor.11:18) there would have been much to discuss about the practicalities of the community's offering. Someone had to know what the outcome of the contributions from households was likely to be and to coordinate the arrangements. Inequalities of financial standing would no doubt get an airing there and would have to be delicately handled. Schedules and accounting processes would have to be established. Untoward circumstances, like a bad season or a drop in trade or additional changes in the taxes or misfortunes affecting particular households, would have to be accommodated. And, above all, two things had always to be closely attended to. One was to maintain harmony within the community in an affair which could easily and for seeming good reason give rise to discord, complaints, and squabbles. How often would a spokesperson have uttered sentiments like those contained in Paul's encouragement to one of these northern communities: "Let each of you look not only to his own interests, but also to the interests of others. Have this mind among yourselves, which you have in Christ Jesus" (Phil.2:4–5)?

The other main concern was maintaining the high spiritual ideal on which Paul was basing the collection. For these Greeks, Jerusalem of the Jews was totally remote, and the idea of a spiritual communion across the islands and the sea and the intervening provinces of the empire was strange and unreal. Only with a keen awareness of being "in Christ" and of Christ as a living bond could they work together in their diverse congregations in one operation for the benefit of a distant people of whom all they knew was that they too were a congregation of the Lord.

Against such ideals and within such constraints we are to weigh the fact that Paul consistently named the undertaking a ministry/*diakonia*. We can see now some of what went to the making of a ministry in the church from his point of view. Just as in his own ministry of preaching, this ministry too was constituted as ministry because it was authorized. Whereas his ministry was authorized by God, this ministry was authorized by the church. We see a glimpse of this in 1 Cor.16:3, where the church is to accredit its delegates, and in 2 Cor.8:18–19, where the famous unnamed preacher has been "appointed by the churches." Thus, what the church declares to be ministry is ministry. Here the ministry is a public activity, namely to travel to another church as a representative of one's own church in the delivery of a gift. Further, the gift-giving is not merely an act of generosity but an expression of the communal experience of faith. In this sense, the ministry is a proclamation and celebration of a shared faith, and one would like to have had the opportunity of reading in these letters of accreditation the churches' varied expressions of their theology of communion in the Lord. As prominent in their local churches as one or other of these delegates were, their ministry on this occasion was temporary. The task done, they became one in membership again with their congregation.

Perhaps the strongest characteristic of their ministry was that it was a totally religious act arising out of a sense of Christian identity and, indeed, out of sensitivity to the demands of that identity. Ministry must conform to that pattern, which has first to be discerned within the needs and possibilities of a group of believers. It will also be tested against the discernment of other groups of believers, in other words, authenticated by its conformity to the common experience of faith, as part of the communion of all churches in the Spirit. The role of Paul, the founder of churches, was not determinative here. The churches had their own responsibility for this ministry, and yet they could only meet the responsibility by collaboration with each other.

Public, organized, accredited, and faithfilled, and whether the giving of a gift or the preaching of God's mystery, ministry enriches both those who establish it and those to whom it is extended. As Paul says, it "overflows in many thanksgivings to God" (2 Cor.9:11).

The Diakonia of the Seven

Select seven men full of Spirit and wisdom. (Acts 6:3)

DEACONS HAVE CONSTANTLY been inspired by the story of the seven Greek men who were presented to the apostles, who in turn "prayed and laid their hands on them" (Acts 6:6). Much of tradition has seen in these men—particularly Stephen, the most famous of them—the forerunners and prototype of the church's deacons.

Tradition

This is the traditional view, as evidenced, for example, in the long entry for December 26 in the eleventh volume of Alban Butler's *Lives of the Fathers, Martyrs and Other Principal Saints* (1866). Here we read that "St Stephen had the primacy and precedence among the deacons newly elected" and, in the words of St Augustine, that "Stephen is named the first of the deacons, as Peter is of the apostles."

Biblical scholars have also taken this view, perhaps most significantly the great English scholar of the nineteenth century, J. B. Lightfoot, in his famous essay *The Christian Ministry.*[1] This study accompanied his commentary on the Letter to the Philippians, where it was natural for Lightfoot to discuss the question of ministry at length since Philippians 1:1 appears to be the earliest written evidence of the existence of officials within a Christian community named "bishops and deacons." In reporting them as bishops and deacons we do need to be honest and add that the Greek words for what we now call bishops and deacons occur at this place, but

---

1. Originally a dissertation appended to his *St Paul's Epistle to the Philippians*, revsd (London: Macmillan, 1891), 181–269, and posthumously as a single volume (1901).

scholars continue to discuss precisely what these terms stood for in the Philippian community. A common translation these days is "overseers and their helpers."

Lightfoot also notes—as do many others—that in the second century, Irenaeus identified the seven men of Acts 6 as the kind of deacons with whom he was familiar from the practice of his own church in Lyons. In addition, Lightfoot reminds us that, out of deference to the Seven of Acts 6, the ancient church of Rome never allowed the number of deacons to exceed seven. On the same grounds, the Council of Neocaesarea enacted a law in 315 limiting deacons to this number whatever the size of a city.[2]

Tradition Disputed

Such ancient authority and nineteenth-century scholarship give to the idea of an original seven deacons the look and feel of authenticity. And yet Lightfoot himself was aware that the idea of deacons so early in the church's life—and in this passage in particular—had been "much disputed."[3] A historian of the modern diaconate, Jeannine E. Olson, notes how the ancient tradition has indeed lived on to the present but "with dissenting views."[4] An eminent successor to Lightfoot in the study of the early church was A. M. Farrer, and he dismissed the whole idea of an original seven deacons as "a very old error."[5] A prominent modern voice here would be that of James Monroe Barnett, a recent champion of the diaconate, who closes his pages on the subject with the plain statement, "We must conclude that the Seven were *not* deacons."[6] This too has been the view which my own study of Acts 6 has demanded. Deacons of today are likely to be interested in following the line of thought that has led to this conclusion. They and the general reader are both likely to be even more interested in how the development of ministry that Luke has sketched

---

2. Ibid., 188–89.

3. Ibid., 188.

4. *One Ministry, Many Roles: Deacons and Deaconesses through the Centuries* (St Louis. Concordia, 1992), 24.

5. *"The Ministry in the New Testament"* in K.E. Kirk, ed., *The Apostolic Ministry* (London: Hodder & Stoughton, 1946, 113–82, citing 138.

6. *The Diaconate: A Full and Equal Order*, revsd ed. (Valley Forge, PA: Trinity Press International), 33.

here can yet remain of value to today's new deacons and to those pursuing the question of ministry more broadly considered.

First, however, a note of reassurance. In recent years many people have experienced moments when they have felt that certain treasured perceptions of theirs have been undermined or demolished by so-called modern biblical experts. Some perhaps have had the encouraging experience of weathering this disappointment and going on to discover within the newer biblical interpretation layers of understanding that are enlightening and enriching. In the same way, I trust that the line of thought we trace here concerning the Seven is by no means detrimental to the deacon's sense of identity today but will rather lead to enlarging reflections on the position of anyone who has been ordained to a role within the Christian community.

A Broad Spectrum

The reason we must ask if these Seven were deacons can be put fairly simply, even though the explanation takes us a little further into how Luke used the Greek words that we normally associate with deacons. Most deacons likely know that what has led people to make a connection between the story in Acts 6 and the diaconate is the way Luke describes the task of the Seven as taking part in "the daily distribution [of food]" and in "serving at tables." These are phrases we read in our modern English translations, although the exact wording can differ from translation to translation.

Most deacons would also be aware that there is a word link between how Luke names these activities in Acts 6 and the title *deacon* itself. The word link is of course the Greek word *diakonia*. It is to this abstract noun that our translations refer in speaking of "the distribution [of food]" in Acts 6:1, just as in speaking of "serving at tables" in 6:2 the translations are referring to the corresponding verb *diakonein*. A third instance of the words occurs in this passage when Luke uses *diakonia* to name "the ministry of the word" (6:4) to which the Twelve decide to make an exclusive commitment.

Thus, according to most of our modern translations of Acts, we have the *diakon-* words identifying (a) distribution of food to needy widows, (b) the activity of serving this food at tables, and (c) the prime responsibility of the Twelve in "the ministry" of preaching the Word. This is a broad spectrum of activities to be named *diakonia*, ranging as it does from social work in something like a soup kitchen to the apostolic proclamation of the gospel. Within this scale, nonetheless, many have been of the opinion that the activities at the kitchen end of the spectrum were what the Twelve ordained the Seven for when they prayed over them and laid hands on them.

The outcome of such a development would make this passage the defining text for the identity of deacons in the church. And this is what it became in some quarters of the historical church, especially under the teaching of John Calvin, for whom social work was the defining activity of deacons. In some sectors of the modern diaconal movement, this is precisely how the modern deacon's identity has been understood, although such is not the case—officially at least—within the Roman Catholic diaconate, where the threefold role remains in place: proclamation of the Word, liturgy, and works of charity.

Where is the Deacon?

The trend to make social work the defining role of deacons has been very strong from the time of the Reformation and on into the various nineteenth- and twentieth-century reforms of the diaconate. A powerful influence in establishing this trend has been Acts 6:1–6. When we look closely at what Luke is doing with this passage within the larger framework of his narrative in Acts, we have reason to pause. Here we discern two features of the narrative that warn us that something could be awry in the seemingly persuasive reading that seven extra Greek men were commissioned to look after the physical needs of Greek-speaking widows who were being overlooked in the social network of the early Christian community in Jerusalem.

The first feature of the narrative is simple in the extreme. Luke does not mention the word *deacon* (*diakonos* in Greek). Although the absence of the deacon's title does not of itself make an argument, it does make us ask why, if Luke was recording the founding of a system of deacons, he does not manage to call the Seven *deacons*. As a writer, Luke was a skilled and sensitive user of Greek and, in regard to what the *diakon-* words stood for in Greek language, religion, and culture, he shows himself to be totally familiar. In addition, his passion for showing his audience the character of the early church was matched only by his passion for presenting his audience with models of the church to build on.

So clearly recognizable are these passions that biblical critics were once inclined to dismiss Luke's version of the growth of the Christian community as an exercise in "early Catholicism." Yet nowhere in the comparatively extensive writings of such an admirer of the early church's development do we come across any explicit mention of a deacon. Thus, we end up with a story about *diakon-* this and *diakon-* that, words which appear to make links with the idea of the *deacon/diakonos,* but the essential link is missing, namely, the title *deacon/diakonos* itself.

The Link to Ministry

The second feature of the passage is somewhat different and consists of the way Luke's use of the *diakon-* words there links back to his uses of *diakonia* earlier in Acts. From a consideration of these links, we will come to recognize that in the *diakon-* words of Acts 6, Luke might be trying to achieve an effect less specific than the establishment of the church's first deacons, an effect that has more to do with the broader question of the nature of the church itself and how it is to cope with changing needs and times. It is clear, for instance, that across the narrative of Acts, Luke is using the *diakon-* words as code words for the kind of ministry by which the Word of God is to spread from Jerusalem. Scholars have recently been paying closer attention to the significance of what initially appears to be a minor feature of his writing. The facts of his usage are simple to record but are impressive to reflect upon.

First, in the upper room, when Peter announces the need to fill the place in the Twelve left vacant by Judas's death, he does so in the context of the commission Jesus laid upon these chosen ones to be "witnesses in Jerusalem, in all Judea and Samaria, and to the ends of the earth" (Acts 1:8). Thus Peter announces the need to fill Judas's "share in this *ministry,*" in Greek "this *diakonia*" (1:17). The word *diakonia* thus embraces the special apostolic mission to take the Word of the Lord abroad. Accordingly, when the Eleven pray for enlightenment on filling "the place in this *ministry* and apostleship," Luke again calls this ministry *diakonia* (1:25).

Luke does not use a *diakon-* word again until Acts 6:1, where he refers to "the daily *ministry/diakonia*" (which we have already met in the phrase of the modern translation, "daily distribution [of food]").There the Twelve rededicate themselves to their original commission of "the ministry/*diakonia* of the word" (6:4). Luke then closes the scene of the Seven with the telltale phrase, "the word of God continued to spread" (6:7).

With these touches Luke keeps us aware of his major theme as he moves into the great preaching event in the brief career of Stephen, one of the Seven (7:2–53). With Stephen's death immediately following, the theme of the progress of the word re-emerges in the account of another member of the Seven, Philip, engaging in a mission to Samaria; Samaria is the first station outside of Jerusalem and Judea according to the stages of the Lord's program outlined by Luke (1:8). This mission leaves Philip poised at Caesarea, the port leading to Rome (8:4–14; 26–40), which is Luke's ultimate objective in the trajectory of the Word of God.

With that great objective of the Lord's program almost in sight, it is not surprising that Luke immediately introduces us to Paul, the one whom the Lord called "an instrument whom I have chosen to bring my name before Gentiles and kings" (9:15). The Lord was to hustle Paul along the road because he "must bear witness also in Rome" (23:11). Having glimpsed this grand geographical and missionary framework, we have no difficulty recognizing that Luke is intending to make Paul an integral part of the master plan which Luke identified in chapter 1 as "this ministry/*diakonia* and apostleship" (1:25) and by which the witness was to reach from Jerusalem to the ends of the earth.

Not surprisingly, when Paul completes his second heroic tour of Asia Minor and Greece and is making his way back to the church in Jerusalem, he leaves the following missionary dedication ringing in the ears of the elders of Ephesus (20:24):

> I do not count my life of any value to myself, if only I may finish my course and the ministry/*diakonia* that I received from the Lord Jesus, to testify to the good news of God's grace.

The striking element here is the reappearance of the ministerial code word *diakonia*. The word is clearly identifying the strenuous mission that Paul had undertaken at the behest of his Lord and by which the word of God's grace has been reaching abroad. Any doubt as to the significance of this wordplay of *diakonia* across Luke's narrative dissipates in the next and last use of the word in Luke. This is when Paul has completed the transit from Ephesus to the mother church in Jerusalem. There in the presence of James, the leader, and of all the elders of the church, Paul makes a report of what "God had done among the Gentiles through his ministry/*diakonia*" (21:19).The word *diakonia* marks the major stages of Luke's history of the Christian mission. In this narrative, the term *diakonia* marks the beginning of the Twelve's mission (1:17, 25); it is there at the peak of their mission to Jerusalem (6:4); it is there to mark Paul's inclusion in the mission (20:24); and it is there when Paul completes his role in the mission (21:19).

Impact of the Word

In the light of this striking pattern of usage, the question arises as to the relevance of the one other instance of the code word where the story of the Seven begins (6:1). If we are persuaded that Luke has worked the code word across his long narrative to indicate how he understands the complementary nature of the roles of the major evangelizers, the Twelve and Paul, we perhaps need to reconsider whether at 6:1 "distribution [of food]" does justice to the idea Luke had in mind for the one remaining instance of the word.[7]

An important part of this reconsideration is to take another perspective on how the narrative works between Acts 1:6 and 6:1. We have been looking at it from the perspective of the mission to spread the Word. Now we turn to the effects the Word was producing among the believers within the first church in Jerusalem. From this perspective we see that Luke is emphasizing the changes brought about in the lives of believers by the impact of the Word. As with the later story of the spread of the Word to Rome, so in this earlier story Luke presents his viewpoint with dramatic emphasis, even though it is intermingled with the higher drama of the proclamation of the Word in the hostile environment of the Temple.

The dimension of danger which the believers' relationship with the institution of the Temple introduces into the mission gives a sharp definition to the picture of the community that is continuously building under the lively power of the Word. Luke's sketches of the affairs of the community under these challenging conditions are familiar. The believers are "constantly devoting themselves to prayer, together with certain women" (1:14); they are "all together in one place" when invested with the power of the Spirit (2:1); they "devoted themselves to the apostles' teaching and fellowship, to the breaking of bread and the prayers" (2:42); they "were together and had all things in common" (2:44–47); they "were of one heart and soul, and no one claimed private ownership of any possessions, but

---

7. Two further instances of *diakonia* at Acts 11:29 and 12:25 designate the mission of the church in Antioch to Jerusalem, as discussed in Chapter 9.

everything they owned was held in common" (4:32); and "there was not a needy person among them" (4:34).

So sacred is this bond between them, welded by the power of the Word, that members of the community sold their possessions, "laid the proceeds at the apostles' feet, and it was distributed to each as any had need" (4:34–35). So sacred is the bond that when it is momentarily broken by Ananias and Sapphira, who keep some of the proceeds of their transaction, the very life of the pair drains away from them (5:1–11). It is as if the pair had stepped outside of the life-giving environment of the community.

Throughout all this building of community, the intensive campaign of the mission proceeded in the Temple, led intrepidly by Peter and John. Flogged and forbidden to "speak in the name of Jesus" (5:40), they merely rejoiced to "suffer dishonour for the sake of the name" (5:41). At this dramatic point, Luke brings to an end his account of the mission to Jerusalem on the part of the Twelve with the statement: "And every day in the temple and at home they did not cease to teach and proclaim Jesus as the Messiah" (5:42).

Good Listeners

In our New Testaments, that statement about proclaiming Jesus marks the end of Acts 5. This division of chapters tends to obscure for us the connection with what immediately follows at the opening of chapter 6. (The chapter divisions were not inserted until the thirteenth century.) Luke proceeds immediately from 5:42 with a phrase which is a typical opener to a new development in the narrative: "In those days" It is as if Luke is writing, "In the course of these activities" Almost indicating as much, Luke's next phrase is, "With the expansion in the number of disciples." And then we have the mention of the complaint from the Hellenists, who were Greek-speaking Jews living in or visiting Jerusalem, that "their widows were being neglected in the daily *diakonia*" (6:1).

What is a reader to make of this? More pertinently, perhaps, what is an audience—for Luke's was largely an aural culture—to make of this, particularly listeners who were attuned to the Greek language and, like Luke, sensitive to the innuendoes created in his narrative by the prior uses of *diakonia* (1:17, 25). Indeed, one is justified in adding that the audience was attuned also to Luke's subsequent uses of *diakonia*, because the audience used this story more than once and was familiar with its development.The ancient audience would also certainly relate *diakonia* in Luke's narrative to other Greek historical and romantic narratives where *diakonia* held a well-known and recognizable place designating sacred commissions of one kind or another. We can thus be confident that Luke was intending to point the audience in this direction by the sheer force of the narrative's momentum.

In other words, the ancient audience would understand at 6:1 that the Greek-speaking widows were being overlooked in the daily preaching of the Word. This is to be understood by us in the sense that, as speakers of Greek and, being widows, without the same freedom as Jewish women, were neither free to attend the large gatherings in the forecourts of the Temple nor linguistically equipped to understand what these Aramaic preachers were saying when they returned from the Temple to speak in the intimacy of the household (5:42). Accordingly, the Hellenists' widows were in need of preachers who could teach them in Greek, preferably at home when Greek speakers came together at their tables (6:2).

A New Group of Preachers

Could the ancient audience have understood the scene of 6:1 in any other way? Could it really have envisaged Luke meaning that the widows were being neglected day by day in "the distribution [of food]" (6:1)? In Luke's outline of the bonding of the community of believers, was not his last story the account of how life drained from Ananias and Sapphira for breaking that bond, and was not his last comment at the end of that story about "the great fear [that] seized the whole church" (5:11) at the very thought that the bond could come under threat?

It would seem impossible that at 6:1 the skilled author Luke could be introducing a situation where the most vulnerable members of the adult society, namely foreign widows, should be exposed to neglect. His whole effort has rather been to establish that alongside the courageous work of proclamation of the Word in Jerusalem—the *"diakonia* and apostleship" received from the Lord (1:25)—another work has been proceeding by which the intimate community of believers has been so nurtured that "there was not a needy person among them" (4:34).

What does this make of the Seven? It makes of the Seven a new group of preachers, directed at first to the needs of the Hellenists—note how happily the story ends at 6:7: "The Word of God continued to spread; the number of disciples increased greatly in Jerusalem"—and then, after the death of Stephen in Jerusalem, to the wide worlds beyond, as begun in Philip's mission (8:5). The only other time we hear of one of the Seven is when Philip is called simply "the evangelist, one of the seven" (21:8).We might reread Luke's account of the Seven in the following (paraphrased) way:

> The Greek-speaking members of the community complained against those who spoke Aramaic that their housebound widows were being overlooked in the great preaching (*diakonia*) that was going on day by day in the environs of the Temple. So the Twelve summoned the whole complement of the disciples and said: "We cannot possibly break off our public proclamation before the huge crowds in the Temple to carry out a ministry (*diakonein*) in the households of these Greek-speaking widows. Brothers, you will have to choose seven men from your own ethnic group who are fully respected, empowered by the Spirit, and equipped for the task. We will then appoint them to the role that needs to be filled. That will mean that the Twelve can get on with attending to worship in the Temple and to our apostolic ministry (*diakonia*) of proclaiming the word there."

PART THREE

Toward Ministry for the Twenty-First Century

Theology of Ministry in the Twentieth Century: Ongoing Problems or New Orientations?

THE CENTENARY IN 2010 of the first World Missionary Conference in Edinburgh rightly occasioned tributes to an initiative that had unforesee-able consequences for the development of ecumenism and for a vigorous reappraisal of where ministry sat, not only in the churches but within the notion of church itself.[1]

At the same time, on revisiting the conference documents, we can be sur-prised at how little the conference had to do with ecumenism as we have known it since 1950. The missionary conference was largely pragmatic in char-acter and very much an in-house Christian affair at the height of European co-lonial involvement in Africa and Asia. Even though the conference lacked the participation of the Orthodox and Roman churches—the latter especially hav-ing a long-standing and vast array of missionary endeavours—its conveners aimed to foster effective coordination among the many different Protestant missionary endeavours in "the cause of worldwide evangelization."[2] This came down to arriving at agreements on sensible, practical arrangements in the mission fields: why build and staff two hospitals, for example, when two denominations working together could better resource just one hospital?

No accord of any kind, however, was envisaged in regard to "differ-ences of doctrine or ecclesiastical polity."[2] In fact, within any association

1. This essay is an expansion of a paper delivered at Trinity College, University of Melbourne, July 7, 2010, at a conference marking the centenary of the Melbourne College of Divinity.

2. W. H. T. Gairdner, *"Edinburgh 1910": An Account and Interpretation of the World Missionary Conference* (Edinburgh: Oliphant, Anderson & Ferrier, 1910), 54.

3. World Missionary Conference, *Report of Commission VIII. Co-operation and the Promotion of Unity* (Edinburgh: Oliphant, Anderson & Ferrier, 1910), 50. In *The World Missionary*

of denominations in mission fields "questions [of doctrine or ecclesiastical polity] on which the co-operating bodies . . . differ shall be ruled out of the discussions of the Association."

The most pious expectation was for "fraternal association and mutual acquaintance."[3] Even so, no such noble aspirations could be entertained in regard to Roman Catholics. The evidence shows that in spite of "individual acts of courtesy," "the representatives of the Roman Catholic Church hold themselves precluded from entering into any agreement or taking part in any practical effort with the representatives of other Christian bodies."[4]

Notably from our point of view, although the World Conference concluded that "schemes of union" were not part of a future agenda, it did bring a measure of humility to such an admission of failure:

> We cannot too often remind ourselves that no large progress either in the unity of the Church or in co-operative effort can be made with our present spiritual conception and capacity.[5]

Fortunately, the "spiritual conception and capacity" broadened. Even amid the horrors of World War I, Archbishop Nathan Söderblom of Uppsala attempted to raise a united Christian voice for peace and—much in the spirit of the new League of Nations—sponsored an interdenominational conference in Stockholm in 1925.

"I propose," he wrote, "an ecumenical council . . . so constructed that it can speak on behalf of Christendom."[6] The ambit, however, was constricted. The council was to be the Christian voice, "not *ex-cathedra*, but from the depths of the Christian conscience" as a Christian contribution toward resolving, in the pursuit of lasting peace, the kinds of political and social problems being addressed by the League of Nations.

Conference, Edinburgh 1910 (Grand Rapids, MI / Cambridge, UK: Eerdmans, 2009), Brian Stanley has documented the tensions produced by this policy at the planning stages between British and American representatives; the British won out (38–41), but the conference created an impetus that was to take the core issue of Faith and Order further (277–81).

3. World Missionary Conference, *Report VIII*, 51.

4. Ibid., 3.

5. Ibid., 142.

6. W. A. Visser 't Hooft, "The Proposal of Archbishop Söderblom," *The Genesis and Formation of the World Council of Churches* (Geneva: World Council of Churches, 1982), 13.

Faith and Order Conferences 1927–63

Söderblom's hopes did not find realization at that time. Two years later, however, a different initiative got under way in the first of a series of world conferences on Faith and Order. The First World Conference convened at Lausanne in 1927, and its agenda marked a dramatic shift from both the Edinburgh and Stockholm conferences. Here, as its title "Faith and Order" suggested, the conference "was to deal exclusively with doctrine and the constitution of the church."[7] Such matters were, of course, the very matters of "doctrine and ecclesiastical polity" that at Edinburgh in 1910 the gathered churches had ruled out.

This authentically ecumenical development organizers attributed to "progress of Church unity on the Mission Fields." This, in turn, pointed to "the imperative demand for unity among the home Churches" as well.[8]

At Lausanne, the voices for unity were irenic—indeed, positively amicable. And voices included representatives of Orthodox churches. At the Second Faith and Order Conference at Edinburgh in 1937, however, those same voices were raised in virulent disagreement on the nature of ministry. Disagreements reverberated from what the historian Slosser identified as an undercurrent of "interdenominational animosities" in the previous decades.[9]

In this atmosphere, the Edinburgh Report advised demurely that the Conference accepted the foundational proposition that "The ministry was instituted by Jesus Christ 'for the perfecting of the Saints...the upbuilding of the body of Christ,' and is a gift of God to the Church in the service of the Word and sacraments." The further three propositions are similarly indeterminate, and following pages of comment are little more than a litany of unresolved differences.[10] So problematic did the very first foundational proposition appear in the aftermath of the Edinburgh conference that at the Third Faith and Order Conference in Lund in 1952, the issue of the church's ministry was not even addressed.

---

7. Ibid., 21.

8. Gaius Jackson Slosser, *Christian Unity: Its History and Challenge in All Communions, in All Lands* (London: Kegan Paul, Trench, Trubner, 1929), 351.

9. Ibid., 372. And see further comment in John N. Collins, *Diakonia*, 26–28, especially note 16 (273) p.273.

10. G. K. A. Bell, ed., *Documents on Christian Unity*, Third Series 1930–48 (London: Oxford University Press, 1948), 267 and 268–69.

Between Lund 1952 and the Fourth Faith and Order Conference in Montreal in 1963, something dramatic occurred. The foundational proposition changed. Instead of speaking of "the ministry" as instituted by Jesus Christ "for the perfecting of the Saints," Montreal concluded that the saints themselves—that is, all the baptized—perform ministry. The Montreal Report on ministry opened with this statement:

> There have been times in the past when the word "layman" was understood to refer to someone who had a merely passive role in the life of the Church, and the word "ministry" referred exclusively to the full-time professional service of the Church. That time is past.[11]

Why was the "layman" no longer just a lay person? The answer had emerged, continued the report, in a "recovery of a true doctrine of the laity." This doctrine leads to the recognition that "ministry is the responsibility of the whole body and not only of those who are ordained." This doctrine arises from the biblical teaching about the royal priesthood of the whole people of God.

The report acclaimed the "recovery" of this doctrine as "one of the most important facts of recent church history."[12] The doctrine of universal or churchwide ministry had found expression within ecumenical circles that very year (1963) in a study by the World Council of Churches' Department of the Laity. There we encounter the new fundamental principle of ecclesiology: Christ "joins in baptism new members to himself, letting them share in his ministry."[13]

The Impact of a "Revolutionary Word"

A leading contributor to this development was Hendrik Kraemer in *A Theology of the Laity* (1958). Kraemer was first director of the World Council of Churches' study center in Bossey, Switzerland. Kraemer recognizes

---

11. P. C. Rodger and L. Vischer, *The Fourth World Conference on Faith and Order: The Report from Montreal 1963* (London: SCM, 1964), 62.

12. Ibid., 63.

13. Madeleine Barot and Ralph C. Young, eds, "Christ's Ministry through his whole Church and its Ministers," *Laity* No. 15 (May 1963), 14.

Christ as "the *Diakonos*, the Servant"—the minister. Because of that, ultimately, "the Church *is diakonia, is* Ministry."[14]

Kraemer wrote:

> The Church then as a whole being ministry or *diakonia*, it follows that, theologically speaking, the ministry of the laity is as constituent for the true being and calling of the Church as the ministry of the "ministry" (the office-bearers or clergy).[15]

Diakonia is thus a "profound, revolutionary word,"[16] but the *diakonic* revolution that Kraemer helped to inflame within ecumenism was already well under way elsewhere. In 1955, within mainstream ecclesiology, Karl Barth had published Part IV/2 of *Church Dogmatics* on the subject of "Jesus Christ, the Servant as Lord." Barth had written:

> Even linguistically, [the church's law] must avoid the fatal word "office" and replace it by "service" [*Dienst/diakonia*], which can be applied to all Christians. . . . either all are office-bearers or none; and if all, then only as servants.[17]

With the same emphasis on these linguistics, Eduard Schweizer had already published *Church Order in the New Testament*,[18] while Ernst Käsemann's "Ministry and Community," which he had developed originally as a German lecture in 1948 under the influence of Schweizer's prelude to *Church Order*, had been translated into English. Here Käsemann closely argued that "all the baptised are 'office-bearers.' "[19] Barth, in his turn, had drawn on Schweizer and Käsemann.[20]

---

14. H. Kraemer, *A Theology of the Laity* (London: Lutterworth, 1958), 149.

15. Ibid., 154.

16. Ibid., 187.

17. Karl Barth, *Church Dogmatics, Vol. 4, Part 2: The Doctrine of Reconciliation*, Eng. trans. (Edinburgh: T&T Clark, 1958, German original 1955), 694.

18. Eng. trans. (London: SCM, 1961); the German original, *Gemeinde und Gemeindeordnung im Neuen Testament*, had appeared 1959.

19. Ernst Käsemann, "Ministry and Community in the New Testament," in *Essays on New Testament Themes*, Eng. trans. (London: SCM, 1964), 63–94, citing 80; the German original is *Exegetische Versuche und Besinnungen*, vol. 1, 2nd edn, 1960.

20. Barth, *Church Dogmatics*, 4, 677.

The authoritative weight of such a scholarly German-language shift in the understanding of where "ministry" sits in the church left little scope for others to argue any other line. Preparing a brief on *The Role of the "Diakonia" of the Church in Contemporary Society* in preparation for the World Conference on Church and Society 1966, staff members of the World Council of Churches Division of Inter-Church Aid, Refugee and World Service drew on "ecumenical discussions [that] had been gradually rediscovering the scriptural background of 'diakonia,'" a process of rediscovery that had been going on "for more than a decade."[21] They produced the following working definition of the term: "The service which the individual Christian as well as the Church as a corporate unit is called to render to every needy person in all kinds of suffering and alienation."[22]

This "rediscovery of the New Testament concept of 'diakonia'" the authors attributed to "the fact that God has always furnished His Church with new scriptural insights when He has revealed to it new needs and challenges."[23] And the insights led to a transformed vision of the nature of the church:

> The Church, which continuously from its pulpits proclaims Jesus Christ the Word of God and Lord of the world, is called to serve mankind in a common responsible corporate ministry.[24]

Thus the ministry of the church is now churchwide and is to be distinguished from—although not divorced from—the church's worship (*leitourgia*).[25]

Roman Catholic ecclesiology of the 1960s was also engaged with *diakonia*. All four sessions of the Second Vatican Council (1962–65) included protracted debates on the nature of the church, and much thinking was also profoundly affected by these newfound *diakonic* values. In *We Who*

---

21. World Council of Churches, *The Role of the "Diakonia" of the Church in Contemporary Society* (Geneva: World Council of Churches, 1966), 11. Participating in the development of this document were the two enormously influential German theologians of "diakonia," Hans-Christoph von Hase and Paul Philippi. Von Hase's paper "Der Auftrag Heute" in H. Krimm, ed., *Das diakonische Amt der Kirche*, 2nd edn (Stuttgart: Evangelisches Verlagswerk, 1965), 555–606, is available in translation (in abbreviated form), "Diakonia: Today's Task," *Scottish Journal of Theology* 20.1 (March 1967), 57–74.

22. World Council of Churches, *The Role of the "Diakonia,"* 16.

23. Ibid., 13.

24. Ibid., 16.

25. Ibid.

Serve, Augustin Cardinal Bea, a leading protagonist at the Council—described by one of its historians as "anything but a radical" but nonetheless "an emblematic figure for the progressives"[26]—identified "service" as a basic theme of if its deliberations.[27] Indeed, the impact of the service theme, which all the "Transalpines" were aware of as being the German conceptualization of "diakonia/*Diakonie*," was one major source of the tensions between traditional sacerdotal understandings of ministry and the newer formulations. The tensions played out during the production of the two constitutions: *Lumen gentium*, on the nature of the church, and *Gaudium et spes*, on the relationship between the church and the world.[28] Significantly, at the Council's end, Hans Küng published his international bestseller *The Church* in which he described the "enormous" consequences of the church embodying the ancient *diakonia* within its ordained orders.[29]

All this new thinking about ministry and *diakonia* drew on lexicography of the 1930s. In Kittel's *Theological Dictionary of the New Testament*,[30] H. W. Beyer described the *diakon-* words on a semantic template developed in 1931 by Wilhelm Brandt in *Dienst und Dienen im Neuen Testament*.[31] Brandt, himself a chaplain to the Lutheran deaconesses serving the disabled in the vast institute at Bethel, was giving academic shape to a German Lutheran tradition of *diakonia* going back eighty years to Theodor Fliedner and his contemporaries who founded the deaconess Motherhouses.[32]

Since World War II to this day, the new *diakonia*, long fully embraced within German Evangelical Churches, has remained the iconic Christian semantic emblem of the lowly, selfless, loving service that characterized

---

26. John W. O'Malley, *What happened at Vatican II* (Cambridge, MA: Harvard University Press, 2008), 115, 114.

27. Augustin Cardinal Bea, *We Who Serve: A Basic Council Theme and its Biblical Foundations* (London: Chapman, 1969).

28. O'Malley, *Vatican II*, traces the tortuous history of *Lumen gentium* and *Gaudium et spes* (see the book's index).

29. Hans Küng, *The Church*, Eng. trans. (London: Burns and Oates, 1967), 392; German original, *Die Kirche*, 1967.

30. Eng. trans., Vol. 2 (1964), 81–93; German original, *TWNT* 2 (1935).

31. Gütersloh: Bertelsmann, 1931.

32. See an expression of Fliedner's conceptualization in his "Gutachen 'Die Diakonie und den Diakonat betreffend'" [1856] in N. Friedrich et al., eds, *Diakonie pragmatisch* (Neukirchen-Vluyn: Neukirchener Verlag, 2007), 25–54.

the life and death of Jesus and that should characterize all ministry performed in his name.[33]

Such ministry was the Spirit's call to all the baptized. And such *diakonic*
theology underpinned ecumenical studies preparatory to and following
upon Faith and Order's agreed statement of 1982, *Baptism, Eucharist, and
Ministry*.[34] Here the statement on ministry exposes its understanding of
ministry as rooted in *diakonic* passages in the New Testament about Jesus
"giving himself as a sacrifice for all" in his "life of service" (para. 1, Mark
10:45), and about "the whole people" called to manifest their charisms "in
acts of service...in word and deed" (para. 5, 1 Cor. 12:4–6).

The statement also evidences an acute awareness of the problem raised
by such a paradigm when one turns to identify the distinctive character
of the ministry attributed to the traditional forms of ordained ministries
(para. 6). In its next paragraph, accordingly, the statement introduces a
new terminology in the hope of clarifying what might be said directly
about the character of the ordained ministry.

Thus "*ministry* in its broadest sense denotes the service to which the
whole people of God is called," while "*ordained ministry* refers to persons
who have received a charism and whom the church appoints for service
by ordination." Not surprisingly, in the course of the following eight years,
as denominational committees reported their evaluations of *Baptism,
Eucharist, and Ministry*,[35] multiple and diverse concerns emerged in regard
to just who exercised ministry in the church. Pre-reformation churches
charged *Baptism, Eucharist, and Ministry* with destroying the order of ministry which the church had inherited and by which it continued to be sustained. On the other hand, numerous churches of the reform hailed the
acknowledgment of the ministerial character of the whole church.[36] We

---

33. For fuller treatments of these linguistic developments, see Collins, *Diakonia*, 5–45;
"From διακονία to Diaconia Today: Historical Aspects of Interpretation," *Diakonian tutkimus,
Journal for the Study of Diaconia* 2 (2009), 133–47, accessible at www.dts.fi and in Chapter 1
of this volume).

34. World Council of Churches, *Baptism, Eucharist, and Ministry*, Faith and Order Paper No.
111 (Geneva: World Council of Churches, 1982).

35. The responses were published in six volumes (1986–88) with their thinking brought
together by the Faith and Order Commission in *Baptism, Eucharist, and Ministry 1982–1990*
(Geneva: World Council of Churches, 1990).

36. See illustrations of such incompatibilities in my "A Ministry for Tomorrow's Church,"
Journal of Ecumenical Studies 32.2 (Spring 1995), 159–78, esp. 161–65.

might call such an outcome a ministerial cul de sac, a situation we see acknowledged in 1998 by the Faith and Order Commission.[37]

Reaction against the Diakonic Consensus

In the same year, Hans-Jürgen Benedict, a professor in Hamburg's *Rauhes Haus*—the training school for *Diakonie* that had developed from the orphanage founded there by Johann Hinrich Wichern in 1833—attended an international conference on *Diakonie* in Finland. There the Norwegian Kjell Nordstokke drew Benedict's attention to the new semantic profile of the Greek *diakon-* words in my 1990 linguistic study.[38] This amounted to the fact that the long-standing academic and ecumenical consensus on *diakonia* as loving service had collapsed. This in turn pointed to the question that Benedict made the title of a paper published in Germany in 2000: "Does the 'Diakonie' of the German Lutheran Churches rest on a Misunderstanding?"[39]

The possibility of a situation like this had been signaled in 1996 when The Hanover Report of the Anglican-Lutheran International Commission on *The Diaconate as Ecumenical Opportunity* announced that, in relation to *diakonia* expressing "a character of humble service," recent exegetical

---

37. Faith and Order Commission, *The Nature and Purpose of the Church: A Stage on the Way to a Common Statement* (Geneva: World Council of Churches, 1998), see esp. 44.

38. It is no accident that a Nordic theologian influenced Benedict. Already in 1997 Birgitta Laghé introduced the re-interpretation into her essay "Diaconia—Ecclesiological Perspectives of Diaconia and Diaconate" in Sven-Erik Brodd et al., *The Theology of Diaconia* (Uppsala: Diakonistiftelsen Samariterhemmet 1999, Swedish original 1997); see especially Sven-Erik Brodd, "An Escalating Phenomenon: The Diaconate from an Ecumenical Perspective," in Gunnel Borgegård and Christine Hall, eds, *The Ministry of the Deacon: 1. Anglican—Lutheran Perspectives* (Uppsala: Nordic Ecumenical Council, 1999), 11–50. In a separate essay in the same volume, "The Deacon in the Church of Sweden," Brodd anticipated that the situation created by the re-interpretation would be "the focus of future debates" (137). Idem, "*Caritas* and *Diakonia* as perspectives on the Diaconate," in Gunnel Borgegård, Olav Fanuelsen, and Christine Hall, eds, *The Ministry of the Deacon: 2. Ecclesiological Explorations* (Uppsala: Nordic Ecumenical Council, 2000), 23–69; Kjell Nordstokke, "The Diaconate: Ministry of Prophecy and Transformation," ibid., 107–30; Kari Latvus, "The Paradigm Challenged. A New Analysis of the Origin of Diakonia," *Studia Theologica* 62 (2008), 142–57.

39. "Beruht der Anspruch der evangelischen Diakonie auf einer Missinterpretation der antiken Quellen? John N. Collins Untersuchung 'Diakonia,'" *Pastoraltheologie* 89 (2000), 343–64, reprinted in his *Barmherzigkeit und Diakonie: Von der rettenden Liebe zum gelingenden Leben* (Stuttgart: Kohlhammer, 2008), 114–28, as well as in V. Hermann and M. Horstmann, eds, *Studienbuch Diakonik, Bd. 1: biblische, historische und theologische Zugänge zur Diakonie*, 2nd edn (Neukirchen-Vluyn: Neukirchener Verlag, 2008), 117–33.

work "has called the earlier consensus into doubt." While the Report recognized in the new research an "historical-philological corrective," it failed to incorporate the corrective into its theological framework.[40]

By contrast, Benedict was blunt, naming the consensus a collection of "discordant scholarship, unquestioned assumptions, and unacknowledged borrowings,"[41] and then, however falteringly, opened a new path for a theology of diaconate aligned with the newer understanding of *diakonia*.[42] In the latter exercise he was one of four scholars collaborating under the auspices of the *diakonic* institute of the University of Heidelberg in evaluating the research in the 1990 volume *Diakonia* and assessing its relevance to the commitment of German Evangelical Churches to their program of "Diakonie."[43] The four studies raised no matters of substance in regard to semantic issues but did attract attention to the problem confronting advocates of the traditional German "Diakonie" and consequently of policies underlying the fostering of new deacons among many churches under the influence of the German tradition.

While the question of the theological legitimacy of "Diakonie" was still being so publicly aired, a new semantic investigation into *diakonia* brought questioning to a close. In a doctoral dissertation of 2005 (published in 2007), Anni Hentschel engaged in close critical dialogue with my semantic and exegetical analysis of ancient Greek sources. She tested this against her own reading of Greek sources and concluded by endorsing my methodology and its semantic outcomes. Although some differences of emphasis in a small number of exegetical issues remain, our readings of the foundational Christian texts (Mark 10:45; Luke 22:27) are identical.[44]

---

40. Hanover Report (London: Anglican Communion Publications, 1996), paragraphs 3–4, 62.

41. "Beruht der Anspruch," 354.

42. "Die grössere Diakonie: Versuch einer Neubestimmung im Anschluss an John N. Collins," in V. Hermann, R. Merz, and H. Schmidt, eds, *Diakonische Konturen: Theologie im Kontext sozialer Arbeit* (Heidelberg: Winter, 2003), 127–35; see further "Diakonie als Dazwischengehen und Beauftragung. Die Collins-Debatte aus der Sicht ihres Anstossgebers," in *Barmherzigkeit und Diakonie*, 129–37 (a lecture of 2005; see in relation to note 58 below).

43. In *Diakonische Konturen*, in addition to Benedict (see previous note), see studies by Stefan Dietzel (136–70), Ismo Dunderberg (171–83), and Dierk Starnitzke (184–212), and the discussion of these authors in Chapter 1.

44. Anni Hentschel, *Diakonia im Neuen Testament: Studien zur Semantik unter besonderer Berücksichtigung der Rolle von Frauen* (Tübingen: Mohr Siebeck, 2007); see esp. 85–89. See my article review of Hentschel, "Re-interpreting *diakonia* in Germany," *Ecclesiology* 5.1 (2009), 69–81 (earlier as Chapter 2).

In a later paper Hentschel addressed the nature of the ancient diaconate under the title "In early Christian communities was the diaconate developed to meet social needs and charitable purposes?"[45] To this question, Hentschel answered in the negative.In addition to these uniquely resourced and well-received monographs about *diakonia*, two lexicographers have endorsed the semantic profile presented in them. Working independently of both myself and Hentschel, and without a particular focus on Christian sources, Elvira Gangutia, who edited volume 5 of the new Greek-Spanish lexicon, described a broad range of ancient usage in terms similar to those in my 1990 *Diakonia*.[46] On the other hand, Frederick Danker, editor of the third English-language edition of the classic Walter Bauer lexicon of early Christian literature, was perfectly aware of the theological implications of removing Bauer's more or less conventional definitions. In their place Danker provided semantic categories close to those described in the 1990 volume.[47]

Re-evaluating Ecclesial Ministry

In the light of such a consolidation of opinion regarding the semantic values carried by the *diakon-* terms in their connection with the theology of ministry, the centenary year of the Edinburgh World Missionary Conference is a particularly appropriate time to reassess the place of ministry in ecclesiology. Indeed, the need for reassessment takes on a degree of urgency when we bear in mind the deep-seated problems that have been hindering further progress in ecumenical accord between major branches of the Christian church.

The reinterpretation of *diakonia* has exposed the inadequate and misleading interpretation within the Brandt/Beyer consensus that has determined the main course of the theology of ministry in the second half of

---

45. Anni Hentschel, "Gibt es einen sozial-karitativ ausgerichteten Diakonat in den frühchristlichen Gemeinden?," *Pastoraltheologie* 97/9 (2008), 290–306.

46. Elvira Gangutia, *Diccionario Griego-Español*, ed. F. F. R. Adrados, Vol. 5, ed. Elvira Gangutia (Madrid: Consejo supereior de invertigaciones científicas, Instituto de Filología, 1997), 984–86.

47. *A Greek-English Lexicon of the New Testament and other Early Christian Literature*, 3rd edn, (BDAG), revised and edited by Frederick William Danker, based on Water Bauer's *Griechisch-deutsches Wörterbuch zu den Schriften des Neuen Testaments und der frühchristlichen Literatur*, 6th edn, ed. Kurt Aland and Barbara Aland, with Viktor Reichmann, and on previous English editions by W. F. Arndt, F. W. Gingrich, and F. W. Danker (Chicago and London: University of Chicago Press, 2000).

the twentieth century. This stricture applies also, of course, to the *diakonic* ecclesiological constructs argued by Karl Barth, Eduard Schweizer, Ernst Käsemann, Hans Küng, and many others.[48]

We can draw two conclusions from a situation of this kind. First, from either an ecumenical or a purely ecclesiological point of view, the theology of ministry as formulated on the premise of the twentieth-century consensus about *diakonia* in the New Testament is not able to furnish the church of the twenty-first century with an authentic connection to some of the foundational insights that brought ecclesial communities to birth through ministry in the first century.

Second, the churches of today need to fashion a theology of ministry characterized by the same semantic elements that drew Christians of the first century to appropriate the *diakon-* words to express essential dimensions of their ecclesial identity.Within church bodies to date, serious reconsideration of ministry in such light has been extremely rare. In October 1990, within a few months of the publication of *Diakonia: Re-interpreting the Ancient Sources*, Cardinal Ratzinger opened a Synod of Bishops in Rome with an address on "The Essence of the Priesthood." There he criticized the degree to which traditional Roman Catholic theology of priesthood had been subject to "desacralisation" through the importation from Protestant theology of "a profane vocabulary" (*diakonia* being so characterized). In the light of a recent reinterpretation, he noted, this categorization could no longer be upheld.[49] It is thus ironic that in undertaking in 1992 a decade-long review of the diaconate, the Vatican's International Theological Commission began by addressing "difficulties in terminology" (*diakonia* and related words) with reference to Beyer and Schweizer (among others) but not to my 1990 linguistic study.[50]

---

48. See a broad selection of contemporary writers in my "Ordained and Other Ministries: Making a Difference," *Ecclesiology* 3.1 (2006), 11–32 (esp. 12–13; also Chapter 12 in this book, esp. 187–89).

49. Joseph Cardinal Ratzinger, *Called to Communion: Understanding the Church Today*, Eng. trans. (San Francisco: Ignatius Press, 1996), 105–31, citing 107, 106. Ratzinger cited the unpublished dissertation of 1976 on which the book of 1990, *Diakonia: Re-interpreting the Ancient Sources*, was based. It is noteworthy that in 2005 in his first encyclical as Pope Benedict XVI, *Deus caritas est*, and treating of *diakonia* as "the ministry of charity" and "part of the fundamental structure of the Church" (paragraph 21), the language and concepts revert completely to those of the German tradition stemming from Beyer and Brandt (notes 30, 31 above). See the account of this transformation in Chapter 3 above.

50. International Theological Commission, *From the Diakonia of Christ to the Diakonia of the Apostles*, Historico-Theological Research Document, Eng. trans. (Chicago: Hillenbrand

The situation in Roman Catholic diaconal circles in the United States has been virtually the same. The added significance of this arises from the fact that the United States Conference of Catholic Bishops (USCCB) has mandated and overseen the largest body of deacons by far. Of the world's thirty-seven thousand Roman Catholic deacons, more than seventeen thousand reside in the United States. Naturally, this ongoing numerical expansion has attracted a considerable theological and pastoral literature,[51] including the comparatively recent National Directory issued by the Conference of Bishops.[52] A minute sector of this literature, however, takes account of the relevance of a reinterpretation of the title *diakonos* or of ministry as *diakonia*. Singular here is the essay in which Richard Gaillardetz, on grounds of the reinterpretation, abandons the iconology of Christ the servant as a rationale for the diaconate.[53]

Similarly, when the publication of the ecumenically framed Hanover Report[54] occasioned a review of the diaconate from the perspective of the EKD, its Study Commission acknowledged the correctness of the 1990 reinterpretation but made no attempt to accommodate this finding within

---

Books, 2003). For documentation on the history of this text, see the *Nota preliminare* published in *La Civiltà Cattolica* 154.1 (February 2003), 253–336 (see 253). And further comment in Chapter 14 below.

51. In *The Permanent Diaconate: Its History and Place in the Sacrament of Orders* (New York/ Mahwah: Paulist Press, 2007), 95, Kenan B. Osborne instances fourteen titles up to 2005. This sample includes my *Diakonia* but not my *Deacons and the Church: Making Connections Between Old and New* (Leominster, UK: Gracewing, 2002). The former book also appears in a short annotated bibliography (p. 209: "very helpful for understanding the meaning of *deacon* as used in the New Testament"), but this note is counterbalanced by the information at p. 140 that the identity and spirituality of the deacon derives from the *diakonia* of Jesus "who came to serve": "the central image of his ministry remains the icon of Jesus washing the feet of his disciples." Although almost universally understood as symbolic of the office of deacon, linguistically speaking the washing of feet is not an activity that falls within the semantic range of the Greek *diakon-* words.

52. USCCB, *National Directory for the Formation, Ministry, and Life of Permanent Deacons in the United States* (Washington, DC: USCCB, 2005). The Directory (no. 37) adopts the formulation from the Vatican's own *Basic Norms for the Formation of Permanent Deacons* (Strathfield, NSW: St Pauls Publication, 1998) that the deacon is to be "a driving force for service, or *diakonia*," this being "an essential part of the mission of the Church" (no. 5).

53. "On the Theological Integrity of the Diaconate," in Owen F. Cummings, William T. Ditewig, and Richard R. Gaillardetz, eds, *Theology of the Diaconate: The State of the Question* (New York/Mahwah: Paulist Press, 2005), 67–97. I support Gaillardetz's proposal that the deacon's ministry is essentially "public service to the apostolic ministry of *episkopē* exercised by the bishop or presbyter" (p. 87).

54. See above note 40.

the traditional German conceptualization of "Diakonie."[55] Ormonde Plater, a leading Episcopalian deacon who participated in discussions leading to the Hanover Report, has noted that in the formulation of the report a compromise had to be struck between the Anglican party, who were informed about the reinterpretation, and representatives of the EKD and other Lutheran churches.[56] The compromise was such as not to disturb the traditional Lutheran correlation between "Diakonie" as social work and diaconate as an ecclesial function.

The level of anxiety in regard to this matter can be gauged, nonetheless, from the headline of "The Theme of the Week" in the Württemberg Sunday church newspaper in July 2005: "Is 'Diakonie' a Big Mistake?" This headed a report of my lecture at the Reutlingen-Ludwigsburg Evangelische Fachhochschule (an institute for *diakonic* studies) and constituted a spirited response from a professor at the institute under the headline, "The Foundations of 'Diakonie' are not Shaking."[57] Even Hans-Jürgen Benedict was unable to resolve the problem presented by the incompatibility in German language and value systems between "Diakonie" and the reinterpretation of the ancient *diakonia*. He recommended at a conference on the problem that "Diakonie" should be retained as a designation for Christian social work in Germany because in the German experience it had the impact of a logo.[58] In accord with this assessment, Anni Hentschel advised German readers of her own paper on the early Christian diaconate that in speaking of "Diakonat" she was not speaking of the "neo-Protestant German expression" ("Diakonie"), which in fact had no grounding in the New Testament, but of the early Christian conceptualization of *diakonia*.[59]

In contrast with such unresolved—mainly unaddressed—problems within the Roman Catholic Church and the German Evangelical Churches,

---

55. Stellungnahme des ÖSTA zu der Studie "Der Diakonat als ökumenische Chance. Hannover-Bericht der Internationalen anglikanisch-lutherischen Kommission," ÖSTA Nr. 21d, October 2000. See section III.1 with footnote 21.

56. Ormonde Plater, "The Collins-Kittel Synthesis," *Diakoneo* 17.3 (Easter 1995), 5.

57. M. Ernst Wahl, "Diakonie, ein grosser Irrtum? Wie ein australischer Katholik die evangelische Sozialarbeit zum Nachdenken zwingt," *Evangelisches Gemeindeblatt* 100.29 (July 17, 2005), 2–3; Annette Noller, "Die Grundlage der Diakonie wankt nicht. Gedanken zur diakoniewissenschaftlichen Diskussion um John Collins," *Evangelisches Gemeindeblatt* 100.35 (September 4, 2005), 7 (add correction entered at *Evangelisches Gemeindeblatt* 100.36 (September 11, 2005), 7.

58. "Diakonie als Dazwischengehen und Beauftragung" (above, note 42), 132.

59. Hentschel, "Gibt es einen sozial-karitativ ausgerichteten *Diakonat*" (above, n. 45), 290–91.

writers and church bodies within the Church of England (UK) have taken a more positive approach to the reinterpretation and have attempted to gain approval from the General Synod of the Church of England to re-vamp their "distinctive diaconate" along lines drawn from the reinterpret-ation.[60] Such initiatives have met defeat along what might be called party lines (a very large body of lay ministers within the Church of England versus the very much smaller number of ordained deacons). But the argu-mentation here reflected, it seems to me, a level of deficiency in a general theology of ministry rather than weakness in the proposed theology of diaconate itself.

An early recognition of such a general deficiency was an essay in which Robert Hannaford addressed the confusion arising when "the same term [viz., ministry] does service both for what is common to all Christians *and* for what differentiates within the Christian community [viz. ordained min-istry]."[61] Drawing on the new delineation of ministry emerging from pas-toral applications of *diakonia* as re-interpreted in the New Testament—and calling this development "a first step towards conceptual clarification"[62]—Hannaford was drawn to distinguish between discipleship as "a common obligation of all the baptised" and ministry as "by its nature a summons to some particular, explicit, work for and on behalf of the church."[63]

Paul Avis has significantly advanced from here toward a more fully developed analysis of ministry as a special public responsibility within the mission that all the baptized share.[64] He has been able to contribute in his role within the Church of England's Faith and Order Advisory Group. This group produced the report *The Mission and Ministry of the Whole Church*[65] for the purpose of clarifying, at a time of confusion among both ordained and non-ordained as to who does what in the church, the high demands of mission which discipleship puts upon all who are baptized and upon all

---

60. *For Such a Time as This: A Renewed Diaconate in the Church of England,* report to the General Synod of the Church of England of a Working Party of the House of Bishops, GS 1407 (London: Church House Publishing, 2001).

61. "Foundations for an Ecclesiology of Ministry," in Christine Hall and Robert Hannaford, eds, *Order and Ministry* (Leominster, UK: Gracewing, 1996), 21–60, citing p. 23.

62. Ibid., 26.

63. Ibid., 43.

64. Paul Avis, *A Ministry Shaped by Mission* (London: T&T Clark, 2005). See especially the nuanced discussion of ministry in relation to baptism, mission, and charism in chapter 2.

65. *The Mission and Ministry of the Whole Church. Biblical, Theological and Contemporary Perspectives,* GS Misc 854 (2007).

who have been charged with special roles within that mission. Among the five largely pastoral and ecumenical reasons adduced for the development of this comprehensive statement, the third was the reinterpretation of "the key Greek term translated 'ministry,'" which "offers some immensely helpful pointers" for a fuller appreciation of what the New Testament has to tell us about ministry in the church.

Theological Motifs of a Re-interpreted Diakonia

Theologians of ministry in the twenty-first century would do well to take their lead from this initiative of the Church of England. A beginning would be to take stock of the new *diakonic* values coloring numerous familiar statements in the New Testament relevant to ecclesiology. In summary, even in the New Testament, *diakon-* words do not display any distinctively Christian value and have no "basic meaning" (here "service at table" is usually designated). Nor are the terms inherently part of servile or slavish usage and thus designations of essentially lowly, humble service. Moreover, the words never express or connote benevolence toward the recipient of an activity.[66] All such characteristics of the usage are at variance with the Brandt/Beyer interpretation embodied in the twentieth-century consensus. In particular, the consensus had identified humble and benevolent service to another as the defining element in Christian ministry.

What should regulate our evaluation of early Christian depictions of ministerial activity are the following characteristics of ancient usage. These characteristics are uniformly evident across a thousand years of

---

66. According to the twentieth century consensus, Matt. 25:44 (NRSV, "When did we not *take care of you?*") is the classic illustration of *diakon-* expressing benevolent service; in fact, the *diakon-* term here is simply an instance of usage descriptive of dutiful expectations of butlers, valets, cupbearers, etc., in grand houses and palaces, as at Anaxandrides, FAC, 2.56 (the heavenly court); Athenaeus, *Deipnosophistai*, 192f (banquet of Homeric heroes); Dio Cassius 54.23.4 (Augustus at a banquet); Heraclides, FHG, 2.96 (the Persian court); Josephus, AJ, 2.65 (Pharaoh's court); 6.52 (King Saul); 7.165 (Amnon, Davidic prince); 8.169 (Solomon); 10.242 (Belshazzar); 11.163, 166 (Xerxes); 11.188 (Artaxerxes); 15.224 (Herod); 18.193 (Agrippa); Lucian, *Dialogi deorum* 4.4;5.2 (heavenly court); Polybius 30.26.5 (Games of Antiochus IV); Plutarch, *Moralia* 174d (court of King Cotys, Thrace); Xenophon, *Hiero*, 4.2 (court of the Tyrants); Xenophon, *Historia Graeca*, 5.4.6 (residence of the Polemarchs). See Collins, *Diakonia*, 64–65 (parable), 156 (royal courts; 7 of 8 instances in LXX in royal contexts: see book's index, 358), 157–68 (religious and formal contexts), 309–15 (further reference); *Deacons and the Church*, 59–65. On angels "ministering/*diakon-*" to Jesus (Mark 1:13), H. B. Swete reported the comment of c. 200 CE, "as if he were already a veritable king" (in Clement of Alexandria's *Excerpta ex Theodoto* 85); see *The Gospel according to St Mark*, 3rd edn (London: Macmillan, 1927), 12.

ancient Greek usage. The *diakon-* terms are not ordinary, everyday words; were that the case, we would have difficulty understanding why they sit so well in philosophic and religious discourse and poetic drama. The terms are in fact comparatively rare and belong to higher levels of language. The fact that they occur in reference to banquets says more about the status attributed to the banquet than to the social standing of the waiters.[67]

Since no "basic meaning" can be identified, the meaning of any individual instance of a *diakon-* term is not always easily discerned, especially when our reading is affected by presuppositions arising from the Brandt/ Beyer consensus. Accordingly, the reader is always dependent on what the context is indicating about the meaning. Such discernment was not a problem for the ancient Greeks.

Usage across the centuries reveals that the words occur in a particular set of contexts which we might name as (a) message, (b) agency, and (c) household duties. Nonetheless, distinguishing between such areas in a particular passage can be a subtle exercise. In whatever context a term occurs, however, *diakon-* will always connote a mandate from a commissioning person or institution.

At the simplest level, this connotation of a mandate can be seen in the instance of the table attendant, who is conceived as functioning at the behest of the person reclining at table. Multiple occasions occur of such agency at even the highest social levels.[68] Many subtler and more complex contexts also occur; where the notion of agency merges into a connotation of mediation. Such contexts are what led me to employ the English expression "go-between."[69] Unfortunately, many have taken my occasional use of this expression as indicating that "go-between" is the "basic" meaning of the word. In certain passages of Paul's rhetorical defence of his apostleship, however, the notion of mediation would be close to the mind of his Corinthian audience (as at 1 Cor. 3:5; 2 Cor. 3:3; 5:18; 6:4).

Usage of this color and subtlety would seem to have rich implications within today's Christian churches for the construction of a ministry of the Word, just as the simpler notion of agency has much to contribute to an understanding of what the first Christians had in mind in designating

---

67. See my analysis of usage in relation to service at tables in *Diakonia*, 154–63.

68. See references to this usage (involving senior officers within the imperial system) in Collins, *Diakonia*, 303–05. See also note 66 above.

69. Note the translation by G. H. Box (1927) of *Testament of Abraham* 9.24 (A) "be the medium of my word" (*diakonēsai moi logon*); see Collins, *Diakonia*, 99.

some of their first ecclesial officers "deacons." Working within such changed semantic parameters—and totally freed from the constricted ambit of lowly service—we will necessarily arrive at ecclesiological conclusions substantially at variance with principles espoused within the contemporary *diakonic* consensus.

In the first place we will have different ecclesial expectations relative to the *diakonia* of the Son of Man at Mark 10:45. In the *diakonia* expressed here, the Son of Man is not modeling loving service of others but defining his commitment to the mission received from God.[70] Similarly, the *diakonia* under which Paul established churches is his divine mandate to deliver the Word of God.[71]

In the light of the new understanding of *diakonia* in the missions of Jesus and Paul, any ecclesial polity of fidelity to scriptures would suppose a commitment to embody the same levels of understanding in regard to what *diakonia* implies for churches today. Thus, in due course, the notion of a distinct and exclusive religious mandate will likely be reinstated within a twenty-first-century theology of ordained or commissioned ministry.[72]

Any reforming instincts directed along these lines might also be inclined toward incorporating a revised evaluation of the significance for church order of what Paul had in mind in speaking of *diakonia* among the

---

70. Collins, *Diakonia*, 248–52, and Hentschel, *Diakonia im Neuen Testament. Studien zur Semantik unter besonderer Berücksichtigung der Rolle von Frauen* (Tübingen: Mohr Siebeck, 2007), 278, with note 438. Compare Beyer, *Theological Dictionary of the New Testament*, 2, 86: "in Mark 10:45 and Matthew 20:28...*diakonein* is now much more than a comprehensive term for any loving assistance rendered to the neighbour. It is understood as full and perfect sacrifice, as the offering of life which is the very essence of service."

71. Compare, by contrast, Andrew D. Clarke, *Serve the Community of the Church* (Grand Rapids, MI/Cambridge, UK: Eerdmans, 2000), 250: "Avoiding the notion of leader, Paul did, however, regard himself as a servant. In this regard he does adopt the pattern modelled by Jesus, who came to serve." Similarly, *A Pauline Theology of Church Leadership* (London: T&T Clark, 2008), 98: "The language of serving and servanthood has long been associated with Christian leadership after the pattern of Jesus. The Gospels record at a number of points an explicit identification between serving and leading in Jesus' own mission. The principal verse is [Mark 10:45]." Clarke maintains this servant ideology in the more recent volume in spite of granting there (p. 100) that Collins "has in large measure overturned a consensus," a claim that he had strongly rebutted in the earlier volume (pp. 233–47).

72. This statement is not to be seen as advocating a replication of hierarchical structures in place in many ecclesial communities. That has been the conclusion some have drawn from my earlier work; see reviews of *Are All Christians Ministers?* (Collegeville, MN: Liturgical Press, 1992) by Ronald J. Nuzzi, *National Catholic Reporter* 29.25 (April 23, 1993), 15, and Gideon Goosen, *Pacifica* 6 (June 1993), 242–43. That book concluded, however, with some wide-ranging reflections on how to release authentic ministry from hierarchical constrictions, a subject not possible to take further here.

gifts of the Spirit. The *diakoniai* Paul identifies as gifts of the Spirit at 1 Cor. 12:5 are not anything and everything any Christian does[73] but will be forms of the ministry to which the Spirit calls some in the church.[74]

The "work of *diakonia*" to be undertaken at Eph. 4:12 is not what "the saints" are called to do but is the work of ministry for which the apostles and pastors are given to the church.[75]

The Reformers of the sixteenth century were never in doubt of the nature of ministry. Reflecting on Eph. 4:12, Calvin recognized "the ministry of men [sic], which God employs in governing the Church." He added, "By the ministers to whom he has committed this office, and given grace to discharge it, he dispenses and distributes his gifts to the Church."

Ominously, he concluded:

Whoever, therefore, studies to abolish this order and kind of government of which we speak, or disparages it as of minor importance,

---

73. We need to distinguish between the broad applications of which the English term *ministry* is capable and the special character and narrower semantic range of the ancient Greek usage of *diakonia*. See my critique of ecclesiological constructs arising from misreading of *diakonia* at 1 Cor. 12 with reference to my exegesis of the passage in "Ordained and Other Ministries" (Chapter 12 in this book).

74. Joseph Fitzmyer now supports this view against Käsemann in particular; see his *First Corinthians*, Anchor Yale Bible Commentaries (New Haven, CT: Yale University Press, 2008), 464–65. Compare the broader view long widespread both in ecclesial documentations concerning lay ministries and in ecclesiological writings. Thus the indiscriminate application of *diakonia* to any kind of ecclesial activity in the statement of the USCCB, *Co-Workers in the Vineyard of the Lord: A Resource for Guiding the Development of Lay Ecclesial Ministry* (Washington, DC: USCCB, 2005), 20. See also Zeni Fox, *New Ecclesial Ministry: Lay Professionals Serving the Church*, rvsd edn (Chicago: Sheed and Ward, 2002), 210–20 (but Fox registers my opposing view as "cogent," 218, note 3). Thomas O'Meara writes of the church being endowed with "a ministerial pleroma (sustained by incarnational charism)"; see *Theology of Ministry*, rvsd edn (New York/Mahweh: Paulist Press, 1999), 222. In finding my view here deficient, Stephen Pickard has not taken into account my fuller expositions in subsequent writings; see his *Theological Foundations for Collaborative Ministry* (Farnham, UK: Ashgate, 2009), 38, note 19.

75. Compare, by contrast, vigorous assertions and argumentation to the opposite effect by Markus Barth, *Ephesians 4–6*, Anchor Yale Bible Commentaries (Garden City, NY: Doubleday, 1984), 477–84. In earlier periods the interpretation above was not subject to debate. In presenting a scenario for the redevelopment of a "diaconal church," David Clark steps lightly across such debated issues, managing not to engage even questions affecting the legitimacy of his "servant" concept; see *Breaking the Mould of Christendom: Kingdom Community, Diaconal Church and the Liberation of the Laity* (Peterborough, UK: Epworth, 2005), esp. 61–67. His writing exemplifies wide-ranging and deep-seated popular views about *diakonia*. Collaborators in a sequel edited by him, *The Diaconal Church: Beyond the Mould of Christendom* (Peterborough, UK: Epworth, 2008), often point to defective aspects of the scenario, and one, Paula Gooder, challenges the underlying notion (see Gooder's assessment concluding this chapter).

plots the devastation, or rather the ruin and destruction, of the Church. [76]

Very shortly after his death, the corporate voice of the Reform echoed such views. Thus the Second Helvetic Confession of 1566:

The priesthood and the ministry are very different from one another. For the priesthood...is common to all Christians; not so is the ministry. Nor have we abolished the ministry of the Church because we have repudiated the papal priesthood from the Church of Christ. [77]

Conclusion

If churches today would like to be confident that their ministry conforms to—but is not required to be a mirror image—what the New Testament has to say about it, perhaps their theology of ministry in the twenty-first century should restart from where the Reformers left off. In the final decades of the twentieth century, an enormous amount of work was accomplished by churches in familiarizing themselves with the character of ministry across the ecumenical span. Almost all of this was achieved without a full realization of the character and style of ministry in the earliest churches that a reinterpretation of *diakonia* has opened up for further investigation.

The main Reformers did not operate under this limitation because they were in accord with the meaning of ministry in Paul's letters. Today, if we can consider the essential linguistic issues about *diakonia* closed, surely we are in a more advantageous position to take our own ecclesiology forward without being distracted by the debilitating controversies peculiar to the earliest Christian times and situations. Rather than such a proposal being dismissed as grossly reactionary, I would venture—although not here as an argued conclusion—that a process of this kind could produce ministerial arrangements which would be manageable within ecclesiologies— whether "high" or "low"—across the vast majority of the 160 churches who responded to *Baptism, Eucharist, and Ministry* in the 1980s. [78]

---

76. John Calvin, *Institutes of the Christian Religion*, trans. H. Beveridge, Vol. 2 (London: James Clarke, 1962), 317 (IV.iii.2).

77. *The Constitution of the United Presbyterian Church in the United States of America, Part I, Book of Confessions*, 2nd edn (New York: Office of the General Assembly, 1970), #5.153.

78. See notes 34, 35 above.

Paula Gooder has put a measure on the transformation which the return of the New Testament *diakonia* to the church implies. Assessing the implications of the reinterpretation of *diakonia*, she observes:

Sea changes in opinion on New Testament subjects usually go unnoticed within the church. Just occasionally, however, a change takes place that has an enormous impact on the life and self-understanding of people within the church—this is one of those occasions.[79]

Sadly, talking about reform of ministry within the churches is, to me, all too like talking about reform from within financial institutions or a city's police force. Within groups whose members have identical optimum objectives in regard to both how they operate and what their social rewards might be, measures that change their modus operandi or reward levels will never eventuate for reasons that it is superfluous to spell out. In regard to churches, bishops and their parallel officers in nonepiscopal churches are not the whole problem. More problematic might well be conservative rumps of pew-sitters. And beside these two bodies lie one mass of the indifferent, another of pious suffering souls, and a third of seething critics, name-callers, enthusiasts, and some prophets.

If this picture appears fanciful to some, it might serve to bring to mind for others the hard words of Thomas S. Kuhn describing what it takes for ideas and practices to change in institutional life. We may glibly refer to paradigm shift without recognizing what his research revealed about the process. Acclaimed scientific outcomes have not arisen simply from "an increment to what is already known."[80] Rather each began as what the community perceived to be an anomaly to the controlling paradigm. Inevitably, each anomaly ran up against the sharp edge of conflict, resistance, and eventually competition. Clearly, "the road to a firm research consensus is extraordinarily arduous."[81] Kuhn even suggested that crises may be induced in institutions "by repeated failure to make an anomaly conform."[82] On the other hand, "discovery commences with the awareness of anomaly...and closes only when the paradigm has been adjusted so that the anomalous has become the expected."[83]

---

79. "Towards a Diaconal Church: Some Reflections on New Testament Material," in D. Clark, ed., *The Diaconal Church*, 99–108, citing 103. See also her "*Diakonia* in the New Testament: A Dialogue with John N. Collins," *Ecclesiology* 3.1 (2006), 33–56.

80. Thomas S. Kuhn, *The Structure of Scientific Revolutions* (Chicago/London: University of Chicago Press, 1962), 7.

81. Ibid., 15.

82. Ibid., xi.

83. Ibid., 52.

Throughout history, churches—like the sciences—have undergone multiple paradigm shifts. Possibly the churches stand now in an ecclesiastical era when the crises they came to recognize in the mid-twentieth century and attempted to meet through the inauguration of the World Council of Churches and of Second Vatican Council have intensified beyond their power to respond effectively. As a consequence, they are adjudged by some as turning more regularly—and with increasing ardor—to a recycling of paradigms characteristic of the churches' earlier ascendancy.

Such a response conforms to what Kuhn observed in science: when confronted by prolonged anomalies, scientists "do not renounce the paradigm that has led them into crisis."[84] The way out of the crisis is not achieved by "an articulation or extension of the old paradigm" but only by "a reconstruction of the field from new fundamentals, a reconstruction that changes some of the field's most elementary theoretical generalisations as well as many of its paradigm methods and applications."[85]

Are we to read a picture of this process playing out in what Joseph Ratzinger observed about voting patterns at the Second Vatican Council during the debate on *Lumen gentium*? The constitution is renowned for having given a priority—of honor, at the least—to the notion of "the People of God" over the hierarchical model inherited from the First Vatican Council. Ratzinger noted that, in regard to seven of the eight chapters of the constitution, a mere ten ballots were taken among the bishops, while on the single chapter dealing with "collegiality" of the bishops (with the pope) no fewer than forty-one separate votes were taken, the more important of these being voted on "sentence by sentence."[86] Thus did the notion of the People of God fade to a dull backdrop while the paradigm of pope and bishops was stage-managed into the footlights. Theology of ministry has struggled ever since to find expression across the broad body of that church. On a macro scale, that says little for the ecumenical prospects for lesser churches.

---

84. Ibid., 77.

85. Ibid., 84.

86. Pope Benedict XVI, *Theological Highlights of Vatican II*, Eng. trans. (New York: Paulist Press, 2009, originally 1966), 162. Throughout *What Happened at Vatican II* (note 26 above), O'Malley traces the extended story of the underlying conflict between advocates of collegiality and of papal primacy across the course of the Second Vatican Council. For example,"The minority bishops [pro primacy]…often seemed to understand primacy in Bismarck's terms as an absolute monarchy possessing all authority in the church."

12

Ordained and Other Ministries: Making a Difference

THE AREA OF pastoral theology known as lay ecclesial ministry[1] has attracted much comment and increasing scrutiny in recent years. Part of this as been an evaluation of my own work,[2] and here I want to re-enter debate at the critical juncture of how we are to understand the relationship between ministry as the essential pastoral activity within the church and those "varieties of gifts (*charismatōn*)" among which are "varieties of services (*diakoniōn*)" (1 Cor. 12:4–5). Until we are able to establish the relationship between these "gifts" and these "services" (alternatively, "ministries") and clarify who in the church receives them, we are left with teasing and frustrating questions about who does what in the church. The setting for the following considerations is Roman Catholic writing in ecclesiology, a factor that helps keep the discussion within manageable limits but, as will be immediately apparent discussion can proceed only in the light of ecumenical influences and ramifications.

---

1. National Conference of Catholic Bishops (NCCB), *Together in God's Service: Toward a Theology of Ecclesial Lay Ministry* (Washington, DC: NCCB, 1998); USCCB, *Lay Ecclesial Ministry: The State of the Questions* (Washington, DC: USCCB, 1999). A final document was approved by USCCB in November 2005 and published a month later, but it was not available to me at the time of writing: *Co-Workers in the Vineyard of the Lord: A Resource for Guiding the Development of Lay Ecclesial Ministry* (Washington, DC: USCCB, 2005). Newsworthy was Avery Cardinal Dulles's intervention in November clearing a path for the term *ministry* to be employed for the non-ordained. See editorial comment in *America* 194.2 (January 16, 2006), including the attempt to clarify terminology: "The call to 'lay ecclesial ministry' is a unique call within the church, distinct from the more common 'lay ministry' that all Catholics are to perform in the secular world, and different from the volunteer work that many generous Catholics offer the church."

2. John N. Collins, "Fitting Lay Ministries into a Theology of Ministries: Responding to an American Consensus," *Worship* 79.2 (2005), 152–167; "Fitting Lay Ministries into a Theology of Ministries," *Worship*. 79.3 (2005), 209–222. See Chapter 13 in this book.

Ministry in the Context of Charism

The most innovative and widely read Roman Catholic writers in ecclesiology over the last forty years have had one idea in common. This is that
all members of the church are called to ministry. In fact, on this schedule,
every Christian is baptized into ministry: "Baptism...initiates a person
into charism and diaconal action, into a community that is essentially ministerial."[3] And yet, before entering theology school, probably only the very
youngest of these Roman Catholic writers could have had such a thought
in mind. The fact is that theology courses of recent decades have cultivated
an idea of universal ministry that emerged in German Protestant theology
in the immediate post–World War II era and from the 1960s soon satu-
rated Roman Catholic ecclesiology. The leading expression of the idea was
a single essay by Ernst Käsemann, "Ministry and Community in the New
Testament," that he first presented in Germany in 1949 but published
in Germany in 1960 and in an English translation in 1964. Käsemann
himself noted that his ideas concurred closely with those that Schweizer
first published in 1946 and later reworked in *Church Order in the New
Testament*.[4] No discussion of ministry today is possible without an understanding of the context that Käsemann established for the flood of publications on ministry in the years following the Second Vatican Council.

Roman Catholic ecclesiologists and writers on ministry who have
been attracted to or have felt obliged to take account of the configur-
ation imposed by Käsemann include many whose names one or two
generations of students of theology have harnessed to their under-
graduate papers on topics like the ministry of the laity, the mission
of the church, the diversity of ministries, and the ministry of the baptized. The names are still mostly familiar,[5] and more recent voices echo

---

3. Thomas F. O'Meara, *Theology of Ministry*, rev. edn (New York: Paulist Press, 1999), 211.

4. Ernst Käsemann, "Ministry and Community in the New Testament," in his *Essays on New Testament Themes*, trans. W. J. Montague (London: SCM, 1964), 63–94, see 63, note 1; Eduard Schweizer, *Church Order in the New Testament*, trans. F. Clarke (London: SCM, 1961), 100–01, 180.

5. Hans Küng, *The Church*, trans. R. and R. Ockenden (Garden City, NY: Image, 1976, originally 1967), 247; Bernard Cooke, *Ministry to Word and Sacraments: History and Theology*
(Philadelphia: Fortress, 1976), 198–99, 203–04, 343–44; Nathan Mitchell, *Mission and
Ministry: History and Theology in the Sacrament of Order* (Wilmington, DE: Glazier, 1982),
124–25; Daniel Harrington, "Ernst Käsemann on the Church in the New Testament,"
in his *Light of All Nations: Essays on the Church in New Testament Research* (Wilmington,
DE: Glazier, 1982), 15–45; O'Meara, *Theology of Ministry*, 62–65, 200–07; Leonardo Boff,
Church: Charism and Power: Liberation Theology and the Institutional Church, trans. J. W.

the central idea represented in these earlier writings on church and ministry.[6]

Why such impact from Käsemann's study? Käsemann was considering the place of the gifts of the Spirit in the church. These are the *charismata* of which Paul writes in 1 Cor. 12–14. In pre-conciliar theology (i. e., Roman Catholic theology up to the 1950s) the *charismata* featuring in Paul's statements were often sidelined as gifts with which the Spirit endowed the church in its younger years for the purpose of sustaining it until its structures of order and authority were in place.[7] Käsemann insisted, to the contrary, that the development of these structures was precisely what choked off the church's connaturally charismatic mode of being. The structures prevented the church from being what it should be. What happened in this historical development was that "elect individuals" hijacked the broad *charisma* that graced the body of the church to make of it their own "distinguishing mark"; these self-made "elect" should have been cultivating within the church at large its "common endowment" of *charismata*.[8] The "elect individuals" made this move because they recognized the threat to their office that the Pauline concept of *charismata* embodied.

Against such ages-long stability of elite ecclesiastical office, however, Käsemann insisted that the Spirit endows all Christians with *charismata*, and as a result the church should understand itself as "the dynamic unity

---

Diercksmeier (London: SCM, 1985), 154–64; David Power, *Gifts That Differ: Lay Ministries Established and Unestablished* (New York: Pueblo, 1985), 100–03; Richard McBrien, *Ministry: A Theological, Pastoral Handbook* (San Francisco: Harper & Row, 1987), 21–22; James and Evelyn Whitehead, *The Emerging Laity: Returning Leadership to the Community of Faith* (New York: Doubleday, 1986), 9–10, 158–60; Eduardo Hoornaert, *The Memory of the Christian People*, trans. R. Barr (Tunbridge Wells, UK: Burns & Oates, 1989), 191–95; Michael Lawler, *A Theology of Ministry* (Kansas City, MO: Sheed & Ward, 1990), 28–34; William Rademacher, *Lay Ministry: A Theological, Spiritual, and Pastoral Handbook* (New York: Crossroad Publishing Company, 1991), 31–34, 40–41.

6. Zeni Fox, *New Ecclesial Ministry: Lay Professionals Serving the Church* (Franklin, WI: Sheed and Ward, rev. edn, 2002), 130–31; Edward Hahnenberg, *Ministries: A Relational Approach* (New York: Crossroad Publishing Company, 2003), 71–75; Margaret Lavin, *Theology for Ministry* (Ottawa: Novalis, 2004), 128–35. See the clearly marked tendency also in "Toward a Theology of Lay Ecclesial Ministry" in the 1999 report to the USCCB, *Lay Ecclesial Ministry* (above, note 1), 12–15; similarly in *Co-Workers*, 20 (also noted there).

7. Thus by Chrysostom's day, the gifts in Paul's list (1 Cor. 12:8–10) were considered to have played out their role in the early church and to be no longer necessary as embellishments of the perennial gift of the apostolic office. See Kilian McDonnell and George T. Montague, *Christian Initiation and Baptism in the Holy Spirit: Evidence from the First Eight Centuries* (Collegeville, MN: Liturgical Press, 1991), 257–60.

8. Käsemann, "Ministry and Community," 73.

of charismata and of those endowed with them."⁹ Thus, those being added to the church by baptism continuously energize its unity with their new and varied gifts. As a result, the church is always at work. In Käsemann's phrase, the unity "exists only *in actu*—in the act of *agape*, of service."¹⁰ Such vibrant activity is the only "church order" known to Paul. Käsemann writes: "The Apostle's theory of order is not a static one, resting on offices, institutions, ranks and dignities; in his view, authority resides only within the concrete act of ministry as it occurs, because it is only within this concrete act that the *Kyrios* [Lord] announces his lordship and his presence."¹¹

The impact of a "concrete act of ministry" upon what we call "church order"—and which in the Roman Catholic theology embraces a sacrament of orders reserved for bishops, priests, and deacons—is immediate. "In such a context, then," concludes Käsemann, "all the baptised are 'office-bearers,'"¹² and "there is no longer any suggestion of the sacred office of the sanctuary."¹³

The Transformation of Ministry

Unsurprisingly, Roman Catholic writers have mostly not followed Käsemann to his stunning conclusion. What they have done is take up the idea undergirding Käsemann's thinking on the Spirit's gifts to the church. This idea is what the English translation of his paper named "ministry" or "service," and this "ministry" or "service" is what theologians have worked into the fabric of post-Vatican II ecclesiology.

In considering the idea of "ministry" or "service," we note that Käsemann was by no means the first to emphasize the central position in ecclesiology that the New Testament concept of "ministry" should occupy. His unique emphasis at the time was to draw out implications from the inclusion of a ministerial attribute or function among the gifts of the Spirit in 1 Corinthians 12. Along with Käsemann, other northern European theologians were beginning to scrutinize "ministry" or "service" and, in

9. Ibid., 70.
10. Ibid., 70.
11. Ibid., 83.
12. Ibid., 80.
13. Ibid., 78.

doing so, found themselves caught up in knots of language. We will look at two of these.

One knot was the tangle of conventional language within their own mid-twentieth-century churches concerning ordination and the church offices deriving from that. Northern Europeans did not have at their disposal a broad word like *ministry*, which English and southern European languages had received from Latin. Within a ministerial terminology one could be an ordained minister; a minister of heaven, as Hermes preeminently was[14] or "minister of hell," so Shakespeare of Joan of Arc;[15] a minister of the crown; or, like Florence Nightingale, a nurse "serving and ministering" to the wounded and diseased of the battlefield of Balaclava.[16] Against this, German, Dutch, and Nordic theologians felt the need to extricate themselves from a dichotomy established through the way their languages designated the role of the ordained minister by a term meaning "office" (the German *Amt* and similar). The limitation of such a term was that in the congregation of a local church only one person could possess the *Amt*. That is the nature of an office. This left a large gap—a linguistically and theologically unbridgeable gap—between the ordained and the non-ordained members of a congregation.

This gap was magically closed, however, with the untangling of a second knot. The untangling came by way of a comparatively recent lexical description of what the first Greek-speaking Christians meant when they spoke of ministry in the church. The preferred terms in the leading sources for ministry and ministerial activities were the Greek word *diakonia* and its cognates. First proposed in 1931 by a lone German Lutheran scholar, Wilhelm Brandt, who was chaplain to an institute of deaconesses,[17] and shortly afterward widely propagated as a result of its inclusion in Beyer's article on the *diakon-* words in Kittel's German *Theological Dictionary of the New Testament*,[18] Brandt's description of *diakonia* as lowly and costly love of one's neighbor soon began to edge out the concept of

---

14. Collins, *Diakonia*, 90–92.

15. *1Henry VI*, V. iv. 93.

16. Mrs Gaskell cited in Cecil Woodham Smith, *Florence Nightingale 1810–1910* (London: Constable, 1950), 158.

17. *Dienst und Dienen im Neuen Testament* (Gütersloh: Bertelsmann, 1931).

18. Beyer, "διακονέω, διακονία, διάκονος," in *Theological Dictionary of the New Testament*, 81–93.

office in theological reflections on ministry. His translation of *diakonia* as "Dienst/service" facilitated this process.

Prior to this development, *diakonia* had always been translated into English as "ministry." As the Germans began switching from Luther's *Amt* to a modern-day *Dienst*, writers in English and translators of the Bible in the second half of the twentieth century began switching from the word *ministry* to the word *service* to give clearer expression to their understanding of what the New Testament writers intended by *diakonia*. Such switches were theologically significant. Whereas the English *ministry* and *service* can operate as synonyms in certain contexts, in German the words *Amt* and *Dienst* were set up as antonyms. *Amt* is for the leader's office and embraces the leader's responsibilities and prerogatives, while *Dienst* is a role or function within anyone's reach.

"A Prize Which Everyone Wants to Own"

The hermeneutical linchpin that had locked ministry historically into the established ecclesiastical order had been the conventional understanding of a statement about ministry in the late New Testament letter to the Ephesians. In the AV of 1611, the text states that Christ gifted the church with teachers "for the perfecting of the saints, for the work of the ministry, for the edifying of the body of Christ" (Eph. 4:12). In 1602, the Geneva Bible—the preferred Bible of the protestantized wing of the English church—had already added a marginal note to this description of how the church should work. It read: "He [the writer] sheweth the end [purpose] of Ecclesiastical functions, to wit, that by the ministeries of men all the Saints may so grow up together, that they make one mystical body of Christ."

Neither of these early Protestant translations left an opening for understanding that the ministry/*diakonia* mentioned in the passage could be anything other than "the work" or office of the teachers. Luther and Calvin translated in the same mode and made much of this element in their own teaching.[19] In 1946, the first edition of the RSV still presented exactly this understanding, but by its second edition of 1971 we read a wholly different message. Here, and in virtually all subsequent translations, Christ gives

19. Collins, *Are All Christians Ministers?* (Collegeville: Liturgical Press, 1992), 17–34.

teachers to the church "for the equipment of the saints for the work of ministry."

Clearly, between 1946 and 1971 someone had pulled the hermeneutical pin and thereby switched claims to ministry from an exclusive clergy to an inclusive body of "saints." Thus, a simple change of translation—in English signified by the removal of a comma between "for the equipment of the saints" and "for the work of the ministry"—registers a seismic change in what a church is and how it operates.

Thus, the preferred twentieth-century translation looses the ministry/*diakonia* given to the church by the heavenly Christ from the control of the clergy, thereby making ministry the call and responsibility of the believers. In a special comment on this passage entitled "The Church without Laymen and Priests," Markus Barth made no bones about what was at stake: "The church's very essence and existence can be described by reference to the order she is given."[20] In the scenario envisaged by Barth, the order supposes "all the saints (and among them, each saint) are enabled... to fulfil the ministry given to them." Further, "This interpretation challenges both the aristocratic-clerical and the triumphalistic-ecclesiastical exposition of 4:11–12."[21] Within such a framework Barth was able to say that the pastor becomes "a minister to ministers."[22]

Reflecting on the advantages of these shifts in ecclesiology but at the same time bemoaning the disadvantages the church has experienced from this shifting terminology, Thomas O'Meara, possibly the most widely read of the contemporary Roman Catholic writers on ministry, has said:

> Ministry's language has ended up confused, sterile, even duplicitous. The word 'ministry' is a prize which everyone wants to own and which the older administration of the church wants to reserve.... Concepts and words from scholastic or Baroque theology have held mastery over ministry while those from charisms and other biblical forms have been relegated to piety. Now diversification in people and ministries questions old regulations.[23]

---

20. Markus Barth, *Ephesians 4–6*, Anchor Yale Bible Commentaries (Garden City, NY: 1984), 478.

21. Ibid., 479.

22. Ibid., 48.

23. O'Meara, *Theology of Ministry*, 144. Compare a milder statement in O'Meara's revised edition (1999), 153.

An Ecumenical Consensus

A glance at initiatives within ecumenical circles in the mid-twentieth century shows how rapidly and deeply the modern shifts in language affected the theology of ministry. In 1948, John A. Mackay, president of Princeton Theological Seminary and prominent in the development of the World Council of Churches, presented a series of lectures on the letter to the Ephesians that was published in 1953 under the title *God's Order*. Of Eph. 4:11–12 he wrote: "No passage in the Bible is more crucial than this for the welfare and mission of the Christian Church today."[24] And the crux of the passage was that "members of the rank and file of the Christian congregation...may render service [read 'ministry,' *diakonia*] to Christ and the Church in the fullest sense of the term."[25]

Not content with that plain assertion, Mackay made sure he discredited the earlier and traditional translation supported by the newly published RSV, in which ministry was the work of the teachers. He claimed that this translation was "without linguistic authority" and reflected "undoubted ecclesiological bias."[26]

By the 1960s, the World Council's Department of the Laity was developing a series of influential studies along lines advocated by Mackay. The papers were all set within the context of what the department's theologians understood as "the conjoint ministry of the whole Church,"[27] and it acknowledged that this context arose largely from "the renewed attention given by biblical scholars to this subject of the ministry...[which had] shaken some of the age-old confessional bias."[28] Members of the department were possibly alluding to Eduard Schweizer's recent study of church order with its still influential chapter on ministry as *diakonia*,[29] but undoubtedly also to Hendrik Kraemer's classic *A Theology of the Laity*,[30] because Kraemer had been the first director of the World Council's Ecumenical Institute at Bossey

---

24. John Mackay, *God's Order: The Ephesian Letter and This Present Time* (London: Nisbet, 1953), 185.

25. Ibid., 186.

26. Ibid., 185.

27. World Council of Churches Department of the Laity, *Laity* 15 (1963), 10.

28. World Council of Churches Department of the Laity, *Laity* 9 (1960), Editorial.

29. Schweizer, *Church Order*, 171–80.

30. Hendrik Kraemer, *A Theology of the Laity* (London: Lutterworth, 1958).

near the World Council's headquarters in Geneva. Central to Kraemer's book are sections where Kraemer expounds how "the church *is* ministry" and "the church *is* diakonia," labeling the Greek term "that profound, revolutionary word...which lies at the bottom of the gospel."[31]

The Department of the Laity's brief had been to prepare for the first discussion of church order by the Faith and Order Commission of the World Council in over twenty-five years. The previous discussion in Edinburgh in 1937 had been inconclusive and generated no little animosity as delegates championed incompatible models of church order. With the reintroduction of the topic of church order at the Fourth World Conference in Montreal in 1963, delegates hailed "the recognition that ministry is the responsibility of the whole body and not only of those who are ordained." And they named this recognition "one of the most important facts of recent church history."[32]

Hans-Ruedi Weber, a former director of the Department of the Laity, would call this accord "a Copernican change."[33] Thirty years later, the ecumenical initiative espoused at Montreal found expression in the Dublin Text ("therefore all are ministers"[34]) that had been prepared for the Fifth World Conference at Santiago de Compostela 1993, whose official report recorded that "Baptism is...the basis of all Christian ministry."[35]A study document of the Faith and Order Commission, *The Nature and Purpose of the Church*, drew attention five years later to the fact that "the location of the ministry of the ordained in, with, among or over the people of God

---

31. Ibid. The sections referred to are 136–55, the final descriptive phrase is cited from 187.

32. P. C. Rodger and L. Vischer, eds., *The Fourth World Conference on Faith and Order* (London: SCM, 1964), 62.

33. World Council of Churches, *Living in the Image of Christ* (Geneva: World Council of Churches, 1986), 71. For vivid illustrations of the pervasive influence of Weber's "Copernican change," see Robin Greenwood, *Transforming Church: Liberating Structures for Ministry* (London: SPCK, 2002). Greenwood instances attempts to renew pastoral strategies in five Anglican dioceses across United Kingdom, United States, South Africa, and Australia based on convictions about "total ministry" (p. 130) in "a post-hierarchical Church" (p. 93) within "a ministering community" (p. 126); the strategy operates on theological perceptions that "baptism is at the centre of a co-ministering Church, rather than clerical hierarchies"; that "through baptism each follower of Christ is called into...ministry and given the gifts required to carry it out" (p. 102); that "the call to ministry begins at baptism, not ordination" (p. 112), etc.

34. *One In Christ* 28.4 (1992), 386, see paragraph 44.

35. Thomas F. Best and Günther Gassmann, eds, *On the way to Fuller Koinonia*, Faith and Order Paper no. 166 (Geneva: World Council of Churches, 1994), 249.

is disputed within and among the churches."[36] The grounds underlying the dispute had been exposed in the six volumes of *Churches Respond to BEM: Official Responses to the "Baptism, Eucharist, and Ministry" text*,[37] which makes at times vigorous assertions of differences of view between Reformed churches supporting a baptismal call to ministry and pre-Reformation churches upholding the specific and exclusive character of ordained ministry.[38]

Roman Catholic Engagement

The Montreal conference took place in July 1963, nine months after the opening of the Second Vatican Council, and in the documentation associated with the development of the council many have observed the pervasiveness of concepts relating to ministry and service within the shadow of the Greek *diakonia*.[39] A historian of the council has in fact noted that this was no accident but the direct result of consultation initiated by the Faith and Order Commission of the World Council of Churches.[40] However, while the ministerial ecclesiology of the World Council did not set the pattern for the Vatican Council's formulation of doctrine on the church, the new ministerial language certainly informed the conciliar rhetoric and deeply characterized virtually all subsequent Roman Catholic writing on the theology of ministry.

The first major statement—and it remains of enduring significance within Roman Catholic circles—was by Hans Küng,[41] whose depiction of ecclesiastical office as ministry/*diakonia*, deriving from H. W. Beyer's account in Kittel's *Theological Dictionary*, held, in his view, "enormous"

---

36. Faith and Order Paper no. 181(Geneva: World Council of Churches, 1998), 44.

37. Faith and Order Papers nos. 129, 132, 135, 137, 143, 144 (Geneva: World Council of Churches, 1986–88.

38. See my report of such differences in "A Ministry for Tomorrow's Church," *Journal of Ecumenical Studies* 32.2 (1995), 163–65.

39. See my account in *Diakonia*, 14–20.

40. C. Moeller, "History of the Constitution" [Pastoral Constitution on the Church], in H. Vorgrimler, ed., *Commentary on the Documents of Vatican II*, trans., vol. 5 (1969), 22, cited in Collins, *Diakonia*, 20.

41. Küng, *The Church*, 496–502; see also *Why Priests?*, trans. J. Cumming (London: Collins Fontana, 1972), 26–27; *On Being a Christian*, trans. (Garden City, NY: Doubleday, 1978), 486–87.

implications for how the church should order itself.[42] Across the next three decades a similar emphasis recurred, usually in conjunction with the charismatic emphasis deriving from Käsemann, as noted above.

Thus, Bernard Cooke framed his study within "that broad area of ministry...in which all the members of the church share"[43] and made strong connections with both its charismatic nature[44] and its roots in Beyer's reading of *diakonia* in the New Testament.[45] Paul Bernier shares similar assumptions about the origins of Christian ministry.[46] In sum, in the words of Nathan Mitchell, "the entire community is...'charismatic' and ministry belongs to *all* members rather than to a hierarchically constituted few."[47]

Depicting the state of the question toward the end of the twentieth century, James Tunstead Burtchaell identified a scholarly Roman Catholic consensus—established independently of any magisterial doctrinal position—according to which the earliest churches did constitute "a normative first era" but were "without authoritative offices."[48] This is clearly in sympathy with the long-established Protestant consensus that recognized "a casual and charismatic community,"[49] including "uncategorised activists as those to whom the early churches deferred."[50] Successors of the latter "were seen to be raised up, not by ecclesiastical designation, but by an infusion of...[the] Spirit."[51] Burtchaell's own position turns out to be not far from either of these. He concludes that in its first pre-office phase, the church sustained itself through "men and women known as apostles and prophets...who carried no titles but whose activist zeal was

42. Küng, *The Church*, 500.

43. Cooke, *Ministry to Word and Sacraments*, 203.

44. Ibid., 198–99, 204.

45. Ibid., 343–44.

46. Paul Bernier, *Ministry in the Church: A Historical and Pastoral Approach* (Mystic, CT: Twenty-Third Publications, 1992), 36, 47–8, 63.

47. Nathan Mitchell, *Mission and Ministry: History and Theology in the Sacrament of Order* (Wilmington, DE: Glazier, 1982), 125.

48. James T. Burtchaell, *From Synagogue to Church: Public services and Offices in the Earliest Christian Communities* (Cambridge: Cambridge University Press, 1992), 137.

49. Ibid., 136.

50. Ibid., 348.

51. Ibid., 349.

accredited by the same divine fire: these were the ones to whom believers most notably deferred."[52]

If we turn from such unfinished business concerning historical, linguistic, and theological initiatives in ministry to look for clarification or enlightenment in recent official Roman Catholic teaching, we will be disappointed. To look back to *Lumen gentium* of the Second Vatican Council would be pointless because its ambiguities on ecclesiological issues are widely acknowledged. Edward Schillebeeckx provided a full account of the tensions playing out from these ambiguities at the Roman Synod on the priesthood in 1971.[53] And in spite of significant post-synodal exhortations by John Paul II in *Christifideles laici* and *Pastores dabo vobis*,[54] a consistent teaching on where ministry and charism sit in the church is yet to be achieved. In the former document, for example, we read in reference to 1 Cor. 12:4 (among other passages) of Christ bestowing upon the church "varied hierarchical and charismatic gifts."[55] This formulation is confusingly clumsy and raises more questions than it can resolve: the expression "charismatic gifts" is tautologous, and the formulation appears designed to separate hierarchical offices from *charismata*. More pointedly, is the concept of hierarchy at all evident in 1 Cor. 12:4 or even in Eph. 4:11–12? Kenan Osborne's claim of a distinct terminology—"apostolate for the unordained and ministry for the ordained"[56]—does not clarify obscurities in such teaching and can hardly be sustained; it also sits oddly with the title *Ministry* for his study of lay ministry.

One constant in teaching since Vatican II has been ongoing support of the laity's participation in the mission of the church, as initially announced in the *Decree on the Apostolate of the Laity* (*Apostolicam actuositatem*): "They have...their own assignment in the mission of the whole People

52. Ibid., 350. Burtchaell's ultimate claim that the offices which did appear in the second century were adaptations from the synagogue will not hold for the office of deacon, of whose title (*diakonos*) he provides an eclectic and wholly inadequate semantic profile (pp. 317–18).

53. Edward Schillebeeckx, *The Church with a Human Face: A New and Expanded Theology of Ministry*, trans. J. Bowden (London: SCM, 1985), 209–58.

54. John Paul II, *Christifideles laici*, trans. (Homebush, NSW: St Paul Publications, 1988); *Pastores dabo vobis*, trans. (Boston: St Paul, 1992).

55. John Paul II, *Pastores dabo vobis*, paragraph 20.

56. Kenan Osborne, *Ministry: Lay Ministry in the Roman Catholic Church: Its History and Theology* (New York: Paulist Press, 1993), 557.

of God."[57] Their part in the mission has frequently been endorsed as, for example, in the subtitle of chapter 3 of *Christifideles laici,* "The Coresponsibility of the Lay Faithful in the Church as Mission." In regard to ministry, however, the language is muddled. On the one hand, we read a comprehensive statement about ordained and lay ministries like the following:

> The Synod Fathers have insisted on the necessity to express with greater clarity, and with a more precise terminology, both the *unity of the Church's mission* in which all the baptised participate, and the substantial *diversity of the ministry* of Pastors which is rooted in the Sacrament of Orders, all the while respecting the other ministries, offices and roles in the Church, which are rooted in the Sacraments of Baptism and Confirmation.[58]

Against such an explicit attribution of ministries to laity, we read earlier in the same paragraph, "A person is not a minister simply in performing a task, but through sacramental ordination."

Some years later a great sensitivity became apparent in relation to the question of who has the call on ministerial terminology. This was in an instruction on the collaboration of lay people with priests that was issued by no fewer than eight Vatican congregations and councils.[59] Article 1 in the document's "Practical Provisions" addresses the "need for an appropriate terminology," but the contortions of the English are perplexing. Nothing is achieved, it seems to me, by trying to resolve here the terminological problem perceived by the multiple dicasterial bodies authorizing this statement. In presenting one paragraph (which happens to be a citation from an address of John Paul II to a 1994 symposium on "The Participation of the Lay Faithful in the Priestly Ministry") I wish merely to illustrate the confusion arising from terminology invoked by ecclesiastical authorities as they seek to safeguard the proprieties of a hierarchical arrangement of ministry:

---

57. A. Flannery, ed., *Vatican II: The Conciliar and Post Conciliar Documents* (Dublin: Dominican Publications, 1997), 768, para. 2.

58. *Christifideles laici,* no. 23; italics original.

59. Congregation for the Clergy and others, *Instruction on Certain Questions regarding the Collaboration of the Non-ordained Faithful in the Sacred Ministry of Priests,* trans. (Strathfield, NSW: St Pauls, 1997).

In some cases, the extension of the term "ministry" to the *munera* [usually translated as "functions"] belonging to the lay faithful has been permitted by the fact that the latter, to their own degree, are a participation in the one priesthood of Christ. The *officia* [offices] temporarily entrusted to them, however, are exclusively the result of a deputation by the Church. Only with constant reference to the one source, the "ministry of Christ" (...) may the term *ministry* be applied to a certain extent and without ambiguity to the lay faithful: that is, without it being perceived and lived as an undue aspiration to the *ordained ministry* or as a progressive erosion of its specific nature.[60]

Frederick Danker Updating Walter Bauer

Having observed, then, the linguistic impasse reached and the theological unease felt in regard to levels at which we apply ministerial terminology among members of the Body of Christ, it is time to remind ourselves that we would not have been distracted in this manner about uses of the word *ministry* had two German Lutheran theologians not been drawn into redefining the Greek word underlying all talk of ministry. The Greek word, of course, is *diakonia*. Wilhelm Brandt (1931)[61] and Hermann W. Beyer (1935)[62] produced a semantic profile of *diakonia* that we can outline in the following descriptive phrases:

- a word from everyday language
- not a word from biblical tradition but secular in character
- part of slave terminology
- basically meaning slavish service at table and applied on this basis to other slavish activities, like the washing of feet
- taken up by early Christians precisely in order to depict a lowly estimation of functions of leadership in their midst, but overlaid by them with the spirit of love with which Jesus imbued all his acts of servant leadership

---

60. Ibid., Article 1:2.

61. See note 17 above.

62. See note 18 above.

Against this linguistic profile, which has supported most of the new theology of ministry,[63] the research in my *Diakonia* of 1990 generated a set of semantic characteristics of an astonishingly different kind:

- not from everyday language and comparatively rare
- belonged to high levels of rhetoric and poetry
- not secular in character
- colored by a profound connection with religion
- not necessarily a slavish connotation but freely applied to activities by people of eminence
- person carrying out the *diakonia* did so as the agent of a superior and with all the authority required for the task
- early Christian usage conformed to standard Hellenistic usage
- no basic meaning relating to service at table; in fact, meaning in particular instances determined only by consideration of literary context

Clearly such disparate and incompatible linguistic profiles will produce disparate and incompatible theological profiles of ministry as *diakonia*. As reinterpreted, *diakonia* will induce meanings within New Testament Greek that we will need to represent in English somewhere along the spectrum of ideas like the following: messenger, spokesperson, representative, go-between, medium, agent, attendant, waiter.

In the Greek understanding, the waiter at table is hardly a "waiter" at all but an attendant who is dispatched time and again by a diner to fetch the various dishes. And most of the mentions of this table attendant occur in relation to banquets of a religious character. In a significant statement, the apologist for ancient Greek religious banquets, Athenaeus (*Deipnosophistae*, 192b), stated that "the one who was to do the waiting (*diakonēsōn*) was never a slave; rather young sons of free men would pour the wine."[64]

I note that the most recent protagonist of the classic Brandt-Beyer linguistic profile of early Christian *diakonia* has been Andrew D. Clarke, who concluded his study of leadership and ministry in the Pauline churches by

63. Exemplified in Michael Glazier's entry "Ministry" in M. Glazier and M. K. Hellwig, eds, *The Modern Catholic Encyclopedia*, rev. and expanded edn (Collegeville, MN: Liturgical Press, 2004), 550–51. "The essence of ministry is service...rooted in a charism, and each Christian derives from baptism some charisms which lead to ministry.... Today...in a more informal, interpersonal way, as when we offer support to others by our daily words and acts of mutual kindness and encouragement. Jesus interpreted his life and work as a service."

64. See the text and discussion in Collins, *Diakonia*, 158.

contesting my reading of Paul's usage and reverted to "a significant emphasis on the servile nature" of the ministries of Jesus and Paul.[65] Apart from wholly discounting the relevance of the literary and cultural setting I described for ancient *diakon-* usage, what has happened in Clarke's interpretative process is, to recall James Barr's phrase, an engagement in "illegitimate totality transfer." This is principally evident in the way that Clarke shifts the contextual values of *doul-*/slave passages along with values he attaches to *diakon-* in the gospels onto Paul's usage where *diakon-* is contextualised in discourse about the Word of God.

Since the publication of Clarke's study in 2000, however, the tendency to endorse the re-interpretation has gathered momentum. In English-speaking theological circles a telling impetus has come from substantial changes to the lexical description of *diakon-* words introduced to the leading lexicon of early Christian Greek by Frederick William Danker in the light of the new linguistic research.[66] In the important area of German theology, where the re-interpretation had gone virtually unobserved for over ten years, the impetus came ironically from Johann Hinrich Wichern's Rauhes Haus in Hamburg, heartland of German Lutheran diakonic theology since the 1830s. Hans-Jürgen Benedict, a professor there, published a challenge to his colleagues in diakonic ministry under the title (to translate): "Does the claim of evangelical [Lutheran] *diakonia* rest on a misinterpretation of the ancient sources? John N Collins' investigation of 'Diakonia.' "[67] In the course of the article, Benedict expresses the view that the re-interpretation had exposed in German writing on *diakonia* its "nonsenses, unquestioned assumptions, and hidden influences."[68]

---

65. Andrew D. Clarke, *Serve the Community of the Church: Christian as Leaders and Ministers,* (Grand Rapids, MI and Cambridge, UK: Eerdmans, 2000), 233–47, citing 245. See further on Clarke's 2008 volume in Chapter 1 (note 45).

66. *A Greek-English Lexicon of the New Testament and other Early Christian Literature,* 3rd edn rev. and ed. Frederick William Danker, based on Water Bauer's *Griechisch-deutsches Wörterbuch zu den Schriften des Neuen Testaments und der frühchristlichen Literatur,* 6th edn, ed. Kurt Aland and Barbara Aland, with Viktor Reichmann, and on previous English editions by W. F. Arndt, F. W. Gingrich, and F. W. Danker (Chicago and London: University of Chicago Press, 2000).

67. Hans-Jürgen Benedict, "Beruht der Anspruch der evangelischen Diakonie auf einer Missinterpretation der antiken Quellen? John N. Collins Untersuchung 'Diakonia,'" *Pastoraltheologie* 89 (2000), 349–64.

68. Ibid., 354.

Benedict's trenchant views sparked a surge of German Lutheran interest in coming to terms with the re-interpretation of *diakonia*. Contributing here were a leading theological committee of the EKD,[69] contributors to the volume published by the Diakonic Institute of the University of Heidelberg,[70] individual theologians,[71] and, in October 2005, a three-day conference in Rummerlsberg, Bavaria, sponsored by the Diakonic Institute and other agencies of the Evangelical Church. This conference addressed the scenario described in its promotional brochure as follows:

What is a deacon? What will characterise this profession in the future? If in the past only a few could give clear answers to these questions, contemporary developments make the task even harder. The Australian theologian John N Collins has put in question the traditional understanding of the biblical term *diakonia*.[72]

Independently of Benedict, the Hanover Report of the Anglican-Lutheran International Commission had already acknowledged the importance of

---

69. ÖSTA [Ecumenical Study Committee of the Evangelical Church in Germany], "Stellungnahme des ÖSTA zu der Studie 'Der Diakonat als ökumenische Chance. Hannover-Bericht der Internationalen anglikanisch-lutherischen Kommission,'" Nr. 21d (2000). The following statement at n. 63, for example, is in striking contradiction to the exegetical principle adopted by Brandt, Beyer, and Schweizer (and represented *passim* in the many studies in Gerhard K. Schäfer and Theodor Strohm, eds, *Diakonie—biblische Grundlagen und Orientierungen*, 2. Auflage, Veröffentlichungen des diakoniewissenschaftlichen Instituts an der Universität Heidelberg, Bd 2 [Heidelberg: HVA, 1994]): "Offenkundig ist... dass für die neutestamentliche Rede von Diakonia ein Verständnis im Sinne des helfenden und Nöte wendenden Dienens am Nächstenliebe, nicht von vornherein vorauszusetzen ist, sondern jeweils im Einzelfall begründet werden muss." (I note that the exception introduced here at the statement's end—that loving service might be discernible in some instances—is a view I strongly contest.)

70. V. Hermann, R. Merz, H. Schmidt, eds., *Diakonische Konturen. Theologie im Kontext sozialer Arbeit* (Heidelberg: Winter 2003); four of the six New Testament studies are in direct dialogue with my reinterpretation, those by H.-J. Benedict (127–35) and Dierk Starnitzke (184–212) strongly supporting it, while S. Dietzel (136–70) and I. Dunderberg (171–83) raise particular issues accounted for in Chapter 1 of this book, section "Reactions."

71. Wilfried Brandt, "Biblische 'Diakonia' contra Evangelische Diakonie? Die Wortgruppe 'diakonia, diakonein, diakonos' im griechischen Neuen Testament, neu interpretiert durch John N. Collins," *Mach's wie Gott werde Mensch!* www.vedd.de/Dokumente (*Impuls* 2004); Annette Noller, "Pfarrer/innen und Diakon/innen," *Deutsches Pfarrerblatt* 12 (2005), 2–4.

72. Einladung/Programm, *Professionalität und Identität Beruf: Diakon/in*. Fachtagung zum Berufsbild und zur Ausbildung von DiakonInnen, October 16–18, 2005. (My translation above.)

the re-interpretation,[73] as had the Church of England's House of Bishops' report, which developed its theology of the diaconate on the "rediscovery of the biblical idea of diakonia."[74] From the beginning of the Anglo-Nordic Diaconal Research Project, Sven-Erik Brodd anticipated that "the focus of future debates" about the diaconate would centre on the re-interpretation,[75] a debate he went on to engage with over the life of the project, with the support of Kjell Nordstokke.[76]

In the United States, where Ormonde Plater, writing within the Episcopal context, had long based his theology of diaconate on the re-interpretation,[77] Benjamin L. Hartley adopted the research as the basis of a diaconal model for the United Methodist Church.[78] And for the first time in Roman Catholic writings in the United States, Richard Gaillardetz worked from the re-interpretation toward a theology of the diaconate free of the limitations of a service-orientated *diakonia*.[79]

On the broader question of what is and is not ministry, Paul Avis drew substantially on the re-interpretation to establish the essentially ecclesial

---

73. Anglican-Lutheran International Commission, *The Diaconate as Ecumenical Opportunity* (London: Anglican Communion Publications, 1996); see the indebtedness expressed to "the historical-philological corrective to earlier understandings of the *diakon-* words provided by John Collins' *Diakonia*," 20, n. 60.

74. B. Rogerson, ed., *For Such a Time as This: A Renewed Diaconate in the Church of England* (London: Church House Publishing, 2001), 30.

75. Sven-Erik Brodd, "The Deacon in the Church of Sweden," in Gunnel Borgegård, Olav Fanuelsen, and Christine Hall, eds, *The Ministry of the Deacon*, vol. 1, *Anglican-Lutheran Perspectives* (Uppsala: Nordic Ecumenical Council, 1999), 97–140, citing 137.

76. Sven-Erik Brodd, "*Caritas* and *Diakonia* as Perspectives on the Diaconate," in Gunnel Borgegård, Olav Fanuelsen, and Christine Hall, eds, *The Ministry of the Deacon*, vol. 2, *Ecclesiological Explorations* (Uppsala: Nordic Ecumenical Council, 2000), 23–69; Kjell Nordstokke, "The Diaconate: Ministry of Prophecy and Transfromation," 107–30.

77. *Many Servants: An Introduction to Deacons* (Cambridge, MA: Cowley, 1991, 2nd edn 2004), 1–3, 13–20, 198–200. See also Plater's many contributions, especially his column "Through the Dust," in the newsletter of North American Association for the Diaconate *Diakoneo*.

78. Benjamin Hartley, "Connected and Sent Out: Implications of New Biblical Research for the United Methodist Diaconate," *Quarterly Review* 24/4 (2004), 367–80.

79. Richard Gaillardetz, "On the Theological Integrity of the Diaconate," in Owen F. Cummings, William T. Ditewig, and Richard R. Gaillardetz, eds, *Theology of the Diaconate: The State of the Question* (New York: Paulist Press, 2005), 67–97. His co-contributors report the reinterpretation but in the substantive issue draw mainly on Walter Cardinal Kasper's diaconal theology which develops along classic lines of the German understanding of *diakonia/Diakonie*; see "The Diaconate" in his *Leadership in the Church: How Traditional Roles Can Serve the Christian Community Today*, Eng. trans. (New York: Crossroad Publishing Company, 2003), 13–44.

character of ministry in the face of the ambiguities arising from the Käsemann-Schweizer consensus.[80] A few years earlier, Robert Hannaford had made the same connection between the reinterpreted *diakonia* and ministry as "ecclesially sanctioned and authorized act," recognizing there "a first step towards conceptual clarification."[81] In France, Charles Perrot similarly based his rich description of the ministry of the word on the research,[82] and in one of his last works, Jean-Marie Tillard, the former Canadian vice president of the Faith and Order Commission, developed his reflections on the bishop as *diakonos* of the Lord "come to serve" on the values projected by the re-interpretation. He claimed these said "infinitely more" than the lowly service of good will projected in the studies of Beyer, Käsemann, and Schweizer.[83]

Rereading Gifts and Ministry

In turning to re-read the central passage in the New Testament about ministry among *charismata*, we engage the diverse range of *diakon-* usage in Paul. Of greatest interest is the usage clustering around his discussion of his own apostleship. This discussion is at its most intense in 2 Cor. 3–6 because Paul is seeking to establish the authenticity of his apostleship in the face of unnamed rivals. A remarkable feature of his apologia is that while the addresses to his letters normally introduce him to his readers under the title of "apostle," in the heat of his exposition across these four chapters he does not once appeal to that title. His whole rhetoric is directed at having the Corinthians acknowledge him as a *diakonos*

---

80. See the chapter "A Ministry Shaped by the Mission of God" in Paul Avis, *A Ministry Shaped by Mission* (London: T&T Clark, 2005), 43–87.

81. Robert Hannaford, "Foundations for an Ecclesiology of Ministry," in Christine Hall and Robert Hannaford, eds., *Order and Ministry* (Leominster, UK: Gracewing, 1996), 21–60, citing 26. Note the contrast between this and Hannaford's earlier estimation of *diakonia* in the Beyer tradition in "Towards a Theology of the Diaconate" in Christine Hall, ed., *The Deacon's Ministry* (Leominster, UK: Gracewing, 1991), 25–44.

82. Charles Perrot, *Après Jésus. Le ministère chez les premiers chrètiens* (Paris: Les Éditions de l'Atelier/Les Éditions Ouvrières, 2000), 230–61. A decade later, however, his views are only faintly discernible in just two (Roselyne Dupont-Roc; Christophe Rimbaud) of six papers in the Dossier *Diakonia. Le service dans la Bible*, Cahiers Évangile 159 (March 2012).

83. Jean-Marie Tillard, *L'Église locale:Ecclésiologie de communion et catholicité* (Paris: Cerf, 1995), 166–79, 183–91 (citing 166, note 1, and 184).

faithfully engaged in the *diakonia* he had received from God, Christ and Spirit.[84]

The import of Paul's sustained use of the *diakon-* words throughout this section is that Greek people of ancient times would recognize the writer was laying claim to a privileged religious title and presenting himself as accredited by a heavenly power to deliver a critically important religious message to those open to receiving it. Further, the hearer of this claim would attribute a particular character to the heavenly message. This would be its in-built guarantee of authenticity; presented as the Word of God, the Word itself would speak clearly within the religious consciousness of each recipient, assuring each individual that the divine Word rests in the heart and speaks its message there. The capacity of the *diakon-* words to express such intimacy of mediation is precisely why Paul chose these words at this juncture in the defense of his apostleship.

The passage about ministry among *charismata* occurs in Paul's earlier correspondence with this same group. At 1 Cor. 12:4–6, the RSV reads:

> *There are varieties of gifts, but the same Spirit;*
> *and there are varieties of service, but the same Lord;*
> *and there are varieties of working, but it is the same God.*

Here we have three lines of an identical type setting up a stylistic pattern that draws the reader's attention to three different terms: *gifts, service* (this term translated variously in earlier eras as "administrations," "ministrations," "services," and only rarely as "ministries"), and *working*. (In Greek, the words are all plural: *charismata, diakoniai*, and *energēmata*.) For Ernst Käsemann and most exegetes, these terms are interchangeable, that is, they are different designations for one and the same thing, namely, the church's mode of operation or its activities.[85] And whatever the nature of the activities, they are all heavenly gifts. To symbolize these relationships, we could link the terms with equal signs, thus: *charismata = diakoniai = energēmata*. By this reading, the whole church performs *diakoniai* or ministries.

---

84. Collins, *Diakonia*, 195–212; see further Collins, *All Christians*, 44–50; "The mediatorial aspect of Paul's role as *diakonos*," *Australian Biblical Rview* 40 (1992), 34–44 (in this book as chapter 6).

85. See Wolfgang Schrage, *Die erste Brief an die Korinther*, 1. Teilband (Einsiedeln: Benziger/Neukirchener-Vluyn, 1991), 1541; Anthony L. Thiselton, *The First Epistle to the Corinthians* (Grand Rapids, MI: Eerdmans/Carlisle: Paternoster, 2000), 931–33.

In my view,[86] Käsemann could not have taken this interpretative stance in 1949 had he been aware of what kind of word *diakonia* really was for the ancient Greeks, how it operates in a Greek sentence, or what values it carried for Paul and his audience in conformity with widespread ancient Greek usage. The *diakoniai* of 1 Cor. 12:5 are designating the same form of "ministry" that Paul had in mind when in 1 Cor. 3:5 he had designated himself and Apollos "ministers through whom you believed" (*diakonoi*). And it is not without significance that in speaking of "ministry" there, he writes of it as gift—"ministers through whom you believed, as the Lord *gave* to each (*edōken*—in the emphatic end position)." This *diakonia* was not a "ministry" given to the whole church but was in fact the privilege, responsibility, and burden of those few chosen to deliver the Word in the name of God, Christ, and Spirit.

The rich history of *diakonia* creates a new and special background for the reading of the sentences at 1 Cor. 12:4–6. In this light we are drawn to understand Paul's Greek as meaning something very like the following:

> *There are varieties of gifts, but the same Spirit:*
> *both varieties of ministries and the same Lord,*
> *and varieties of workings but the same God.*

What is happening here is that we are reading the first sentence as a generic statement about "gifts" and then reading the two succeeding sentences as being about two species of gifts, first, "ministries" (for the likes of Paul and Apollos) and, secondly, "workings" (which are distributed church-wide: as the passage goes on to say, "It is the same God who inspires them all in every one."[87]) The sense of "both…and" is a normal function of the Greek "*kai…kai.*" In recognizing two species here and in distinguishing one from the other within the genus of gifts in the first sentence, I note that I am not alone. E. Earle Ellis came to the same conclusion without

---

86. Collins, *All Christians*, 120–30 (in this book as chapter 8); "Ministry as a Distinct Category among Charismata (1 Corinthians 12:4–7)," *Neotestamentica* 27.1 (1993), 79–91; "God's Gifts to Congregations," *Worship* 68.3 (1994), 242–49; *Deacons and the Church*, 81–85.

87. RSV, but its translation "inspires" (for *energōn*) breaks the link with the preceding "activities" (*energēmata*); the Greek maintains the link by keeping the same stem (*energ-*), which is to say that God "activates" all the "activities" among all, but which is not saying that God "inspires" specific "ministries" among all.

the advantage of recognizing the full semantic value carried by *diakoniai* in this passage.[88] To sum up, I present my own translation of this critical passage:

> *Divisions exist among gifts, although the Spirit is one and the same:*
> *both divisions of ministries, the Lord too remaining the same,*
> *and then divisions of activities, with God of course remaining the same,*
> *the one who activates all these things among all of us.*[89]

In this compact statement Paul was at pains to distinguish among gifts to the church by separating out gifts named *diakoniai*. Designated by this standout term, this set of gifts would at once be recognized by Corinthians as comprising ministerial functions of a heavenly quality pertaining to those who had come among them delivering the Word of God. Paul was explicit at verse 28 about the distinctive character of these "ministers"—so named at 1 Cor. 3:5 (*diakonoi*)—and strongly emphasized their unique and irreplaceable role within the church: "God has appointed in the church first, apostles, second prophets, third teachers, then workers ... healers,

---

88. E. Earle Ellis, *Pauline Theology: Ministry and Society* (Grand Rapids, MI: Eerdmans; Exeter, UK: Paternoster Press, 1989), 35. See further references in this sense to Beza and Estius in Schrage, *Der erste Brief*, 141, note 156. While Estius noted that the Latin exegetical tradition favoured ecclesiastical offices here for the Vulgate's *ministrationes* (not *ministeria*!), Estius himself sought any opportunity in his era of Counter-Reformation to uphold biblical support for the three major orders; see my "Ministry as a Distinct Category," 90 (above, note 86; similarly in regard to Lapideus, 80–81); "God's gifts," 248–49. I note also that J. A. Fitzmyer, without explicitly endorsing the rhetorical pattern identified above, accepts that the reinterpretation has established the designation of distinctive and exclusive functions through the term *diakoniai* in this passage ("*pace* Käsemann," as he observes); see *First Corinthians*, Anchor Yale Bible Commentaries (New Haven, CT: Yale University Press, 2008), 465.

89. Collins, *All Christians*, 126. This book of 1992 was the first occasion on which I developed this interpretation. The following year I elaborated the exegesis in the paper "Ministry as a Distinct Category" (see especially 83–89), where I also noted the earlier difficulties experienced with the passage while writing *Diakonia* (232–33, 258–59), and today I remain of the view that "we are yet to disabuse ourselves of the myth created among us in our time that these words [*diakon-*] were part of ordinary and everyday language" (86): "To Paul's high world of godly *diakonia*, through which ancient Corinthians anticipated receiving heaven's mysteries written large on their hearts (to borrow Paul's later imagery of the process involved in *diakonia*, 2 Cor. 3:3), we now bring the banal inadequacies arising from Kittel's lexicography of the 1930s. By the weight of this 1930s learning Paul's high rhetoric has been brought down to the lowlands of short horizons where mysteries are beyond the range of vision, and the divinely commissioned *diakoniai*, by which churches are constituted, became ... 'everyday acts of service.'" (89)

helpers" His further rhetoric in verse 29—"Are all apostles?"—reinforces the priority of these teaching roles as it also emphasizes the rich and irreducible diversity of gifts within the congregation.

Ministry and Ministries Within Churches Today

In focusing on the ecclesiological relevance of 1 Cor. 12:4–6 I have sought to emphasize that in the latter half of the twentieth century a particular reading of Paul's leading statement about gifts in the church generated a comprehensive shift in the theological understanding of the place of ministry within the church. The shift has been from an understanding of ministry as endowed by ordination (or commissioning) to an understanding of ministry as deriving from baptism. As such, ministry has come to be recognized as a gift that is universal among the baptized or churchwide.

One also refers to this contemporary understanding of the modus operandi of the church as "every member ministry,"[90] a once-novel concept that has become a driving force for pastoral strategies in the face of a depleted clergy and a more informed and pastorally equipped laity. I have pointed out that this repositioning of ministry as churchwide instead of as coterminous with ordained or official ministry found the main part of its justification in Ernst Käsemann's understanding of *charismata* in the first Christian churches and Eduard Schweizer's broad view of *diakonia* within the first churches. Accordingly, a re-interpretation of *diakonia* in early Christian language, where it designates the preeminent role of those delivering the Word of the gospel, inevitably demands that we reassess how we envisage the giftedness of the church today. Given the prominence long attained by questions about ministry in the broader question of what is church, one can hardly exaggerate the significance of determining what is ministry and what is not.

One part in the exercise of discernment of ministries is to make allowance for the correlation between ministries so named in the English language and *diakonia* in early Greek. In alluding earlier to one difference at this point between English and German, we noted that in the German dichotomy of *Amt/office* versus *Dienst/service*, the ecclesiologists aligned *diakonia* exclusively with the latter. In English, by contrast, the main traditional translation, "ministry," is a word that readily accommodates

---

90. Greenwood, *Transforming Church*, 132.

application to official roles, most obviously in the once standard phrase "minister of religion" and the contemporary "cabinet minister." The official status of such functionaries is clear, and in English we create no ambiguity by extending the usage to ecclesial situations where non-ordained members of a congregation hold appointments—short or long term—of a pastoral or liturgical character.

The same happened in Paul's Greek when, for example, he designated Phoebe a minister (agent, delegate) of the church in Cenchreae (Rom. 16:1) or when he designated the Asian delegation to Jerusalem a *diakonia* (ministry, mission, delegation). Among our churches of the earlier modern era, any one of the pastoral or liturgical roles now commonly filled by non-ordained members could have been seen as the exclusive prerogative of the ordained minister, but neither singly nor as a group were such roles likely to have been identified as the essential reason the minister of religion had had to undergo ordination or commissioning.

Precisely this constitutive element of the ordained ministry is what corresponds to the ecclesial *diakonia* in Paul's ecclesiology. In fact, in both Paul and in Luke the essential ecclesial *diakonia* is the ministry of the Word. The same is true, of course, of the ecclesiology of Luther and Calvin and of the Baptist and Pentecostal praxis of more recent times. The pre-Reformation churches, by contrast, had compromised the priority due to this ministry by the application of a profoundly sacerdotal and hieratic character to the mode in which the primal ministry was delivered. In either case, it seems to me, the Word of God was obscured, and the ministry—as Paul warned (2 Cor. 6:3)—had obstacles in its way. In the pre-reformation churches this was by way of a ritual removed from the people and in a language not of the people, and in reformed churches in the worldly authority attaching to the minister via a largely fundamentalist hermeneutic.

Against both these models, an examination of Paul's ministry suggests that today's churches are unlikely to achieve the renewal they seek without undertaking a challenging and dangerous journey of discovery into how "the word increases" (Acts 6:7). In 1992, I attempted to describe this journey:

> Paul had no control over the reception of his ministry or over the measure of authority which the Corinthians might attach to it. And in fact he knew that the authority carried by ministry was not a coercive, political, or legal authority but an authority arising from the

power of the gospel which ministry made available to believers. The ministry had a capacity to effect change in the lives of individuals and in the lives of their organizations only in so far as it opened believers to the summons of the gospel. One might say that of itself ministry did not possess authority but that it transferred authority to those being ministered to. Theirs were the decisions, and the decisions became authoritative in so far as they conformed with the gospel.[91]

In saying this about the authentic nature of official ministry, my view remains that early Christian *diakonia* clearly points in the direction I named as "the higher ground of thinking about ministry."[92] However, such is not to be understood as simply endorsing the status quo of heavily historicized hierarchical arrangements such as those we see in the Roman Catholic Church and elsewhere. More than once such an agenda has been read into my re-interpretation of the original ministry/*diakonia*.[93]

As a higher view of ministry than is general in ecumenical circles, the revised *diakonia* points to the responsibility of the churches to equip themselves with the kind of ministers who can maintain the lively interplay of the Word of God among members of a congregation and in communion with the broader church. All manner of gifts across the congregation and from within the broader church will contribute to harmonious interplay. Enriching also will be challenges from changing cultural and social environments.

No such interplay is possible, however, so long as familiar obstacles are left to stand in ministry's way. My list includes the exclusion of women, marginalization of the Word of God in the interests of sacramental ritualism, mandatory celibacy, lifetime appointments, large congregations or congregations of any size that inhibits two-way communication, global uniformity at the expense of regional inculturation, exclusivist language, lack of ecumenical will. This is a sizable list of substantive issues and

---

91. Collins, *All Christians*, 134.

92. Collins, *Diakonia*, 262.

93. Joseph Ratzinger, "On the Essence of the Priesthood," in *Called to Communion: Understanding the Church Today*, trans. A. Walker, (San Francisco: Ignatius Press, 1996), 106; See Timothy Radcliffe's reflections on balancing the re-interpretation against historical and social realities in *The Tablet*, July 11, 1992, 865–66; Gideon Goosen, "Review of J. N. Collins, *Are All Christians Ministers?*," *Pacifica* 6.2 (1993), 242.

practices—and it still leaves much unaccounted for—but it brings forward some of what one commentator called "hardened institutional polarizations" that the new understanding of *diakonia* could remove to reveal "the radical newness of the New Testament."[94]

In its deepest reality, this radical newness is "the dispensation/*diakonia*/ministry of the Spirit" (2 Cor. 3:8) that leads to a dynamic outcome in the sublime "ministry/*diakonia* of reconciliation" (2 Cor. 5:18), what William Tyndale correctly perceived as and happily named in his 1526 New Testament "the office to prreache [sic] the atonement," this word designating nothing less than the state of "at-one-ment" with God.

---

94. Robert Imbelli, "Is There a Minister in the House?," *Commonweal*, March 12, 1993, 21.

13

Fitting Lay Ministries into a Theology of Ministry

Part 1: Critiquing an American Consensus

First-world churches have been struggling to articulate a theology that will make sense of widespread and increasingly professional lay engagement in pastoral activities. This broadening engagement continues to take its impetus from the enlivening vision of the People of God that the Second Vatican Council projected, and it replaces a pre-conciliar "lay apostolate" whose function was understood in terms of specific mandates from the hierarchy. *Apostolicam actuositatem* (Decree on the Laity), a title that itself speaks of "apostolic activity," asked all members of the church to recognize the sacramental connection with Christ and the Spirit by which "they are assigned to the apostolate."[1]

The pastoral implications of this have been working themselves out ever since, with no little difficulty and some baffling initiatives. Much inspiration sprang at first from developments within Base Ecclesial Communities in third-world situations. Inspirational as this remains, first-world pastoral leaders soon recognized that their own situations differed from those in the third world. Third-world pastoral initiatives developed in clergy-poor environments that suggested a primary focus for lay involvement should lie within the ministry of the Word. A leading instance here was the paper "Celebration of the Word and New Ministries" issuing from the Latin American Episcopal Council's (CELAM) Department of Vocations and Ministries in 1977.[2] Through this ministry the local

---

1. "Apostolicam actuositatem 3," in *Vatican Council II: The Conciliar and Post Conciliar documents*, ed. Austin Flannery (Dublin: Dominican Publications, 1977), 768.

2. Consejo episcopal latinoamericano, Departamento de vocaciones y ministerios, *Celebracion de la palabra y nuevos ministerios* (Bogotá: CELAM, 1977).

community sought to discover its strength and vision while waiting on a fuller sacramental support from visiting ordained leaders.

By contrast, in first-world countries, the cultivation of lay pastoral involvement first occurred at a time when there was no significant clergy shortage. This tended to mean that lay engagement was initially more commonly an embellishment to liturgies presided over by presbyters, and only gradually did it begin to stretch to leading responsibilities within the liturgy and pastoral responsibilities beyond it. Once the now familiar shortage of clergy pointed to an inevitable rundown of some traditional pastoral functions within parishes, roles of lay assistants expanded to make up part of the shortfall. In this experience, however, lay assistants eventually came up against the inability of the clericalized system to take full advantage of the talents and energies of the new amateur and largely part-time collaborators.

For many of these collaborators, the realization dawned that a genuine understanding of their role required a fundamental rethinking about church structures. Soon enough it was an open secret that a theological hole stood between the practice of the past and the new vision and needs of the present. This was the period—mid-1970s through 1980s—that saw a rainstorm of books, journal articles, and conference reflections on ministry. This was the rush to fill the hole. That the input was not of a consistency to take the weight that had to be put on it became clear as the years passed, with the result that the problem of who did what in the church went essentially unresolved.

In the process, however, one overriding and enormously powerful idea was let loose that appeared to have the capacity to bring ordained and lay pastoral activities together again as operations of the one body of Christ. This idea was simple and attractive: ministry is something for which the church as a whole is responsible and is a calling that falls upon each Christian in baptism.

On the face of it, the concept of churchwide ministry would appear to be another way of saying with the Decree on the Laity that all "are assigned to the apostolate." Subsequent statements from the magisterium, however, can hardly be said to have enshrined any such new pastoral strategy. Indeed, if we take the implications of the *Instruction on Certain Questions Regarding the Collaboration of the Non-ordained Faithful in the Sacred Ministry of Priests*, the teaching would seem to point in an opposite direction. In asserting the different roles of "the common priesthood" and "the ministerial priesthood," the *Instruction* described the exclusive "ministry" of the ordained as "the mission received by the Apostles from Christ," comprising "the functions of teaching, sanctifying and governing the faithful."[3]

Multiplying Ordinations

While any new magisterial pastoral strategy is yet to appear—at least something more specific than the general proposition of evangelization in *Novo millennio ineunte*—individuals and groups within ecclesial cultures of particular regions have ventured some projections on the basis of what has been developing on the ground. Most specific—as well as radical—would be Bishop Fritz Lobinger's carefully developed model for multiple ordained leaders within local communities.[4] This would issue in a team-leadership of ordained eucharistic presiders, each of whom would be the animator of a section of the community, and among whom one would be more highly educated in the Christian tradition and thus the animator for the other leaders. Clearly, the model owes much to Lobinger's experience in the bush stations of South Africa—also, as he acknowledged, to the earlier proposal by William R. Burrows[5]—but the model has much to offer to pastoral care in first-world suburban or rural spreads as well.

By comparison, first-world thinking has been more conservative. Clearly wary of canonical and bureaucratic obstacles to developments along lines envisioned by Lobinger, first-world pastoral theologians have sought to develop theory on the basis of lay pastoral praxis since the Second Vatican Council. In German-speaking lands, this led Winfried Haunerland to recommend the creation of a new lay level of ordained ministers that would not appear as a threat to the traditional threefold order.[6] In France, Bernard Sesboüé considers that such a solution would be premature: We lack the language for what is a new reality that we should

---

3. *Instruction on Certain Questions Regarding the Collaboration of the Non-ordained Faithful in the Sacred Ministry of Priests*, Eng. trans. (Strathfield, NSW: St Pauls Publications, 1997), 18–19 (sections 1 and 2).

4. Fritz Lobinger, *Like His Brothers and Sisters: Ordaining Community Leaders* (New York: Crossroad Publishing Company, 1999).

5. William R. Burrows, *New Ministries: The Global Context* (Melbourne: Dove Communications 1980) 125–131.

6. Winfried Hauerland, "The Heirs of the Clergy? The New Pastoral Ministries and the Reform of the Minor Orders," *Worship* 75/4 (July 2001), 305–20.

not try to classify too quickly. We have not yet reached the point where we can begin to commission such people sacramentally; the time is not yet ripe, either for the people concerned or for the hierarchical Church. We are still in the phase simply of the existential reality. This is what we have to cope with and manage.[7]

The experience of Paul Zulehner, a professor of pastoral theology in Vienna, seems to suggest that this is the only course left open to local churches. He was led to this conclusion by experience of interventions by Roman congregations which reduced locally developed proposals for the expansion of lay participation to "a largely ineffective appeal to the laity to involve themselves in a clerically led Church."[8]

Expanding Ministry

In the United States, the process has been different again. Here, pressures have mounted for practical pastoral measures in response to the de-priesting of parishes and under the impact of the concurrently well-developed system of Lay Ecclesial Ministries.[9] Notwithstanding calls for more radical initiatives from groups like Call to Action, CORPUS, FutureChurch, and Voice of the Faithful, North American theologians have largely turned aside from theologizing directly about the new lay ministries in the interests of re-theologizing the inherited official ministries of bishop, priest, and deacon. This would be true even of Paul Lakeland's *The Liberation of the Laity*.[10]

By such procedure they hope to find room within the theology of ordination for the inclusion of at least the leading ministries currently entrusted to non-ordained women and men. This article aims to take up the main issues arising in this line of thinking, and claims that the approach has been less than discerning in its scrutiny of the sources of the theology of

---

7. Bernard Sesboüé,"Lay Ecclesial Ministers: A Theological look into the Future," *The Way* 42/3 (July 2003), 57–72, see 69.

8. Paul Zulehner, "Deaf to the Faithful," *The Tablet*, May 17, 2003, 9.

9. See Zeni Fox, *New Ecclesial Ministry: Lay Professionals Serving the Church*, rev. edn (Kansas City, MO: Sheed and Ward, 2002).

10. Paul Lakeland, *The Liberation of the Laity. In Search of an Accountable Church* (New York/ London: Continuum, 2003). See, for example, 106 and indexed references to topics like church structures, clergy, bishops, priesthood.

ministry. The critique is largely from the vantage point established in my own research into the origins of the Christian concept of ministry.[11]

Lakeland's basic appeal to what he conceives as the early church's understanding of ministry[12] is a stark contemporary reminder that the first problematic area remains the sphere of ministerial language that I described in 1990 in the first chapter of *Diakonia*.[13] These pages continue to be relevant to any modern discussion of ministry. Their significance arises from the fact that over the last fifty years the word *ministry* has ceased to mean what it used to in ecclesiology. Once always referring to the ordained leadership and pastoral practice of a church, the term was actually only lightly used within Roman Catholic circles, and there more often than not had a reference to ministry in Protestant practice. This made it possible for Roman Catholics to refer to the "minister" of a local Protestant church without appearing to compromise the unique Catholic understanding of their own leader as the "priest."

Within a few years of the conclusion of the Second Vatican Council, such ingrained usage quickly underwent a full circle of change. Observers had noted how the pastoral language of council documents was deeply imbued with ministerial language whether in regard to bishops, priests or lay people. The words *mission, apostolate,* and *ministry* applied indiscriminately to hierarchical and lay participation in the pastoral life of the church. Of these two levels of participation we read, for example, in *Gaudium et spes*:

> The gifts of the Spirit are manifold: some men are called to testify openly to mankind's yearning for its heavenly home and keep the awareness of it vividly before men's minds; others are called to dedicate themselves to the earthly service [Latin *servitio*] of men and in this way [Latin: *suo ministerio*] to prepare the way for the kingdom of heaven.[14]

---

11. Collins, *Diakonia*.

12. Lakeland, *Liberation*, 144, 284–85.

13. Collins, *Diakonia*, 14–20.

14. Austin Flannery, ed., *Vatican Council II: The Conciliar and Post Conciliar Documents* (Dublin: Dominican Publications, 1977), 937.

Here, ministerial words apply only—but pointedly—to the laity (in spite of the way the English translation obscures this aspect of the paragraph). In the same document (paragraph 51),[15] such secular "ministry" of the laity extended even to responsibilities connected with procreation: "God, the Lord of life, has entrusted to men the noble mission [Latin: *praecellens ministerium*] of safeguarding life." Other expressions extend to mission and apostolate:

> The church's mission is concerned with the salvation of men...The apostolate of the Church therefore, and of each of its members, aims primarily at announcing to the world by word and action the message of Christ...[16]

Usage in regard to the hierarchy barely needs illustrating except for one instance that provides us with an unmistakable clue as to where the ministerial emphasis has suddenly come from. In *Lumen gentium* we read that the office of bishops is "in the strict sense of the term, a service [Latin *servitium*], which is called very expressively in sacred scripture a *diakonia* or ministry [Latin '*diaconia*' *seu ministerium*, with 'expressively' as *significanter*]."[17] Here we encounter the Latin version of the Greek word *diakonia*; traditionally, as in the Vulgate translation of Paul's discourse on his "ministry/*diakonia*" in 2 Cor. 3:1–6:13, this term had been translated into Latin as *ministerium*. The conclusion to the famous preface introducing *Gaudium et spes* takes us to the biblical source from which these words *diakonia*, *ministerium*, and *ministry* derive their newfound theological significance:

> The Church is not motivated by an earthly ambition but is interested in one thing only—to carry on the work of Christ...for he came into the world to bear witness to the truth, to save and not to judge, to serve and not to be served.[18]

---

15. Flannery, *Vatican Council II*, 955.

16. Flannery, *Vatican Council II*, 772.

17. Ibid., 378; on this term, see note 42 in chapter 3 of this book.

18. Ibid., 905.

The final biblical reference here is to Mark 10:45 (the Greek verb "to serve" is *diakonēsai*), and the citation not only imbues the idea of service or ministry with the values attaching to the life-giving action of the Son of Man but signals that ministry/*diakonia* is essentially a process whereby a minister engages with the needs of another.

The most widely read application of this linguistic perception to the theology of ministry is probably in the pages Hans Küng devoted in 1967 to "Ecclesiastical Office as Ministry" in *The Church*.[19] These pages were farther reaching in their immediate impact upon the church at large than were the conciliar statements themselves on church and ministry. At the same time, Küng's was not an original perception but an adaptation of a view already circulating in non-Catholic writings on ministry and deriving its academic respectability from the 1935 lexical description of the *diakonia* words in Kittel's *Theological Dictionary of the New Testament*.[20] The popularity of the notion predated the Second Vatican Council and had already reached its peak expression in 1959 in the original edition of Eduard Schweizer's *Church Order in the New Testament*.[21] In particular, the notion was already permeating new thinking about lay ministry in the World Council of Churches and other ecumenical circles, largely through Hendrik Kraemer's *Theology of the Laity*. Here we encounter the programmatic statement:

> Remoulding the laity involves an equally drastic remoulding of the ministry and of the theologians...under the light of that profound, revolutionary word: *diakonia*.[22]

---

19. Hans Küng, *The Church*, Eng. trans. (Garden City, NY: Image Books, 1976; German original and first edition in English 1967), 495–502.

20. H. W. Beyer, "*diakoneō, diakonia, diakonos*," in *Theologisches Wörterbuch zum Neuen Testament*, ed. G. Kittel, vol. 2 (Stuttgart: Kohlhammer, 1935), 81–93.

21. Eduard Schweizer, *Church Order in the New Testament*, Eng. trans. (London: SCM, 1961); originally *Gemeinde und Gemeindeordnung im Neuen Testament* (Zurich: Zwingli, 1959).

22. Hendrik Kraemer, *A Theology of the Laity* (London: Lutterworth Press, 1958), 187. A rare example in North American literature of a confrontation with conventional theology on the basis of these foundational writings was William J. Rademacher, *Lay Ministry: A Theological, Spiritual, and Pastoral Handbook* (New York: Crossroad Publishing Company, 1991). The orientation here is radical: "There is no ministry apart from the Holy Spirit and her creative activity continually empowering the minister....There is also no ministry apart from needs. Need antecedes ministry and shapes and defines it....Ministry does not need to be empowered by mandate or delegation of a superior possessing power.... 'Ministry,' or *diakonia*, is a nonsacral word. The early church leaned heavily on this secular term to describe its main ministering activity" (46–47). Perhaps the deep-rooted hierarchism at work within the

Thus the ecclesiological pedigree of the word *ministry* in the modern sense is not long. I contend that the pedigree is questionable and holds no joy in the way of ecclesial outcomes. On the one hand, too much is easily read into its uses in the discourse of the Second Vatican Council while, on the other hand, many are aware of theological difficulties embedded in ecclesiological statements about ministry when read within the modern framework. Some theologians attempt to identify a rationale in the broad-ranging usage within the conciliar documents,[23] but ultimately the exercise is unrewarding. At one point in the Vatican documents we may certainly identify a distinction between "lay apostolate" and "pastoral ministry" (the latter of the ordained),[24] but at other points we encounter the mix of terms that we noted above. And the issue has hardly been clarified in subsequent official documents, beginning with Paul VI's 1972 motu proprio *Ministeria quaedam*, where we read that "minor orders" have been abolished and "are henceforth to be called ministries."[25] On the other hand, the *Instruction on Certain Questions* (paragraph 2) reversed this apparent stylistic tendency twenty-five years later in announcing that "a person is not a minister simply in performing a task, but through sacramental ordination."[26]

North American church and its theological institutes prevented ministerial thinking venturing further along these lines; as Joan Chittester commented in her foreword (ix), "He has done the church a great favor. All may not call it so."

23. Elissa Rinere, "Conciliar and Canonical Applications of 'Ministry' to the Laity," *The Jurist* 47 (1987), 204–27; Russell Shaw, *Ministry or Apostolate? What Should the Catholic Laity Be Doing?* (Huntington, IN: Our Sunday Visitor, 2002). Contrary to Rinere's analysis, Kenan Osborne recognizes in the conciliar documents a usage that identifies the term *apostolate* as designating activities of disciples both ordained and lay, and the term *ministry* as designating activities of ordained disciples. See *Ministry. Lay Ministry in the Roman Catholic Church: Its History and Theology* (New York/Mahwah: Paulist Press, 1993), 556–57. The common ground between the two would be the sharing through baptism in the three functions ("tria munera") of Jesus as priest, prophet, and king. On this basis he envisaged the possibility of a church with "ordained ministers," "non-ordained ministers," and other baptized who were neither of these (598); such "'lay' ministry" would arise from "a specific call" (560). More recently, in the context of a consideration of my own work, he has written of "the common ministry that belongs to all Christians," insisting that until its relationship to the ordained ministry is clarified, "a solid theology of lay ecclesial ministry will remain a non-reality." See "Envisioning a Theology of Ordained and Lay Ministry: Lay/Ordained Ministry—Current Issues of Ambiguity," in Susan K. Wood, ed., *Ordering the Baptismal Priesthood: Theologies of Lay and Ordained Ministry* (Collegeville, MN: Liturgical Press, 2003), 195–227, citing 207.

24. Flannery, *Vatican Council II*, 773: "The lay apostolate and the pastoral ministry complete each other."

25. http://www.romanrite.com/Churchdoc.html (accessed June 1, 2004).

26. *Instruction on Certain Questions* (see note 3 above), 19.

The Diakonic Faultline

A more helpful view of the interplay in conciliar documents of the *ministry* words with the pre-conciliar terms *mission* and *apostolate* is that many participants in the council, especially certain *periti*, were aware of the emergence into ecclesiological discourse of the ancient Greek term *diakonia* and wished to see conciliar statements reflecting new contemporary insights, especially if the insights had potential for shared ecumenical understandings of church and ministry.[27] In subsequent decades, however, the issue has hardened and now may even seem to be intractable.

Thus Thomas P. Rausch has drawn attention to the discordant readings proffered in regard to *diakonia* by me and the mainstream "modern scholars."[28] A critical factor contributing to this stage of the discussion is the way the modern ecclesiological reading of *ministry/diakonia* is being indiscriminately read back into the New Testament sources of ministry and church.[29] There are many ecclesiologists, church leaders, lay ministers, and synod members who have known no other translation of Mark 10:45 than that of RSV/NRSV: "The Son of Man came...to serve." The same have had no other view of Ephesians 4:12 than that the heavenly Christ gave gifts of apostles and teachers to the church "to equip the saints for the work of ministry," or of 1 Corinthians 12:4 than that among gifts of the Spirit are "varieties of services." These are critical passages for any theology of church and ministry, and more than once I have drawn attention

27. Of this interplay, in *Diakonia*, I wrote (20): "Charles Moeller has recorded that the emergence of the idea of service in the Pastoral Constitution on the Church in the Modern World was 'no accident, but the result of collaboration with the separated brethren.'" The collaboration was initiated by the April 1963 letter from Lukas Vischer (of the Faith and Order section of the Wold Council of Churches) that spoke of "the trilogy: communion (*koinonia*), *diakonia* and witness," a theme that, as Moeller notes, had been running through the World Council and its commission on Faith and Order. See further my sketch of the provenance of the diakonic aspect there (20–24).

28. Thomas P. Rausch, "Ministry and Ministries," in Wood, ed., *Ordering the Baptismal Priesthood* (note 23 above), 52–67, see 53 and 57. Rausch notes the new reading of *diakonia* on its first publication, even if he appears to have been uncertain of the extent of its relevance; see *Priesthood Today: An Appraisal* (New York/Mahwah: Paulist Press, 1992), 23 (but compare 133). On the other hand, Osborne's comments in "Envisioning a Theology" (note 23 above) do not adequately represent my reading of *diakonia*, and in *Orders and Ministry* (Maryknoll, NY: Orbis, 2006), Osborne reverts to the Brandt/Beyer amalgam (See chapter 1 of this book) of *diakonia* as service (41–42), although partly obscured there by the misuse of the term *dikaiosynē* for *diakonita*.

29. See my reflections on such a dysfunctional hermeneutic in *Deacons and the Church: Making Connections Between Old and New* (Leominster, UK; Gracewing/Harrisburg, PA: Morehouse, 2002–03), 132–37.

to Markus Barth's commentary on Ephesians[30] for the purpose of illustrating how profoundly the modern understanding of *diakonia* can be made to affect ecclesiology:

> The traditional distinction between clergy and laity does not belong in the church. Rather, the whole church, the community of all the saints together, is the clergy appointed by God for a ministry to and for the world.[31]

Here, whereas the introductory statement about "clergy" and "laity" can be argued on several other grounds—as Herbert Haag has made abundantly clear[32]—the second statement marks an ecclesiological watershed.

Recent North American Roman Catholic ecclesiology appears to be poised atop this watershed, having got itself there along the familiar *diakonic* faultline. What can theologians do to make an inclusive church out of a church that is already hierarchically constituted and that carries in its long memory and embodies in its institutions, architecture, ritual, language, and law an ecclesiology that is certainly not the one Barth saw in the *diakonic* description of the church in the New Testament? In addressing this conundrum, Paul Lakeland curiously echoes Barth's own phrasing ("If we are all called to be ministers, whether ministers to the church or ministers in the world, does that mean that there are no laity any longer?"[33]) but dodges the implication of a univocal sense of churchwide ministry by suggesting that ordination of the one kind of minister could be seen as establishing a "qualitative" difference between that person's ministry and the ministry of the non-ordained.[34]

The Sacrament of Ministry

Other recent books, one by Edward Hahnenberg and the other edited by Susan Wood for the Collegeville Ministry Seminar, work more closely within a context of a sacramental theology and share two fundamental principles. The first is in accord with "an emerging consensus in

30. Collins, *Diakonia*, 274, note 36; *Are All Christians Ministers?* (Collegeville, MN: Liturgical Press, 1992), 17–34.

31. Markus Barth, *Ephesians*, vol. 2, The Yale Anchor Bible Commentaries (Garden City, NY: Doubleday, 1974), 479.

32. Herbert Haag, *Clergy and Laity: Did Jesus Want a Two-Tier Church?* Eng. trans. (Tunbridge Wells, UK: Burns and Oates, 1997).

33. Lakeland, *Liberation of the Laity*, 282.

34. Lakeland, *Liberation of the Laity*, 269–71.

contemporary Catholic theology," which "recognizes baptism as the fundamental sacrament of ministry."[35] In her "summary of the consensus" Susan Wood puts this view in the following terms:

> Pre-conciliar theology identified ministry with the sacrament of orders and distinguished the various degrees of orders by the sacramental powers proper to each. The seminar proposes a broadening of the understanding of ministry to include the laity and to view ministry in terms of distinct ecclesial relations that further specify the exercise of discipleship grounded in baptism.[36]

The second principle supports this in seeing charisms or "gifts of service given by the Spirit of God," as Elissa Rinere identifies them in reference to 1 Corinthians 12:5,[37] being realized in the range of pastoral activities in which lay people engage themselves. Wood puts this:

> We assume our place in the order of the Church according to our state in life and the charisms we bring for the upbuilding of the community and Christian discipleship.[38]

In Hahnenberg's view, "charisms mediate the Spirit to the individual and lead outward to active service; their source is Christ's Spirit and their goal is ministry."[39] He further observes: "The view of charisms leading to ordinary ministry in the church has become common."[40] David Power concludes his contribution to Wood in similar vein:

> We are in a period comparable to New Testament times, when charisms were given by the Spirit, some listings of charisms and services made, but no definitive count taken. Counting may be one of the ways of quenching the Spirit.[41]

---

35. Rausch, "Envisioning a Theology," 62.

36. Wood, "Conclusion: Convergence Points toward a Theology of Ordered Ministries," in Wood, ed. *Ordering the Baptismal Priesthood*, 257.

37. Rinere, "Canon Law and Emerging Understandings of Ministry," in Wood, ed., *Ordering the Baptismal Priesthood*, 68–84, see 77.

38. Wood, ibid., 257.

39. Edward P. Hahnenberg, *Ministries: A Relational Approach* (New York: Crossroad Publishing Company, 2003), 61.

40. Ibid., 71.

41. David Power, "Priesthood Revisited: Mission and Ministries in the Royal Priesthood," in Wood, ed., *Ordering the Baptismal Priesthood*, 87–120, see 118. Power's emphasis here echoes

On grounds of a consensus regarding the broad range of ecclesial activities called ministry/*diakonia*, Hahnenberg proposes expanding ordination to include women and men, married and single, as well as expanding the roles that women and men would be ordained for: ordination not just for the presbyterate but for the ministerial activities which he reports the present laity is already engaged in. "The question is not," he writes, "how to fit new ministries into the clerical system as it currently exists, but whether the current system is the only way in which the church can structure its ministries."[42]

This vision is undoubtedly inviting, and perhaps Hahnenberg convinces us that a restructuring of ministerial arrangements is exactly what our age-old church needs if it is to be a twenty-first-century institution capable of providing meaning and vibrancy from youth to old age for hundreds of millions of human beings. The alternative scenario is not attractive. At the present apparent rate of attrition in the first world—the latest estimate in my city is of a 13 percent decline in church attendance over the last five years—the Great Church of the West would appear to be diminishing within a few short generations to the scale of a Galapagian cultural wreck on the rim of human memory. While the new century waits to decide on this, many of us may feel that Hahnenberg's agenda will provide the shove we need to get us through the first decade. And yet the revised Article 6 on "The Sacrament of Holy Orders" in *Catechism of the Catholic Church* stands in opposition : "Only a baptized man (*vir* [as our official English translation laboriously adds]) validly receives sacred ordination."[43]

Nonetheless, Hahnenberg carries an impeccable North American pedigree, reaching back over twenty and thirty years to Richard McBrien, David

---

his much earlier writing on gifts in the light of his reading of *diakonia* in the New Testament, as in *Gifts That Differ: Lay Ministries Established and Unestablished* (New York: Pueblo, 1985), 103: "In Christ there are no official limits to the outpouring of the Spirit. The spirit blows both where and how he wills, so that it is the free gift of the Spirit which determines the nature of the ministry to be conferred, as well as the person to be gifted with it. From such an understanding of the charismatic, it follows that unexpected services may arise at any time. It also follows that breaches may be created in the firm walls of canonical and theological formulations which restrict ministry by imposing specific forms and conditions." In his later study, *Mission, Ministry, Order: Reading the Tradition in the Present Context* (New York: Continuum, 2008), 140, and in response to my position on *diakonia*, Power firmly upholds this understanding of gifts in relation to Ephesians 4:11.

42. Hahnenberg, *Ministries*, 205.

43. *Catechism of the Catholic Church*, Eng. trans (Homebush, NSW: St Pauls, 1994), 394, nos. 1536–1600 (1577 cited).

Power, and Thomas O'Meara—all influential voices in broadening the current understanding of what ministry is in the church and from where it originates. It is from the lush ground of what O'Meara has called "the potentiality of a ministerial pleroma"[44] that Hahnenberg's projections arise. That is to say, he shares with the earlier generation of ecclesiologists the conviction that, baptism "initiates a person into charism and diaconal action, into a community that is essentially ministerial."[45] To talk of ministry, Hahnenberg sets out to focus on the body of the baptized, namely, the laity.

In all this we are dealing almost as much with O'Meara as we are with Hahnenberg, O'Meara's doctoral student of lay ecclesial ministry in 2002. O'Meara had made it his main struggle in the first edition of his book (1983) to release the hierarchical grip on the play of ministry in the church. He probed the theological roots of ministry in a church acknowledged to be universally ministerial, laying open untapped lifelines for vibrant growth. But he also alluded to some dangers: "When all is ministry, ministry fades away."[46] He was insistent not only on following through the axiom of the day that ministry is a charism but also on tracing charism back to where it can be seen as the opening upon the divine, which Jesus effected in announcing the Kingdom of God. Thereby, ministry is deinstitutionalized, desacralized, demythologized, and located within the baptized, summoning each Christian to become a revealer in his or her life of the presence of God.[47]

For the historical failure of the church to embody such a ministerial capacity, O'Meara turned on "church bureaucrats" for using the language of ministry to "control definitions and people":

> Concepts and words from scholastic or Baroque theology have held mastery over ministry while those from charisms and other biblical forms have been relegated to piety.[48]

44. Thomas F. O'Meara, *Theology of Ministry* (Ramsey, NJ: Paulist Press, 1983; rev. edn, Mahwah, NJ: Paulist Press, 1999), 222.

45. O'Meara, ibid., 211.

46. O'Meara, *Theology of Ministry* (1983), 159.

47. Compare how David Power wrote in 1985 of some effects of the desacralization of *diakonia* in the New Testament (*Gifts That Differ*, 132): "In the last few decades, some desacralization of the office of bishop and presbyter has taken place. This not only does not threaten seriously the place of the sacrament of order in the church, but it is a necessity if the more basic symbol and reality of the service of God's people and the general outpouring of the spirit are to be retrieved and allowed to revivify the sense of the mission of the whole body."

48. O'Meara, *Theology of Ministry* (1983), 144. Compare his discussion in the revised edition (1999), 151–57.

As a result, "the word 'ministry' is a prize which everyone wants to own and which the older administration of the church wants to reserve."[49]

Reverse Cycle

Not many have put the modern problem of ministerial language so force-fully. By such boldness O'Meara cleared the path for Hahnenberg to walk the extra mile with the laity. Indeed, the dialogue between the two eccle-siologists has something of the air of a common-room discussion at the University of Notre Dame. So long as the conversation remains within members of such schools the construct appears to work well and invites assent. But who else is part of the dialogue? Included we find Congar's fifty-year-old work on the laity,[50] but is the dialogue open to taking *diakonia* all the way with Hendrik Kraemer, who first argued that the laity live in a ministerial stratum? We have David Power on charism, but are we given an opportunity to suspect that Paul's teaching on charism and ministry in 1 Corinthians 12 may not be so neatly packaged as Power needs it to be?[51] We are told to listen to Jean-Marie Tillard on the nature of the local church,[52] but does anyone tell us what Tillard had to say about the nature of ministry in the first Christian communities? Tillard wrote about aspects of ministry (*diakonia*) in the New Testament in the following terms:

> We have to see the *diakonia* [ministry] as essentially a responsibility endowed by the Spirit, an office that Christ freely assumed to carry out his Father's plan, a mandate tied to a mission given by God and implying a special position within the community, a responsibility coming from on high and bringing with it a specific authority.[53]

Clearly the originating Christian "ministry/*diakonia*" identified here is essentially different from the "ministry" deployed by the consensus across

---

49. Ibid. Compare revised edition, 153.

50. Hahnenberg, *Ministries*, 37; Zeni Fox, "Laity, Ministry, and Secular Character," in Wood, ed., *Ordering the Baptismal Priesthood*, 121–51, see 125–29. Lakeland's endeavor in *The Liberation of the Laity* derives from Congar.

51. See Collins, *All Christians*, 120–30 (chapter 8 in this book); "Ministry as a Distinct Category among Charismata (1 Corinthians 12:4–7)," *Neotestamentica* 27/1 (1993), 79–91; *Deacons and the Church* (note 29 above), 81–85; Joseph F. Fitzmyer, *First Corinthians*, Anchor Yale Bible Commentaries (New Haven, CT: Yale University Press, 2008), 465.

52. Hahnenberg, *Ministries*, 119–20.

53. Jean-Marie R. Tillard, *L'Église locale* (Paris: Cerf, 1995), 167 (my translation).

the range of all the baptized. On Tillard's reading there is no such thing as an "essentially ministerial" church, but he nonetheless works toward a church that holds within it an ample supply of essential ministries.

It may not be apparent to all readers, but Tillard sourced his thinking here on the linguistic research in my *Diakonia*, the semantic findings of this investigation being now embodied in Frederick Danker's third English-language edition of Bauer's *Greek-English Lexicon of the New Testament*.[54] For a number of years, these findings have been part of the conversation in many quarters, notably in the Hanover Report of the Anglican-Lutheran International Commission,[55] in the Church of England report to the House of Bishops *For Such a Time as This*,[56] its follow-up, *The Mission and Ministry of the Whole Church*[57] and, within the context of the Anglo-Nordic Diaconal Research Project, Sven-Erik Brodd on *caritas* and *diakonia*.[58] In France, Charles Perrot has reflected profoundly on the new *diakonia* in relation to ministry of the word,[59] and Fabien Blanquart has readdressed the nature of ministry within the diaconate.[60] Increasingly in Germany, largely as a result of Hans-Jürgen Benedict's strong critique of consensus theology,[61] the question of the nature of the deacon's ministry has also come under close scrutiny, as in the symposium published

54. *A Greek-English Lexicon of the New Testament and other Early Christian Literature*, 3rd edn, (BDAG), rev. and ed. Frederick William Danker, based on Water Bauer's *Griechisch-deutsches Wörterbuch zu den Schriften des Neuen Testaments und der frühchristlichen Literatur*, 6th edn, ed. Kurt Aland and Barbara Aland, with Viktor Reichmann, and on previous English editions by W. F. Arndt, F. W. Gingrich, and F. W. Danker (Chicago and London: University of Chicago Press, 2000).

55. Hanover Report, *The Diaconate as Ecumenical Opportunity* (London: Anglican Communion Publications, 1996).

56. Church of England, *For Such a Time as This: A Renewed Diaconate in the Church of England* (London: Church House Publishing, 2001).

57. [55] The Faith and Order Advisory group of the Church of England, *The Mission and Ministry of the Whole Church: Biblical, theological and contemporary perspectives*, GS Misc 854, General Synod of the Church of England (London: 2007).

58. Sven-Erik Brodd, "*Caritas* and *Diakonia* as Perspectives on the Diaconate," in Gunnel Borgegård, Olav Fanuelsen, and Christine Hall, eds, *The Ministry of the Deacon*, vol. 2: *Ecclesiological Explorations* (Uppsala: Nordic Ecumenical Council, 2001), 23–65.

59. Charles Perrot, *Après Jésus: Le ministère chez les premiers chrétiens* (Paris: Éditions de l'Atelier/ ÉditionsOuvrières, 2000), 229–61.

60. Fabien Blanquart, *Quel serviteur?* (Paris: Cerf, 2000).

61. Hans-Jürgen Benedict, "Beruht der Anspruch der evangelischen Diakonie auf einer Missinterpretation der antiken Quellen? John N. Collins Untersuchung 'Diakonia,'" *Pastoraltheologie 89* (2000), 349–64.

by the *Diakoniewissenschaftliches Institut* of the University of Heidelberg.[62] This exercise has been exposing problems arising for the diaconate when its ministry is treated generically instead of as specific to deacons, as in my *Deacons and the Church*—which is to be distinguished from Owen Cummings's later book of the same title.[63]

To compose a theology of ministry for today, one can no longer ignore the deeper levels at which early Christians were thinking when they called ministry *diakonia*. It seems that pastoral theology is missing something when it bypasses the Pauline understanding of ministry as both gift to the church and commissioned responsibility for the Word of God. Should the church of the new millennium once again engage that understanding, might it not be drawn to conjure up the enriching and versatile ministries for women and men which it needs and for which many yearn?

---

62. Volker Herrmann, Rainer Merz, and Heinz Schmidt, eds, *Diakonische Konturen: Theologie im Kontext sozialer Arbeit* (Heidelberg: Winter, 2003). A series of reports and position papers addressing the issues include "Stellungnahme des ÖSTA [Ecumenical Study Committee of the German Evangelical Church]" on the Hanover Report (2000); Wilfried Brandt, "Biblische 'diakonia' contra evangelische Diakonie" (2003); Jürgen Gohde, president of the Diakonic Organisation of the German Evangelical Church, "Die Aufgabe der Diakonie im zukünftigen Europa," available at http://www.diakonie.de/de/downloads/Gohde-Promotion2003.pdf (an address on the occasion of Dr Gohde's doctorate *honoris causa*); Annette Noller, "Diakonat und Pfarramt: Biblische und professionstheoretische Überlegungen," in R. Merz, U. Schindler, and H. Schmidt, eds, *Dienst und Profession: Diakone und Diakoninnen zwischen Aspruch und Wirklichkeit* (Heidelberg: Winter, 2008), 84–95.

63. Owen F. Cummings, *Deacons and the Church* (New York/Mahwah: Paulist Press, 2003). See my *Deacons and the Church* above at note 29.

Part 2: Making a Fit

So old is the classic threefold form of Christian ministry that its historical origins cannot be precisely determined. The fact that the titles and inter-relationships of bishop, presbyter, and deacon are observable early in the second century does not tell us as much as the information appears to offer. The principal factor here is our lack of further information about the character of the congregation and of its operations. Nonetheless, it seems wholly unrealistic to anticipate that, in the interests of making itself more pastorally relevant in the early stages of the third millennium, the Great Church of the West might refashion the order of its ministry in any way substantially different from the order it has inherited.[64] Thus, it is not going to be reducing its threefold ministry to a single univocal ministry with multifunctional operatives sustaining the congregations in their faith and works.

The church's ecumenical interests bolster this position. Among the Orthodox churches the threefold nature of the ordained ministry is simply not negotiable, and the Latin church would never threaten this link between the two traditions. Inside the West itself, the Latin church has also been taking encouragement from the ecumenical expressions of interest in establishing a level of accord on the issue of a threefold ministry, a situation we have long been familiar with as a result of the Faith and Order paper *Baptism, Eucharist, and Ministry*.[65]

Similarly, so soon after having restored the diaconate as a permanent office, the Latin church is not likely to consider pruning the ministry back to the pragmatically shaped twofold model of bishop and presbyter that operated since the Middle Ages. Too much papal and conciliar authority, along with theological reflection and ecumenical hope, has been invested

---

64. Note the general observation made by John Paul II as he confronted this issue in *Novo millennio ineunte*, note 29, "We ask ourselves today the same question put to Peter in Jerusalem immediately after his Pentecost speech: 'What must we do?' (*Acts* 2:37)...We are certainly not seduced by the naive expectation that, faced with the great challenges of our time, we shall find some magic formula. No, we shall not be saved by a formula but by a Person...It is not therefore a matter of inventing a 'new programme.' The programme al-ready exists: it is the plan found in the Gospel and in the living Tradition, it is the same as ever...This is a programme which does not change with shifts of times and cultures, even though it takes account of time and culture for the sake of true dialogue and effective com-munication." (Translation at http://www.vatican.va/holy_father/john_paul_ii/apost_letters)

65. Faith and Order Commission, *Baptism, Eucharist, and Ministry*, Faith and Order Paper no. 111 (Geneva: World Council of Churches, 1982). See section III, esp. note 22.

in this redevelopment of diaconate for there to be any reversal. In addition, ecclesiastical authorities simply do not like tinkering in such ways. Their preferred modus operandi is to leave things in place in the hope that gradual theologizing will reveal a workable solution or at least a face-saving compromise.

If it will not trim the model back, will the hierarchy attach add-ons to its ministerial constitution for the purpose of recognizing and accommodating contemporary lay ministries within the arc of official ministry? Part I of this article referred to recommendations to this effect.[66] Thomas F. O'Meara, who is probably the most widely read current writer on ministry, has reflected deeply on the rationale for extending ordination to anyone engaged in pastoral ministry,[67] while Edward Hahnenberg has recommended introducing grades of commissioning and ordination that will take account of temporary and permanent roles but will also sidestep the problems immediately raised by the prospect of ordaining women.[68]

On the other hand, we also encountered Bernard Sesboüé's opinion that the body of the church is not yet ready for a multiplicity of ordained ministries.[69] More significantly, a move in the direction of multiplying ordinations would be oat odds with the policy enunciated in Paul VI's 1972 motu proprio, *Ministeria quaedam*.[70] This was to curtail—indeed, eliminate—"minor" ordinations, a policy developed in the interests of heightening the profile of the "major" ordinations and at the same time intensifying their focus on the work of ministry. Further, the purpose of the subsequent 1997 *Instruction on Certain Questions Regarding the Collaboration of the Non-ordained Faithful in the Sacred Ministry of Priests*, which was issued in the names of no less than eight Vatican congregations and councils, was precisely to advance the exclusive

66. William R. Burrows, *New Ministries: The Global Context* (Melbourne: Dove Communications, 1980); Fritz Lobinger, *Like His Brothers and Sisters: Ordaining Community Leaders* (New York: Crossroad Publishing Company, 1999); Winfried Haunerland, "The Heirs of the Clergy? The New Pastoral Ministries and the Reform of the Minor Orders," *Worship* 75/4 (July 2001), 305–20.

67. O'Meara, *Theology of Ministry*, rev. edn(Mahwah, NJ: Paulist Press, 1999), 219–24.

68. Edward P. Hahnenberg, *Ministries: A Relational Approach* (New York: Crossroad Publishing Company, 2003), 176–209.

69. Bernard Sesboüé, "Lay Ecclesial Ministers: A Theological look into the Future," *The Way* 42/3 (July 2003), 57–72.

70. Paul VI, *Ministeria quaedam*, http://www.romanrite.com/Churchdoc.html (accessed June 5, 2004).

character of the responsibilities for ministry of ordained men.[71] Bestowing titles like "chaplain" and "co-ordinator" on non-ordained collaborators in ministry was banned, and the document adopted the restricted terminology of ministry apparent in the new Code of Canon Law, as described by Elissa Rinere, rather than the looser style that she identified in the usage within conciliar documents.[72] The current discussion underway in North America, as in the Collegeville Ministry Seminar,[73] appears to have taken little account of this specialist usage in the magisterial documentation, and this situation once again brings to the fore the question of what ministry is.

What is Ministry?Before any progress can be made on the question of where lay ministries fit among ordained ministries, we need to revisit the issue of whether ministry is a baptismal charism, and thus an inherent capacity of any Christian, or a pastoral function restricted to those who are ordained. Since all are agreed that ministry in the church today is the ministry that important New Testament passages about pastoral activities name as *diakonia*, we must take a lead from the thinking there.

In looking to this Greek source, we do need to leave behind the broad associations clustering today around the English word *ministry*. These all arise from legitimate uses of the English word, but they are not necessarily of a uniformly theological weight. That is to say, if Paul were writing today about life in the church, he would not apply the *diakon-* words across the broad range of activities that we refer to in speaking of ministry. And yet the much narrower range of his applications of the *diakon-* words indubitably applies to the kind of ministry that is essential to the establishing and sustaining of the life of a church. Indeed, one can go so far as to say that a church needs no more ministry than what Paul intended to denote by way of the *diakon-* words.

Paul's principal statement about ministry/*diakonia* is in 2 Corinthians 2:14–6:13. Over more than three chapters, Paul mounts a spirited apologia for the authenticity of his own apostolic status in the face of visiting critics of his work. While the title of apostle is fundamental to his self-understanding, as he indicates in the address of each of his letters in such phrases as "Paul,

---

71. *Instruction on Certain Questions Regarding the Collaboration of the Non-ordained Faithful in the Sacred Ministry of Priests*, Eng. trans. (Strathfield, NSW: St Pauls Publications, 1997).

72. Elissa Rinere, "Conciliar and Canonical Applications of 'Ministry' to the Laity," *The Jurist* 47 (1987), 204–27. See also her "Canon Law and Emerging Understandings of Ministry," in Wood, ed., *Ordering the Baptismal Priesthood*, 68–84.

73. Wood, ed., *Ordering the Baptismal Priesthood*.

an apostle of Christ Jesus by the will of God" (2 Corinthians 1:1), in his defense of this apostleship he does not once call upon that primary title. Instead, in the course of reviewing the activities his calling has engaged him in and urging the Corinthians to reflect on their experience of the process he initiated, Paul consistently designates his essential task as *diakonic* in character. Thus we read of his "competence from God" to be a minister (*diakon-*) of a new covenant (2 Corinthians 3:6); of a ministry (*diakon-*) that dispenses the Spirit of God, justification, and glory (3:6–9); and of the divine condescension that engaged him in this ministry (*diakon-*) (4:1), which is "the ministry (*diakon-*) of reconciliation" (5:18). His role in delivering this heavenly message constitutes him an "ambassador" for Christ (5:20).

A reading of the passage in the light of Paul's rhetoric reveals—even in translation—how Paul's concept of ministry supposes an engagement in a process whereby a divine word is committed to the accredited minister and passes entire, under the minister's proclamation, to the recipient, who in turn is conscious of communing in that word with the divine. This is the point of Paul's appeal to "the conscience" of everyone (4:2), for Paul is challenging his readers to recognize that their very experience of his ministry among them in Corinth is their best guarantee of the authenticity of his ministerial activity as compared with their experiences under the methods of others who have arrived among them.

Because the *diakon-* words were deeply entrenched in Greek religious discourse—Hermes was the minister/*diakon-* par excellence—they served Paul's purpose here to perfection.[74] Paul could take for granted that the terms were recognizable among Greek-speakers as having singular semantic values, including those attaching to the notion of mediating messages from heaven to earth. For this reason he played upon their potential to the full, confident that the audience would register every nuance. This is why he can in one move change from ministry/*diakon-* terms to the ambassador term (5:20). Either as ambassador or minister Paul is an accredited spokesperson for a deity who delivers a word that is the deity's own. Indeed, as he concludes the passage, Paul easily reverts to his preferred terms. At 6:3–4 we read (NRSV):

We are putting no obstacle in anyone's way; so that no fault may be found with our ministry (*diakon-*), but as servants (*diakon-*) of God

74. Collins, *Diakonia*, 203–05; *All Christians*, 44–50; "The Mediatorial Aspect of Paul's Role as *Diakonos*," *Australian Biblical Review* 40 (1992), 34–44 (in this book as chapter 6).

we have commended ourselves in every way: through great endurance, in afflictions, hardships.

The NRSV's sense is not that "we have commended ourselves as servants of God" but that (to borrow Ralph Martin's rendering) "we commend ourselves as ministers do."[75] This reading is required because Paul uses the Greek accusative for "ourselves" but a nominative for "ministers/*diakonoi*." Compare Victor Furnish: "as ministers of God should."[76] Bultmann translates similarly[77] and,this is common, except in translations of the New Testament.

The import of this grammatical nicety is that Paul is modeling himself upon preexistent expectations of what an authentic minister/*diakonos* is. And what that is he proceeds to delineate in the following verses (6:4b–10), particular features being exposure to physical dangers from travel in strange places and restraints imposed by those opposed to his message ("beatings, imprisonments, riots"), but also his own qualities ("patience, kindness") and endeavors ("labors"). At the center of this profile of the minister/*diakonos* is the "truthful speech" of the spokesperson and "the power of God" enabling the minister/*diakonos* to be faithful to his mandate in the midst of such disabling possibilities (6:7; Martin refers neatly to this catalogue as an "Identi-kit picture.")

Ministry Under Mandate

What emerges from Paul's apologia is a depiction of a minister operating under a mandate. In Paul's own case, the mandate is under Christ or God, and it imposes a responsibility upon the minister different from the responsibilities of other members of a believing community. In fact, I consider this differentiation between the mandated minister and the believing member of a community the essential factor determining Paul's analysis of gifts in the church (1 Corinthians 12:4–7). Having argued this reading elsewhere,[78] I note here only the difference it makes to our understanding of the charismatic endowment of the church.

---

75. Ralph P. Martin, *2 Corinthians* (Waco, TX: Word Books, 1986), 172.

76. Victor Paul Furnish, *II Corinthians* (Garden City, NY: Doubleday, 1984), 343.

77. Rudolf Bultmann, *Der zweite Brief an die Korinther* (Göttingen: Vandenhoeck & Ruprecht, 1976), 171: "wir empfehlen (erweisen) uns so, wie es einem Diener Gottes zukommt."

78. Collins, *All Christians*, 125–30 (as in chapter 8 in this book); "The Mediatorial Aspect of Paul's Role as *Diakonos*," *Australian Biblical Review* 40 (1992), 34–44 (chapter 6 in this book);

When Paul states that "there are varieties of gifts, but the same Spirit" (1 Corinthians 12:4), he issues a programmatic or generic statement about each church, namely, each church is replete with gifts of the Spirit. He implies in fact that the gathering is church only in so far as it lives and acts within the Spirit. When Paul proceeds, however, to two further statements about "varieties of services" and "varieties of activities" (12:5–6), his intention is to divide the generic set of gifts into two groupings, namely, those to do with "services" and those to do with "activities." The first grouping, designated "services" in the NRSV, Paul calls *diakoniai*, by which he means the mandated apostolic activities or ministries that he would soon describe in 2 Corinthians and to which he had already alluded in 1 Corinthians when identifying the functions of Apollos and himself (1 Corinthianns 3:5, "Servants/*diakonoi* through whom you came to believe, as the Lord assigned to each.")

In emphasizing Paul's consistent patterns of thought and expression in all matters relating to apostolic ministry/*diakonia*, I draw attention to Andrew Clarke's attempt to downgrade the *diakonic* terminology when discussing the same material.[79] In gospel narrative he recognizes lowly connotations attaching to instances of the *diakon-* words and proposes that these values should apply to the *diakon-* words Paul introduces into his discussion of ministerial activities. This reading would see Paul placing "a significant emphasis on the servile nature" of his ministry.[80] Such a proposal would be acceptable, however, only insofar as it is a legitimate hermeneutical exercise to transfer values of the *diakon-* words as they occur in a context of narrative or ethical instruction in the gospels to the same words as they occur in the different level of discourse upon which Paul operates in his discussion about apostolic ministry. Paul's ministerial discourse creates its own context and imposes its own semantic contours on the *diakon-* words there. In addition, these contours coincide precisely with stylistic and semantic characteristics evident in other Christian and non-Christian rhetoric about the delivery of messages to and from heaven

---

"Ministry as a distinct category among charismata (1 Corinthians 12:4–7)," *Neotestamentica* 27/1 (1993), 79–91; "A Ministry for Tomorrow's Church," *Journal of Ecumenical Studies* 33/2 (Spring 1995), 172–73; *Deacons and the Church*, 81–84.

79. Andrew D. Clarke, *Serve the Community of the Church: Christians as Leaders and Ministers* (Grand Rapids/Cambridge: Eerdmans, 2000), 233–47.

80. Ibid., 245.

and about the mediation of effects (e. g., light and sound) from one environment to another.[81]

Mandated Ministry in Luke

New Testament writers later than Paul evidence the same sense of a mandated ministry within the church. We see this at Ephesians 4:12, where—contrary to understandings represented in translations and most commentaries—the ministry/*diakonia* is not predicated of the "saints" but of the teachers given to the church by Christ on high.[82] This is the ministry/*diakonia* whose mandate the writer urges Timothy to fulfil (2 Timothy 4:5).

In this respect Luke is of particular interest for today's churches. His narrative of the re-constitution of the Twelve after the death of Judas opens with Jesus mandating "the apostles" (Acts 1:2) to be witnesses "to the ends of the earth" (1:8), and develops with Peter advocating a replacement for Judas "in this ministry/*diakonia*" (1:17). In due course, the eleven pray over the two qualified candidates (1:24–25):

> Lord, you know everyone's heart. Show us which one of these two you have chosen to take the place in this ministry/*diakonia* and apostleship.

After the casting of lots, Matthias was accepted as "chosen" by the Lord to enter into ministry.

In a remarkable development later in Luke's narrative, Paul himself—who, like Matthias, had not received a mandate for ministry with the Eleven from the risen Lord—expresses to the Ephesian elders at the end of his career in Asia (Acts 20:24) his prayer to "finish my course and the ministry/*diakonia* that I received from the Lord Jesus, to testify to the good news of God's grace." By the careful deployment of this ministerial codeword, Luke indicates that the founding apostolic mandate was extended in the case of Paul by heaven's intervention—the Lord designated Paul "an instrument whom I have chosen" (9:15)—and, in the instance of Matthias, by the church's own devices.

The mandate of Paul and the Twelve was, as Luke named it, "the ministry/*diakonia* of the word" (6:4). And this was the mandate that the church as a body, after due consideration and in consultation with the

---

81. Collins, *Diakonia*, 203–05; "The Mediatorial Aspect" (in this book as chapter 6). For further comment on Clarke, see index.

82. Collins, *Diakonia*, 233–34; *All Christians*, 17–34.

Twelve, brought the Seven under in the midst of prayer and through a commissioning ritual (Acts 6:1–6). That we subsequently hear of the Seven Hellenist men only as evangelists—in the persons of Stephen (Acts 7) and Philip (8:5; 21:8)—must suggest that their original mandate in Jerusalem was not the physical care of the Hellenist widows but the nurturing in them, through their own language, of the word of God.[83]

Ministry Versus Prophecy

Each of these three scenarios of the ministries of the Twelve, the Seven, and Paul places at center stage a mandate from the Lord or from the church that is constitutive of the respective ministries. Minor details of this characteristic of early church life are observable in regard to other individuals as well, for example, Phoebe, the church's delegate to Rome (Romans 16:1); Stephanas (1 Corinthians 16:15); Archippus (Colossians 4:17); Tychichus (Ephesians 6:21; Colossians 4:7); Onesiphorus (2 Timothy 1:18); and, I would suggest, Onesimus (Philemon 13). An ecclesial mandate is also clearly in evidence in relation to the ministry/*diakonia* mentioned in Paul's references to the Asian collection for Jerusalem (Romans 15:22–29; 2 Corinthians chapters 8 and 9) and in Luke's references to the Antiochian delegation to Jerusalem (Acts 11:27–30; 12:24–25). Certainly such sources would not lead us to suspect that the early Christian groups were reliant on charismatic inspirations before ministry arose among them. The known ministers among them had been sent. That is the point of the ministerial terminology they elected to use.[84]

That prophecy was also a feature of early Christian praxis and is recognizable as charismatic in the modern sense is clear from Paul's discussion in 1 Corinthians 14, but prophecy in this sense was an intra-church phenomenon for the enrichment of the community and with inbuilt controls as recommended there by Paul. There is no indication that it was the basic instrument of evangelization. That prophets appear here and there in the broader narrative (Acts 6:27; Romans 12:6; Ephesians 4:11; Didache, etc.) does little to inform us of their role and significance for the development of the early churches, and the very obscurity speaks rather of a practice and process that was soon superseded.

---

83. Collins, *All Christians*, 36–40; *Deacons and the Church*, 47–58 (in this book as chapter 10).

84. See the chapter "Emissaries in the Church" in Collins, *Diakonia*, 217–26 and chapter 9 in this book..

Ministry and Threefold Order

All we eventually know of the established ministries structured into the early church is what we can construe from the threefold order of bishop, presbyter, and deacon that entered history. Before the accommodations of the fourth century, this threefold order established itself as the instrument of the church's growth. Therefore, one course open to us in our desire to work from an authentic tradition toward a reformation of contemporary church order is to trace a connection between ministerial processes we have identified in the New Testament and the established threefold order. Those few ancient ministerial processes were sufficient to found and to sustain Christian groups that saw themselves in a dynamic relationship with both the past and a future into which they envisaged the tradition expanding.

What the threefold order was attempting to maintain in the church was due observance of the Lord's mandate to witness to his word. Prior to its emergence, Pauline ministry had already demonstrated that churches developed through activities centered on the ecclesial implications of the ministry/*diakonia* of the Word. Mission for witness was central to the apostolic endeavor that the New Testament called ministry/*diakonia* (as it underlay also the prophetic activity just alluded to). How bishop and presbyter were understood to function as instruments of this elemental responsibility of the church is not difficult to surmise. It was as holders of the Word and teachers of the community, and in both capacities an essential connection was with ritual, in particular with entry into the Christian body through baptism and with proclaiming the mystery of the Lord's death and abiding presence in the assembly. Determining the respective roles of bishop and presbyters in these small congregations is beyond the scope of the present article and is of less import than their shared focus on the Word of God (evident in the remains of later apses which had provided chair and benches for the presider and the presbyterate).

When and for what purpose the diaconate attached itself to this order is not at all clear, nor is it clear that its role within the Roman church of the fourth century—so strongly criticized in the anonymous pamphlet *On the Arrogance of Deacons*[85]—was connatural with its origins. One constant in the documentary evidence is the linguistic affinity between the *diakonos*

---

85. "De iactantia Romanorum leviticorum," in *Corpus Scriptorum Ecclesiasticorum Latinorum* 50 (1908, Johnson Reprint, 1963), 193–98.

and the *episkopos*. This appears in both early and later writings in the New Testament (Phil. 1:1; 1 Tim. 3:1–13), and speaks at once of a strong relationship between a superior or senior figure of a community and an associate executive, but to what precise purpose other than the support of a Christian community it is difficult to determine.

The Deacon's Ministry

The strong relationship between deacon and bishop remained, however, and accompanied the future development of the office of deacon until its effective demise. So obvious is the relationship that it is futile to attempt to find the rationale for the early deacon in works of charity, even if these were to be understood as operations in the name of the bishop. Nowhere in ancient sources is it possible to establish an innate correlation between the diaconate and works of love, and likewise nowhere in Christian sources are there grounds to argue that the deacon's title makes of the deacon a symbol par excellence of Christ the Servant, which would appear to be the preferred understanding in most modern theology,[86] including that of the International Theological Commission.[87] My book *Deacons and the Church*—which is to be distinguished from the later book by Owen Cummings of the same title[88]—attempts to expose the inadequacy of this approach.

Because in recent years the question of diaconate has occasioned much discussion of its availability for women, a particular theological evaluation by Gerhard Müller warrants comment. He has argued that the close association of deacon and bishop has established an inherently sacerdotal orientation of the diaconate, a consequence of which would

---

86. Hervé Legrand, "Le diaconat dans sa relation à la théologie de l'Église et des réception et devenir du diaconat depuis Vatican II," in André Haquin and Philippe Weber, eds, *Diaconat XXXIe siècle* (Brussels: Lumen Vitae/Cerf/Novalis/Labor Fides, 1997), 13–41; Theodore W. Kraus, *The Order of Deacons: A Second Look* (Hayward, CA: Folger Graphics, 1997), 112–15; Dorothea Reininger, *Diakonat der Frau in der Einen Kirche* (Ostfildern: Schwabenverlag, 1999), 629–31; Walter Kasper, *Leadership in the Church: How Traditional Roles Can Serve the Christian Community Today*, Eng. trans. (New York: Crossroad Publishing Company, 2003), 25–28; Paul M. Zulehner, *Dienende Männer—Anstifter zur Solidarität: Diakone in Westeuropa* (Ostfiildern: Schwabenverlag, 2003), 27–43. Such literature has expanded exponentially.

87. International Theological Commission, Historico-Theological Research Document, *From the Diakonia of Christ to the Diakonia of the Apostles* (Chicago: Hillenbrand Books, 2004), 85.

88. Owen F. Cummings, *Deacons and the Church* (New York/Mahwah: Paulist Press, 2004). For my *Deacons and the Church*.

be the ineligibility of women for ordination as deacons.[89] The argument would appear to lose much of its relevance, however, when we consider that sacerdotal understandings of bishop and presbyter developed only subsequently to the association of deacon and bishop. Of course, the early conviction that the deacon was ordained "not unto the priesthood, but unto the ministry [*diakonia*]" (cited in *Lumen gentium*)[90] adds substance to this critique of Müller,[91] and strongly suggests that we look elsewhere for an explanation of the relationship. What the linguistic factors point to is, in fact, a diaconal role that consists in a relationship of agency between deacon and bishop. The deacon would emerge as the associate executive already referred to. And of course, outside of the Christian tradition, the whole literary history of the *diakonos* as agent—of heavenly prime movers as of political and military officers—is immediately relevant to this understanding of deacon and bishop.[92]

The concept of the deacon as an agent in sacred affairs takes on a greater relevance when we link it with the fact that the deacon receives a sacramental ordination, especially in light of the permanency of the diaconate. No longer the step to priesthood or episcopacy that it was for most of its history nor a career path, it must answer to the church for the sacrament through which it has come about. In one sense, the Second Vatican Council expected much of the new diaconate as "a proper and permanent rank of the hierarchy" and in assigning it roles in "the service of the liturgy, of the Gospel, and of works of charity" (*Lumen gentium*) These assignations, however, were never more closely described,[93] and the result has been that a diversity of diaconates coexist in today's church—but in those places only where bishops have felt confident enough about its role description to institute some form of it.

---

89. Gerhard Ludwig Müller, *Priestertum und Diakonat: Der Empfänger des Weihesakramentes in schöpfungstheologischer und christologischer Perspektive* (Freiburg: Johannes Verlag, 2000), 35–36.

90. Flannery, *Vatican Council II*, 387.

91. See also Phyllis Zagano, *Holy Saturday: An Argument for the Restoration of the Female Diaconate in the Catholic Church* (New York: Crossroad Publishing Company, 2000), 65–68.

92. Collins, *Diakonia*, 133–49.

93. The list of eleven functions in Paul VI's General Norms of 1967 is representative only and was not presented as constituting the pastoral role of deacons. In the light of concluding remarks above, however, we can read here a full pastoral program for a team of deacons in any parish. See Appendix 1, General Norms for Restoring the Permanent Diaconate in the Latin Church, in Patrick McCaslin and Michael G. Lawler, *Sacrament of Service* (New York/

Deacons and Lay Ministries

The new situation of a church inadequately resourced to meet its pastoral responsibilities in terms of word and sacrament is now making a nonsense of recent developments. On the one hand, the diaconate has been restored as a major initiative for the renewal of the church's vitality but remains underresourced and indeed dysfunctional (see evidence in the overview by Sherri Vallee[94])—I direct this comment at the institution and not at individual deacons, who so often embody the highest ideals of the gospel. On the other hand, a raft of lay ministries has taken shape in response to genuine pastoral demands, and yet these new ministers have no assured future in the church. In the unlikely event that the rundown in priest numbers is reversed, what prospects would lay ecclesial ministers look to?

In the face of any such conundrum, the new ecclesial situation actually carries the key to its resolution. Instead of introducing a new tier of hierarchical order to accommodate the new ministers, the ecclesial authorities could extend to the new ministers an invitation to receive sacramental ordination as deacons. Of its nature, which is within the field of agency in the name of the gospel, the diaconate is a commodious and versatile facility that for far too long most ecclesial authorities have misunderstood and underrated. The most honest contemporary attempt on the part of a major church to move in this direction has been in the report *For Such a Time as This*.[95] The sad history of this report, which was sidetracked in the name of preexisting lay ministries (specifically, the Anglican Lay Readership),[96] stands as one more warning to advocates

---

Mahwah: Paulist Press, 1986), 135–36 (number 22). The account of "The Diaconal Ministry" in the *Directory for the Ministry and Life of Permanent Deacons* (Strathfield, NSW: St Pauls, 1998), 100–18, marks no advance on this; in acknowledging the "different forms" diaconal ministry takes, the directory eschews any attempt to draw up a definitive description of diaconal ministry, its listings mainly clarifying what is canonically permitted.

94. Sherri L. Vallee, "The Restoration of the Permanent Diaconate: A Blending of Rules," *Worship* 77/6 (November 2003), 530–52.

95. Church of England Working Party of the House of Bishops, *For Such aTime as This: A Renewed Diaconate in the Church of England* (London: Church House Publishing, 2001).

96. See Peter Owen's report "General Synod of the Church of England—November 2001 Group of Sessions 12 to 15 November 2001," November 25, 2001: "There was concern that distinctive deacons, as described in the report, seemed very little different from readers and other lay ministers. Synod was asked to commend the report for study and ecumenical responses but declined to do so; instead the report was returned to the Archbishops' Council so that the roles of Readers, pastoral assistants and Church Army Officers could be examined

of innovation in the church's order to do their homework closely. To cap
the attractiveness of this innovation within the Roman Catholic Church
in its increasingly dire situation, the theology of diaconate—in the light
at least of the ancient *diakonia*—generates no impediment to the ordination of women.[97]

as well." (Accessed at http://anglicansonline.org/news/articles/2001/CofEsynod1101.html,
June 5, 2004.)

97. For comments on the versatility of the diaconate, see the closing observations of Kyriaki
Karidoyanes FitzGerald in *Women Deacons in the Orthodox Church: Called to Holiness and
Ministry* (Brookline, MA: Holy Cross Orthodox Press, 1999), 193–98; also my own reflec-
tions concluding *Deacons and the Church*, 128–38, as well as in chapter 14 in this book.

14

Ties that Bind: Deacons Today in the Grip of Yesteryear

"THE TIES THAT bind" speak to us about bonding: as between a mother and her infant, or within the broader span of family ties. John Fawcett's famous hymn of 1772 applied the phrase to Christian life: "Blessed be the tie that binds Our hearts in Christian love." In that same sense, there is a powerful bond between deacons of the churches. Deacons today are highly conscious of being servants together after the manner of Christ the servant, or—as they like to say—of Christ the deacon.

"Ties that bind" thus has a positive slant. Over recent decades, however, I have come to see bonding of this kind among deacons as limiting. The bonding claims a biblical base, and I have long disagreed with the interpretation that forged such bonds. Accordingly, this paper seeks to expose them for what I believe they are: bonds of captivity, if that is not too strong—at least bonds that hold deacons back and inhibit bold evangelical initiatives on the part of those who have the say in our churches. They are ties, in other words, that hold us all bound to an inherited paradigm of the diaconate.

The paradigm is embedded in the dominant semantic profile of the deacon's title—the Greek word *diakonos*—and of the designation for the deacon's professional or ecclesial avocation, diaconate or, in the Greek, *diakonia*. Theology of the diaconate and job descriptions for the deacon have been constructed on the basis of a servant theology of the church that arises from a servant theology of Jesus the Lord which, in turn, is said to be exemplified in the role of servant deacons.

A Sharp Theological Divide

My own linguistic research and exegetical investigations have sought to challenge this paradigm, and to date the challenge has met with only partial agreement. The title of my research volume of 1990 was *Diakonia: Re-interpreting the Ancient Sources*,[1] and the re-interpretation it offered of ancient Greek sources of all literary genres has been widely acknowledged as ground-breaking.[2] Of interest here, however, is that in theological circles that share this generous assessment there is often a reluctance to share what I see as the inevitable implications for theology of ministry as a whole or for the ministry of deacons in particular.

While I will not be attempting here to take the challenge further, it may be helpful to draw attention to the sharp divide that has opened up in the theology of diaconate.[3]

The "re-interpretation" of my title was implying, of course, that the received understanding of *diakonia* and the servant theology that developed around it were in error. The book and later writings state unequivocally that at no point in ancient Greek usage, Christian or other, did *diakonia* mean loving service to those in need. In Germany in 2007, Anni Hentschel argued in her published doctoral thesis that this re-interpretation was correct both in the methodology that generated it and in its major exegetical outcomes.[4] In 2008 Hentschel turned explicitly to the question, "In early Christian communities was there ever a diaconate designed specifically for social and charitable activities?" She answered this emphatically in the negative.[5]

---

1. New York: Oxford University Press (reprinted 2009). The linguistic investigation has been taken further into patristic literature in "A Monocultural Usage: *diakon-* words in Classical, Hellenistic, and Patristic Sources," *Vigiliae Christianae* 66.3 (2012), 287–309.

2. For reference to a number of reviews see John N. Collins, "A Ministry for Tomorrow's Church," *Journal of Ecumenical Studies* 32.2 (1995), 159–77 (in particular, 167–69). Introducing a later evaluation of the study, David P. Scaer called it "a scholarly avalanche whose conclusions are inescapable." See "Ministry in the Lutheran Church Today," *Semper Reformanda,* 2000, http://SemperRef.homestead.com/.

3. I have described this divide in so far as it affects ministry generally in "Ordained and Other Ministries: Making a Difference," *Ecclesiology* 3.1 (2006), 11–32 (See chapter 12 in this book); "Theology of Ministry in the Twentieth Century: Ongoing Problems or New Orientations?," *Ecclesiology* 8.1 (2012), 11–32 (See chapter 11 in this book).

4. *Diakonia im Neuen Testament. Studien zur Semantik unter besonderer Berücksichtigung der Rolle von Frauen* (WUNT 2.226; Tübingen: Mohr and Siebeck, 2007). And see my article review, in "Re-interpreting *Diakonia* in Germany," *Ecclesiology* 5.1 (2009) 69–81 (see also chapter 2 in this book).

5. Anni Hentschel, "Gibt es einen sozial-karitativ ausgerichteten Diakonat in den fruehchristlichen Gemeinden?," *Pastoraltheologie* 97.9 (2008), 290–306. See also her "Diakonie in der Bibel" in K.-D. Kottnik and E. Hauschildt, *Diakoniefibel: Grundwissen for alle, die mit Diakonie zu tun haben* (Rheinbach/Guetersloh: CMZ/Guetersloher Verlag, 2008), 17–20.

Similarly, in 2001, a working party of the Church of England presented to the General Synod its assessment of what it called the "rediscovery of the biblical idea of *diakonia*" in the following terms: "These findings have major implications for our understanding of the 'diaconal' aspect of the Church's mission and for the office of deacon in particular."[6] In 2007, the Faith and Order Advisory Group of the Church of England recognized what it called "immensely helpful pointers" in regard to what matters most, namely, the meaning of *diakonia* in the New Testament.[7] In an essay contributed in 2008 to David Clark's book, *The Diaconal Church*, Paula Gooder expressed the view that if the re-interpretation was right, "we have before us a new way of viewing not only the diaconate but ministry as a whole."[8] For more than a decade now the semantic profile of *diakonia* presented in the re-interpretation has underlain the lexicographical description in the Bauer-Danker lexicon of the early Christian Greek.[9]

On the other hand, representing the controlling paradigm, Herbert Haslinger published his extensive 2009 study on "foundations for the social work of the church" under the title of the German loanword *Diakonie*. In two of the book's 450 pages, Haslinger dismissed the re-interpretation along with Hentschel's endorsement of it.[10] Next, in 2011, Dierk Starnitzke, director of one German diaconal foundation and professor of New Testament at another, published a study on the biblical background of *diakonia*. The blurb announced that the study proceeds in

---

See further her latest study, *Gemeinde, Ämter, Dienste: Perspektiven zur neutestamentlichen Ekklesiologie* (Neukirchen – Vluyn: Neukirchener Verlag, 2013).

6. *For Such a Time as This: A Renewed Diaconate in the Church of England*. A report to the General Synod of the Church of England of a Working Party of the House of Bishops, GS 1407 (London: Church House Publishing, 2001), 31.

7. Faith and Order Advisory Group, *The Mission and Ministry of the Whole Church: Biblical, Theological and Contemporary Perspectives*, GS Misc 854, citing 16.

8. Paula Gooder, "Towards a Diaconal Church: Some Reflections on New Testament Material," in David Clark, ed., *The Diaconal Church: Beyond the Mould of Christendom* (Peterborough: Epworth, 2008), 99–108, citing 103.

9. *A Greek-English Lexicon of the New Testament and other Early Christian Literature*, 3rd edn, (BDAG), rev. and ed. Frederick William Danker, based on Water Bauer's *Griechisch-deutsches Wörterbuch zu den Schriften des Neuen Testaments und der frühchristlichen Literatur*, 6th edn, ed. Kurt Aland and Barbara Aland, with Viktor Reichmann, and on previous English editions by W. F. Arndt, F. W. Gingrich, and F. W. Danker (Chicago and London: University of Chicago Press, 2000).

10. Herbert Haslinger, *Diakonie: Grundlagen für die soziale Arbeit der Kirche* (Paderborn: Schoeningh, 2009), see 348–49. I reviewed the book in "A German Catholic view of Diaconate and Diakonia," *New Diaconal Review* no. 2 (May 2009), 41–46.

the light of the re-interpretation by Collins, but the book itself argues that the re-interpretation is half right and half wrong: right in regard to Paul's understanding of *diakonia* as an essential expression of his mission as proclamation, but wrong in regard to what *diakonia* means in the Gospels, where Jesus expresses and establishes the diaconal character as lowly and loving service.[11] Andrew Clarke had developed a similar critique in his studies of early Christian leadership in his books of 2000 and 2008.[12]

These are just a few names in illustration of the unresolved issue of what the deacon's title means and what the deacon's avocation might consist in. I do not aim to force those issues further. Instead, this chapter sketches the emergence of a particular understanding of the diaconate across what is now approaching two hundred years of modern church life. It identifies the origins of this understanding in what was little more than pious—certainly pre-critical—reflection upon what was considered the biblical tradition of the diaconate. The survey also illustrates how the modern diaconate has remained largely impervious to recent attempts to replace the older pervasive understanding with a re-interpretation of *diakonia*. The survey will shift from denomination to denomination, and this is as it has to be because the foundational notion of the modern diaconate has crossed virtually all denominational barriers, with a significant exception in the Orthodox tradition.

The Greek Orthodox Experience

In an address of July 2010 to the Sixteenth Clerical Symposium of the Greek Orthodox Archdiocese of America, John Chryssavgis made a set of observations about the standing of the diaconate in today's Greek Orthodox tradition.[13]

I summarize these as follows:

- In the Greek Orthodox Church, the diaconate is considered the first office of the ministry, but today has merely symbolic status.

---

11. Dierk Starnitzke, *Diakonie in biblischer Orientierung: Biblische Grundlagen, Ethische Konkretionen, Diakonisches Leitungshandeln* (Stuttgart: Kohlhammer, 2011), 11–37.

12. Andrew D. Clarke, *Serve the Community of the Church: Christians as Leaders and Ministers* (Grand Rapids, MI/Cambridge, UK: Eerdmans, 2000), see esp. 233–47; *A Pauline Theology of Church Leadership* (London: T&T Clark, 2008), 63–71; on Clarke, see further in the index.

13. http://ancientfaith.com/specials/sixteenth_biennial_clergy_symposium/the_diaconate, accessed July 6, 2011.

- Once a permanent office, it is now just a step to priesthood and beyond.
- A deacon, if he is to be anything in the church, is expected to move on.
- In fact, one hears that deaconship is not thought well of either by people or by priests.
- Indeed, its virtual disappearance is not a matter of regret.
- And this is hardly surprising when we confront the fact that the diaconate's theological profile is difficult to detect.

Such are the views of a deacon theologian reporting on the Greek Orthodox diaconate in 2010. These views echo those of George Khodr in a report to a consultation hosted by the Faith and Order Commission in 1964 on the diaconate in the Orthodox Church, and they illustrate the singularity of the Orthodox tradition in standing outside of the servant paradigm dominant in the West. In fact, Khodr was almost apologetic in recording that "the deacon is the minister who concerns himself with the litanies or antiphonal prayers" without consideration being given to any "social aspect" of a diaconal ministry.[14] Even the recommendation from an Orthodox consultation on diaconia in 1978 "to renew the role of deacons and deaconesses in the total life and witness of the Church" appears not to have had any lasting impact.[15]

About-turns in Pre-Reformation Churches of the West

This consultation, embracing views on the diaconate from nine major churches, marked the high point of mid-twentieth-century quandaries in relation to the diaconate. However, from Lukas Vischer's overview of the ecumenical scene—significantly titled "The Problem of the Diaconate"—and in spite of the commonly accepted principle that the deacon's office represents "in a special way...the characteristic of *diakonia* amidst the

---

14. George Khodr, "The Diaconate in the Orthodox Church," in *The Ministry of Deacons*, World Council Studies No. 2 (Geneva: World Council of Churches, 1965), 40–44 (citing 41). For a more academic description of the deacon in Orthodox churches—centering nonetheless on liturgy—see Peter Plank, "Der Diakonat in den orthodoxen Kirchen," *Internationale Kirchliche Zeitschrift* 95.4 (October 2005), 234–47 (with English summary).

15. "Report of the Consultation" in *The Orthodox Approach to Diaconia: Consultation on Church and Service*, Orthodox Academy of Crete, November 20–25, 1978 (Geneva: World Council of Churches Commission on Inter-Church Aid, Refugee and World Service, 1980), 13. The extensive keynote address by Alexandros Papaderos, "Liturgical Diaconia" (17–52), delivered in German, is heavily dependent on the German tradition of *Diakonie* discussed below.

variety of functions," we learn that no ecumenically agreed-upon theo-logical basis for the modern diaconate had yet emerged.[16] Already in 1957, initiatives within a small sector of the Roman Catholic Church were cut short by a concern in the Vatican that the theological groundwork was insecure. In October of that year, Pope Pius XII addressed a congress on lay apostolate. It is relevant to reflect on the fact that the expression *lay apostolate* was about the only expression available within the culture of the Roman Catholic Church in that period for what its congress was about; *lay ministry* was unheard of, and the term *ministry* itself was in practice reserved exclusively for the preaching and works of Jesus, and for the preaching of the Gospel and dispensation of the sacraments by the church's ordained members.

Within this context, then, Pope Pius XII noted the existence of moves to promote a permanent diaconate as "an ecclesiastical office independent of the priesthood."[17] This concept of a permanent diaconate he rather curtly dismissed, declaring that the time was not yet right.[18]

To say as much in 1957, it seems to me, was to anticipate what John Chryssavgis would still be saying fifty years later: the historical diaconate of the West was, to put it bluntly, of symbolic value without relevance to pastoral ministry within the church.

Seven years later, however, in October 1964, the Second Vatican Council voted 1903 votes to 242 in favor of restoring the diaconate as a full-time order.[19] As an about-turn in Vatican policy, a mere seven years is note-worthy—might one even say unprecedented? The policy was implemented by Paul VI in the 1967 Apostolic Letter *Sacrum diaconatus ordinem.*[20]

---

16. Lukas Vischer, "The Problem of the Diaconate" in *The Ministry of Deacons*, (see note 14) 14–29, citing 19.

17. "Guiding Principles of the Lay Apostolate," Address of His Holiness Pope Pius XII to The Second World Congress of the Lay Apostolate, October 5, 1957, available at http://www.papalencyclicals.net/Pius12.

18. See William T. Ditewig, "The Contemporary Renewal of the Diaconate," in James Keating, ed., *The Deacon Reader* (New York: Paulist Press, 2008), 27–55, esp. 35–36.

19. See accounts of the restoration in William T. Ditewig, *The Emerging Diaconate: Servant Leaders in a Servant Church* (New York: Paulist Press, 2007), 109–19; votes cited from 118, where Ditewig notes that in a separate vote on admitting married men to ordination, the 242 votes *contra* blew out to 629. On the theological debates, see Tim O'Donnell, "How the Ecclesiological Visions of Vatican II Framed the Ministry of Permanent Deacons," *Worship* 85.5 (September 2011), 425–46.

20. See the English text at the Vatican website: http://www.vatican.va/holy_father/paul_vi/motu_proprio/documents/hf_p-vi_motu-proprio_19670618_sacrum-diaconatus_en.html.

By contrast, a Working Party of the Church of England's Advisory Council for the Church's Ministry concluded its reflections in *Deacons in the Church* with the proposal that "the diaconate be allowed to lapse."[21]

And yet, as in the Roman church, there was another remarkable turn around within comparatively few years. In spite of the recommendation of 1974, in 1987 the General Synod of the Church of England enacted legislation enabling the creation of "an ordained distinctive diaconate" for both men and women.[22]

Thus, between 1964 and 1988, the two major pre-Reformation churches of the West sought to reactivate a diaconate that had been dormant for almost fifteen hundred years. Both churches established the diaconate as an individual church order, calling it permanent or distinctive.

In Churches of the Reformation

If we glance, now, at churches of the Reformation we find a different story about deacons. The early reformers set about totally recasting the shape of ministry in the church and, not surprisingly, found the medieval diaconate something of an anomaly. On the one hand it appeared to have a scriptural foundation—largely because of Acts 6 and 1Tim. 3—but on the other hand it appeared to have totally lost its bearings.

Luther dismissed its liturgical function as irrelevant, and as for feeding the poor after the manner of Acts 6, he came to think that in a Christian nation it was the Ruler who should take up that responsibility.[23]

Calvin was much more particular about what the scriptures appeared to enjoin, and he concluded there were two types of deacon, both conformable with Acts 6 and with what is said about widows at 1 Tim. 5:10: The widow "must be well attested for her good works, as one who has...washed the saints' feet, helped the afflicted, and devoted herself to doing good in every way."

Accordingly, one type of deacon would be male, whom Calvin thought should receive the imposition of hands; these would be charged with

---

21. *Deacons in the Church* (Westminster: Church Information Office, 1974), 33.

22. This development was influenced by the recommendation of the report to the House of Bishops (not published until January 1988), *Deacons in the Ministry of the Church*, GS 802 (London: Church House Publishing, 1988), citing above 119.

23. See early developments under Luther in J. E. Olson, *One Ministry Many Roles: Deacons and Deaconesses through the Centuries* (St Louis: Concordia, 1992), 97–104.

administering moneys dedicated to almsgiving. The other type would be female, would not receive imposition of hands, and would be responsible for care of the sick.

Not surprisingly, for the next two hundred years and more, the Calvinist tradition experienced much uncertainty and repositioning on such arrangements.[24]

In fact, across the Protestant tradition well into the nineteenth century, the story of the Protestant deacon had more or less petered out. James Monroe Barnett even went so far as to state of post-Reformation centuries, "The office of the deacon historically has not been a part of either Lutheranism or Methodism. The Presbyterians, Reformed, Congregationalists, Baptists, and Disciples have a diaconate that would appear to be a lay ministry."[25] (Barnett is referring here to a continuing commitment on the part of these churches to social welfare.)

In this context we better understand what led a United Methodist book on the diaconate to open in 1987 with the questions: "What is going on in the United Methodist Church, and what is this diaconate that is causing such a stir?"[26]

Ecumenical Intervention

In short, by considering the diaconate in 2011, we are taking further a vibrant discussion that had resumed in the 1950s, a period when discussion of all aspects of ministry largely occurred within the context of ecumenical relations. Enthusiasm for ministry was greatly raised by the level of accord achieved at the Fourth International Conference on Faith and Order in Montreal in 1963.In 1982, the Faith and Order Commission of the World

---

24. John Calvin, *Institutes of the Christian Religion*, Eng. trans. H. Beveridge, vol. 2 (London: John Clarke, 1962), 322, Bk IV.iii.9. Further, Olson, *One Ministry*, 97–119; E. A. McKee, *Diakonia in the Classical Reformed Tradition and Today* (Grand Rapids, MI: Eerdmans, 1989), 61–82; *John Calvin on the Diaconate and Liturgical Almsgiving* (Geneva: Droz, 1984), 127–37.

25. *The Diaconate: A Full and Equal Order*, rev. edn (Valley Forge, PA: Trinity Press International, 1995), 156.

26. R. S. Keller, G. F. Moede, and M. E. Moore, *Called to Serve: The United Methodist Diaconate* (Nashville: Division of Diaconal Ministry of the General Board of Education and Ministry, 1987), 1. A chart at 52–53 illustrates the variety and complexity of "The Diaconate in North American Churches." See further developments in Ben. L. Hartley and Paul E. Van Buren, *The Deacon: Ministry through Words of Faith and Acts of Love* (Nashville: The United Methodist Church, 1999).

Council of Churches published its statement on ministry in the booklet *Baptism, Eucharist, and Ministry*, a document it described as "the fruit of a 50-year process of study."[27] Perhaps surprisingly, the document described the church's ministry as "threefold,"[28] comprising, that is, bishops, presbyters, and deacons. The commission was aware that not all churches possess such a pattern of ministry but dared to ask such churches, nonetheless, "whether the threefold pattern ... does not have a powerful claim."

Given the uncertain history of the diaconate and its uneven representation among forms of ministry across the churches, *Baptism, Eucharist, and Ministry* was perhaps inviting controversy by giving the threefold pattern of ministry such prominence. Some churches get by on a theology of one order of ministry, with ministry of Word and sacrament and ministry of service being forms within this. Shadows of controversy on the issues did in fact fall across some pages of the published report.[29]

Whatever of such still-unresolved controversy, the fact that the diaconate had advanced from its relative historical obscurity to feature so prominently in the leading ecumenically agreed statement on ministry demands explanation.

A Pastoral Explanation

This sketch of the diaconate's rise to prominence since the 1960s could easily suggest that the impetus came from the enormous and revitalizing gathering of Roman Catholic bishops at the Second Vatican Council (1962–65). As noted, here was the first reinstatement of an ordained diaconate that was not just part of a process through which, as Chryssavgis remarked, deacons were expected to move on to higher things.

In its initiative, however, the Second Vatican Council had itself been open to two influences. The first was from within a sector of its own experience, and this—to be honest—was an increasingly bad experience.

This was the era when, with two World Wars now out of the way, the church in parts of Western Europe had been taking reality checks on the efficacy of its mission. The new sociology of religion was revealing the gap

27. World Council of Churches, *Baptism, Eucharist, and Ministry*, Faith and Order Paper no. 111 (Geneva: World Council of Churches, 1982).

28. Ibid., 25 (para. 25).

29. Ibid., 125–26.

between the ambit of the mission and the realities in the suburbs and the countryside.

Awareness of the realities was especially keen in Belgium and France, where new forms of pastoral endeavor were being pioneered. Roman Catholic minorities in anglophone countries stood by in horror as reports circulated of a de-Christianization of France. France—they heard whisper—was the church's "eldest daughter"! Widely read in the 1950s was Maisie Ward's *France Pagan?*

In fact, *France Pagan?* was a translation and adaptation of a book of 1943, *France, Land of Mission.* Its authors, Henri Godin and Yvan Daniel, exposed a de-Christianized proletariat; its millions were untouched by the church's traditional pastoral strategy. In addition, the authors declared the bishops' policy of a workers' Catholic Action futile, and laid the blame for the impasse upon "current conditions governing the priesthood."[30]

A French Dominican, Michel-Dominique Epagneul, observed the same estrangement throughout the vast French rural communities. The crisis inspired him—also in 1943—to found a religious order of priests and auxiliary brothers to represent the Christian gospel exclusively among these rural communities. The members went forth under the name of "Missionary Brothers of the Countryside."[31]

Experience soon saw "auxiliary brothers" carrying out pastoral functions within areas traditionally associated with priests: "They collaborated," he wrote, "in building the unity of faith, love and worship among the living members of the body of Christ."[32] Before long, Epagneul was wondering why such pastoral workers were not being ordained as deacons, and in February 1957 published an article to this effect in the influential journal from Louvain *Nouvelle Revue Théologique* under the title (translated) "The Role of Deacons in Today's Church."[33]

---

30. Henri Godin and Yvan Daniel, *La France: pays de mission* (Lyon: Abeille, 1943), 106 (cited from amazon.com). For the period, see Gerd-Rainer Horn, *Western European Liberation Theology 1929–1959* (Oxford: Oxford University Press, 2008).

31. The website is under their French name, Frères missionnaires des campagnes.

32. "Der Diakon in den 'Religiösen Instituten': Wie ich dazu kam für einige unserer 'Frères Auxiliaires' den Diakonat in Erwägung zu ziehen," in Karl Rahner and Herbert Vorgrimler, eds, *Diaconia in Christo: Über die Erneuerung des Diakonates,* Quaestiones Disputatae 15/16 (Freiburg: Herder, 1962), 398–401, citing 400.

33. "Role des diacres dans L'Église d'aujourd'hui," *NRT* 79.1 (1957), 153–68.

As noted earlier, it was in October of this year that Pope Pius XII acknowledged the existence of moves for a permanent diaconate but adjudged them premature. The pope's principal objective in this was to uphold the demarcation of hierarchical powers in the context of a developing situation of lay collaboration. On the evidence of Epagneul's call to have his "auxuliary brothers" ordained deacons so that they could carry out most of the normal pastoral and liturgical activities of the priests, the demarcation might be seen as already under threat, and Pope Pius was not sure what further effect the introduction of a permanent diaconate might have upon the clarity of this definitive demarcation. He certainly knew of Epagneul's article, which had appeared in February, and Epagneul had himself forwarded a copy to Pius. By April, Epagneul had already been informed by the Vatican that the pope had passed the article to the Holy Office (today's Congregation for the Doctrine of the Faith) for assessment.[34]

Thus, in France the initial moves for a permanent Roman Catholic diaconate were driven by pastoral needs. The same motivation was at work in Latin America. Here profound concerns attended the totally unmanageable shortage of priests. The pain of the shortage was exacerbated by knowledge of the burgeoning Protestant missionary activity. Similarly, in debates on the question of the diaconate at the Second Vatican Council, arguments were driven mainly by the pastoral potential of the diaconate, especially in places ewhere priests were in short supply. The council bishops supportive of the notion of a permanent diaconate stemmed mainly from mission lands of that era (Africa, Asia) but also from Latin America.[35]

A German Alternative

Parallel to Epagneul's pastoral initiative, a second major idea was at play in France. This was the vision Jean Rodhain, the founder of French Catholic Aid (*Secours catholique*) during World War II, cultivated of a diaconate of charity. In 1959, two months after Pope John XXIII had announced his intention to call an ecumenical council, Rodhain organized and chaired

34. See the editorial note to Paul Winninger and Joseph Hornef, "Le Renouveau du diaconat: Situation présente de la controverse," *Nouvelle Revue Théologique* 83.4 (1961), 337–66.

35. For a dramatic account of motivations of council members supporting and opposing the restoration of a permanent diaconate see Tim O'Donnell, "Ecclesiological Visions."

a meeting at Royaumont near Paris which canvased the concept of a permanent diaconate and advocated petitioning forthcoming council members to promote the project. The main focus, as the petition expressed it, was "the offices of charitable work."[36] In 1960, Rodhain expressed his vision in a vibrant letter to a seminary rector urging the creation of the diaconate as "a specialist body charged with the service of tables."[37] His support in this appeal he identified as the German bishops who favored offering diaconal ordination to the many men already engaged in the tasks of the German *Caritas* organization.The exotic product was clearly in evidence by 1961. In opening their account of the renewal of the diaconate, Winninger and Hornef reported the upsurge and provenance of this alternative product with these words: "The idea of bringing the diaconate back to life is relatively recent...and is expanding rapidly. It began in Germany."[38]Moreover, the upsurge took its rise from developments outside the Roman Catholic ecclesial tradition. This ministerial product is of a Protestant provenance, specifically German Lutheran and Reformed. Hence its "exotic" character in the face of the influences we have been considering.

Given the limited context we are working within, the story is most conveniently sketched against the background of the man who was consumed by a discovery he had made. The man was Hannes Kramer (1929–2001), a Roman Catholic forest worker turned social worker from Freiburg in the mountains of southwest Germany.

Freiburg was the headquarters of the Roman Catholic Bishops' Caritas organization, which Kramer was early attracted to because of its work on behalf of the disadvantaged. This was post–World War II Germany. Inevitably, Kramer was exposed to the parallel endeavours of the (Lutheran) Evangelical Churches (EKD) of the various German states. In its outreach, the EKD did not operate under the Roman Catholic Latin term *caritas* but under the German logo of "*Diakonie.*"

---

36. See the petition in Appendix 2 of Patrick McCaslin and Michael G. Lawler, *Sacrament of Service* (New York: Paulist Press, 1986), 141–50; the identity of the eighty-two prominent theologians who signed the petition accompany the text in its earlier publication in *Worship* 37 (1963), 513–20. Names include F. X. Arnold, Yves Congar, Bernard Häring, Josef Hornef, Hubert Jedin, Karl Rahner, Wilhelm Schamoni, and Paul Winninger.

37. The text of the letter is accessible on the site of the French national committee of the diaconate, http://www.diaconat.cef.fr/documentation/4_Documents_historiques.

38. Winninger and Hornef, "Le Renouveau," 337 (see note 34).

Diakonie

Within Germany *Diakonie* was an undertaking of both a federal office within the EKD and of each state church within the EKD. There are twenty-two of these. *Diakonie* remains today a vast organization, employing upwards of five hundred thousand people in Christian social service.

A small proportion of these are *Diakonen* and *Diakoninnen* (deacons and deaconesses). The German titles warrant mention because through these terms, *Diakonie*, *Diakonen*, and *Diakoninnen*, we have a direct link with the origins of the diaconate in the New Testament and with the Greek terms used there. For simplicity's sake, we will represent these with the one word: *diakonia*.

In the New Testament, *diakonia* actually applies directly to church officers in only two passages (Phil. 1:1; 1 Tim. 3:8), with a third passage also usually brought into play (Acts 6:1–6). Of crucial significance, however, is that in ninety-seven other passages *diakonia* is commonly understood to carry values arising from humble and loving service to people in need, be that physical or spiritual need.

Not unnaturally, perhaps, these values of humble and loving service are then read into the passages about these church officers, inviting us to think of them as deacons extending the Christian community's loving services to those in need of them.

Nineteenth-century Origins of Diakonie Within the EKD

Such ideas about deacons began to take on institutional shape in the 1830s under the prophetic initiatives of men like Johann Hinrich Wichern in Hamburg, Theodor Fliedner (and his wife Friederike) in Kaiserswerth, and other mainly Lutheran pastors elsewhere in the regional churches of Germany. These men founded communities—of women mainly—which engaged in diaconal activities toward the needy.[39]

Over the next century, *Diakonie* was as familiar to Germans as the combined operations of organizations like the Brotherhood of St Lawrence,

---

39. Numerous websites provide information on these developments. See my summary account in *Diakonia*, 8–11. Very interesting as a near contemporary view is the essay from the September 1860 *Quarterly Review* by John Saul Howson, reprinted (c. 2005) by Elibron Classics (www.elibron.com) as *Deaconesses or The Official Help of Women in Parochial Work and in Charitable Institutions*. Florence Nightingale's experience at Kaiserswerth is recounted in Cecil Woodham-Smith, *Florence Nightingale 1820–1910* (London: Constable, 1950).

the St Vincent de Paul Society, and the Salvation Army are to us. One effect of these swathes of social service across the German states was to make virtually unbreakable linkages between *Diakonie* and the reading of passages in the New Testament where the *diakonia* words occurred.

Thus if Jesus tells a story about royal attendants failing to feed the hungry, and the story includes one of the *diakonia* words, then Jesus is taken to be equating *diakonia* with loving service of the hungry, the sick, and the abandoned people of our worlds (Matt. 25:44). If Jesus says of himself that he has come to engage in a *diakonia* that will involve giving up his life as a ransom, then *diakonia* takes on an absolute value that the church must embody in its own way of life and in its structures of ministry (Mark 10:45). The hermeneutical process operating here was described as early as 1965 by Bo Reicke in an essay on deacons in the following terms: "The concept of *diakonia* receives a new meaning through the fact that Jesus describes himself as the model of service to one's neighbor and of *sacrifice* for many."[40] In accord with this line of thinking, when Paul proclaims himself to be an apostle of the Gentiles, he must conform to this *diakonic* pattern. Hence we read of him identifying his mission as his *diakonia* (2 Cor. 5:18).[41]

This powerful message from the New Testament about *diakonia* as a summons to members at all levels of the church, and exemplified in the daily life of the communities of deaconesses and deacons, led to an increasingly extensive library of theology about *diakonia*. A dozen or two new books on *Diakonie* still appear annually from German publishers.

The Diakonic Consensus

More significant, perhaps, is the fact that once the custom of equating *diakonia* with loving and humble service was established in German culture, German dictionaries of Greek New Testament words included service values in their definitions. Deaconesses, pastors, theological students—of whom there were many thousands in Germany—were all invited to embrace the new servant theology.

---

40. Bo Reicke, "Deacons in the New Testament and in the Early Church," *The Ministry of Deacons*, World Council Studies No. 2 (Geneva: World Council of Churches, 1965), 8–13, citing 8.

41. In more recent years, Andrew D. Clarke has strongly advocated this line of argument in *Serve the Community of the Church: Christians as Leaders and Ministers* (Grand Rapids, MI/Cambridge, UK: Eerdmans, 2000), see esp. 233–47; *A Pauline Theology of Church Leadership* (London: T&T Clark, 2008), 63–71.

Some names and titles associated with this will be familiar to many: Kittel's *Theological Dictionary of the New Testament*; Eduard Schweizer's *Church Order in the New Testament*; Ernst Käsemann's essay, "Ministry and Community in the New Testament"; Karl Barth's "The Order of the Community" in *Church Dogmatics* Part IV, Hans Kung's *The Church*, and so on.[42]

A Roman Catholic Convert to Diakonie

In Freiburg of the 1950s, Hannes Kramer was totally enthused—as well as challenged—by *diakonia*. The *diakonia* emerging from the nineteenth-century German Lutheran deaconess movement provided Kramer with both rationale and inspiration for the kind of social work he had committed himself to in the Roman Catholic *Caritasverband*. From our viewpoint sixty years later, we can surmise that, under this persistent *diakonic* influence, Kramer would inevitably have had to begin thinking of the possibility of a new kind of deacon in the Roman Catholic Church.

Tragically, Kramer and his wife Erika—who was especially dedicated to care for the homeless—died together in a car accident near Freiburg in 2001. He was seventy-two and left no major study of the diaconate. Through the journal *Diaconia Christi* of the International Diaconate Centre—for decades he was on the committees of both the journal and the Centre (then in Freiburg)—we can, nonetheless, piece together a record of his critical contribution to the establishment of the Roman Catholic permanent diaconate, including its connection with the understanding of *diakonia* that had underpinned the Lutheran deacon movement since the 1840s.

In his obituary for Karl Rahner in 1984,[43] Kramer recalled his first meeting with the theologian in Innsbruck in 1948. Kramer was not yet twenty years of age and was, as he recalled, a simple woodcutter who did not know to whom he was talking. He confided to the theologian that he wanted to become a permanent deacon, and was relieved Rahner did not think him crazy, as others did to whom he mentioned the dream.

By 1955, Kramer had brought together his first "deacon circle" in Munich, and Rahner delivered to this informal and unconventional group

---

42. Such names recur in discussions throughout Chapters 1, 3, 11–13.

43. "Professor Pater Karl Rahner, SJ, beg. 5.3.1904 in Freiburg, gestorben 30.3.1984 in Innsbruck," *Diaconia Christi* 19.2–3 (August 1984), 64–67.

his first theological paper on the contemporary renewal of the diaconate in the Roman Catholic Church.Kramer felt he was in a position a few years later to request Rahner to publish a major collection of studies on the diaconate. In 1962, forty papers by international scholars appeared as the 650-page volume *Diaconia in Christo*.[44] This was the very eve of the Second Vatican Council. For Kramer the publication was "the breakthrough" he needed. The volume gave theological credibility to the petition his group had circulated among all the bishops prior to the council.[45]

Kramer reported that he and his many colleagues "had nothing else in mind but the renewal and recreation of a permanent office of service which would consist in and by reason of the praxis of the *diakonia* of Jesus Christ and of the communities of the New Testament era."[46]

Collaboration with the EKD

One contributor to the volume *Diaconia in Christo* was the Lutheran scholar Herbert Krimm, who wrote on the Lutheran diaconate. Krimm had already published the first of his volumes collating sources on the history of *diakonia* as understood within the German Lutheran tradition.[47] In his preface Krimm was precise about what that understanding was: *Diakonie,* far from being a marginal factor in church life, was a concept necessarily emerging from the heart of the message about the Kingdom of God.[48]

Kramer's later chronicle of Roman Catholic developments prior to and within the Second Vatican Council puts his association with this Lutheran *diakonic* framework in a broader context.[49] In the early 1950s,

44. See note 32 above.

45. This "formal request" (see note 36 above) was supported by French colleagues—Rodhain in particular—but was made in the name of "the original deacon circle" of Munich; see McCaslin and Lawler there, 141. See also the historian of the German initiative, Margaret Morche, *Zur Erneuerung des Ständigen Diakonats* (Freiburg im B.: Lambertus, 1996), emphasizing the close association of the movement with the German *Caritas* office in Freiburg. Extracts from the book do the same in "Persönlichkeiten im Caritasbereich und ihr Einsatz für den Diakonat," *Diaconia Christi* 31.1/2 (1996), 58–65.

46. "Professor Pater Karl Rahner," 22.

47. *Quellen zur Geschichte der Diakonie: I Altertum und Mittelalter* (Stuttgart: Evangelisches Verlagswerk, 1960).

48. Ibid., 8.

49. "Chronik: Beitrag der Caritas zur Erneuerung des Ständigen Diakonates," *Diaconia Christi* 21.2/3 (July 1986), 15–19.

he recorded, contacts were begun with the *Diakonisches Werk*, the head-quarters of the whole *diakonic* undertaking of EKD; with Lutheran insti-tutes for the education and training of deacons (there are some fifteen of these within EKD); with Krimm, the director of the flagship Institute for *Diakonic* Studies at the University of Heidelberg; with the broader European Association of Lutheran Deacons; and with the World Council of Churches' Faith and Order Commission, whose support for the diac-onate has already been noted.

Over many years Kramer insisted on the ecumenical character of the theological investigations undertaken within the Roman Catholic International Diaconate Centre.[50] To his mind, ecumenical collaboration was of the nature of the diaconate because *diakonia* was itself an expres-sion of the heart of the gospel. Indeed, a later decision by the Vatican to put an end to the close collaboration—a recurrent anxiety on this matter is evident in issues of the Diaconate Centre's journal *Diaconia Christi* across the years 1992–95—was a cruel blow to Kramer and his ecumenical col-leagues. The Vatican required the German Bishops Conference to curtail its financing of the International Diaconate Centre unless the ecumenical bond was broken.[51]

Current Situation

In this outline of current developments, I have not mentioned ordin-ation. In English-language discussion, an ordained deacon can be male or female, while one can assume that a deaconess is not ordained. A dea-coness, so called, is or was normally a member of a community or at least of an ecclesial body of women dedicated or commissioned to diaconate understood as works of charity and justice.

Briefly, pre-Reformation churches ordain deacons; post-Reformation churches vary, even within their own tradition. Thus, Swedish Lutherans ordain deacons, but the state churches of Germany do not. Similarly, the Evangelical Lutheran Church in America reviewed the question closely but

---

50. Claude Bridel, the Reformed theologian with special interests in diaconate, was a long-standing member of the board of the International Diaconate Centre; in the same issue as Kramer's "Chronik" (preceding note), Bridel wrote on the subject of "Der Diakonat als ökumenische Erfahrung" (20–24), concluding with a warm recognition of collaboration with Kramer.

51. Conversation with Margaret Morche in Freiburg, September 1997.

responded negatively in a conference vote, whereas the Missouri Synod has never sought to ordain deacons.

Within the EKD, especially throughout the 1990s, there was much painful soul-searching on the issue.[52] In 1996, the EKD's theological committee, comprising some twenty-five theologians, pastors, and senior church officers (nearly half of these being professors of theology), was commissioned to examine the possibility of ordaining deacons. The committee made a positive recommendation. In 2002, however, with this recommendation having been "overwhelmingly" rejected in some state churches, the EKD synod passed the decision back to the member churches. This was to be no small consultation: EKD comprises some twenty-two state churches.

In the EKD's sister church in Sweden, by contrast, the processes worked along cleaner lines. Over the same time period, the Swedish diaconate had rather painlessly achieved the status of "an ordained ministry in the Church." Indeed, as the chief architect of its theology, Sven-Erik Brodd, put it in 1999, "Today it is absolutely clear. The Church of Sweden *ordains* bishops, deacons and priests."[53] Brodd finds in the Swedish Church's ordination the raison d'etre of the diaconate. Ordination establishes the person as an ecclesial officer whose activity in the name of the church is thus necessarily diaconal, whatever the nature of the activity.[54]

Ordained or not, Protestant deacons devote themselves to the same works of charity and justice. In the Roman Catholic Church there is no deacon without ordination, and women are excluded from diaconal ordination (although this exclusion is not "definitively" established as it is in regard to presbyteral ordination).[55] Constant questions revolve, however, about the *proprium* or identity of the deacon.

---

52. For historical documents and theological comment of this period, see links at http://www.diakonie.de/studien-und-referate-2975.htm. See further discussion in Wilfried Brandt, *Für eine bekennende Diakonie: Beiträge zu einem evangelischen Verständnis des Diakonats* (Neukirchen-Vluyn: Aussat, 2001).

53. "The Deacon in the Church of Sweden," in G. Borgegård and C. Hall, *The Ministry of the Deacon* (Uppsala: Nordic Ecumenical Council, 1999), 97–140, citing 132, 121.

54. Sven-Erik Brodd, "A Diaconate Emerging from Ecclesiology: Towards a Constructive Theology on the Office of Deacon," *Internationale Kirchliche Zeitschrift* 95.4 (October 2005), 266–88.

55. Benedict XVI's motu proprio *Omnium in mentem* of October 10, 2009, introduced changes to Canon Law (nos. 1008–09) that bring it in line with the revised *Catechism of the Catholic Church*: no. 875 declares that, whereas bishops and presbyters have "the mission and faculty to act in the person of Christ the Head," deacons "receive the strength (*vim*) to serve the people of God in the *diaconia* of liturgy, word and charity." Were women to be

The Constraining Idea

The Second Vatican Council described deacons as "dedicated [by ordin-ation] to the People of God in the service/*diaconia* of the liturgy, of the Gospel and of works of charity."[56] This statement, broad as it is, has been central to all formulations of the identity of the deacon and of the nature of the deacon's role. However, the inclusion within the Latin text of the Greek loanword *diaconia* has invited an extraordinay emphasis upon the diac-onate as "a service (*diakonia*) of love" (to borrow the phrase used by a US study committee).[57] This appeal to *diakonia* and the understanding given to it can only be attributed to the influence of the conventional German understanding of *Diakonie*. Hannes Kramer's record of the conferencing and lobbying in Rome at this period of the council is a sure sign of such influence at work.[58]

A further and unmistakable sign is the phrasing adopted by Walter Kasper, longtime patron of the International Diaconate Centre at Regensburg during his time as bishop there. In one of the most widely cited papers on the diaconate, delivered as a lecture at an international con-ference organized by the International Diaconate Centre in Bressanone in 1997, Kasper clearly alludes to the phrase from *Lumen gentium*—"the *dia-conia* of liturgy, of the Gospel and of works of charity"—but lists the three tasks of the deacon as "liturgy, preaching, and *diaconia*." Here, the term *diaconia* replaces *Lumen gentium*'s phrase "works of charity."[59] Kasper was thus not only misrepresenting *Lumen gentium* but he was also exposing the German conviction that *diakonia, Diakonie,* and "works of charity" are synonymous.

---

ordained deacons, this teaching would imply that they would not thereby receive that cap-acity to act "in the person of Christ the Head" with which the sacerdotal orders (episcopal, presbyteral) are endowed.

56. *Lumen gentium* 29: "in diaconia liturgiae, verbi et cartitatis."

57. Catholic Theological Society of America, "Restoration of the Office of Deacon As a Lifetime State: A Report to the U. S. Bishops," *Worship* 45.4 (April 1971), 186–98, citing 193.

58. "Chronik," 18.

59. Walter Cardinal Kasper, "The Diaconate," *Leadership in the Church: How Traditional Roles Can Serve the Christian Community Today,* Eng. trans. (New York: Crossroad Publishing Company, 2003), 13–44, citing 40. The German: "Durch seinen Dienst in Liturgie, Verkündigung und Diakonie…"; see "Der Diakon in ekklesiologischer Sicht angesichts der gegenwärtigen Herausforderungen in Kirche und Gesellschaft," *Diaconia Christi* 32.3–4 (1997), 13–33, citing 30.

In 1990, Kasper's former fellow German theologian, Joseph Ratzinger, stepped away from this widespread conviction. In fact, Ratzinger saw it as damaging to the theology of ministry that underpins the ordained ministries. Opening an address to the Synod of Bishops on the theology of priesthood in October of 1990, Ratzinger asserted that Roman Catholic theologians had undermined the theology of priesthood by uncritically adopting the consensus view of ministry/*diakonia* current in Protestant ecclesiology. In a note supporting his assertion he drew on the re-interpretation of *diakonia* made available through the linguistic research in the thesis that was to become *Diakonia: Re-interpreting the Ancient Sources*.[60] In more recent writings during his papacy, Joseph Ratzinger's predilection for his native German *Diakonie* shows through, strongly coloring the thinking about charity throughout part 2 of his first encyclical, *Deus caritas est*.[61]

Kasper concluded his own address with the comprehensive statement—echoing so much of the encomiums of *diakonia* over the last sixty years—"The church cannot exist without *diaconia*, and the church indeed has a particular office for *diaconia*."[62]

Speakers of English are not so immediately aware of how widely embraced these perceptions of *diakonia* now are. I have emphasized their German provenance, but loanwords like the German *Diakonie* inhabit the speech of churchworkers, deacons, and church leaders across central and northern Europe. Why the same has not happened in the

---

60. Joseph Ratzinger, "On the Essence of the Priesthood," *Called to Communion: Understanding the Church Today*, Eng. trans. (San Francisco: Ignatius Press, 1996), 106; "Vom Wesen des Priestertums," *Zur Gemeinschaft gerufen: Kirche heute verstehen* (Freiburg: Herder, 1991/2005), 101–24, see 103.

61. See nos. 20–25; at no. 25, the explicit alignment of "the ministry of charity/*Dienst der Liebe*" with *diakonia*. The English-language website of the Pontifical Council *Cor Unum* for Human and Christian Development states that its objective is "to strengthen the Christian roots of Charity," which the German-language website states as "*um die christlichen Wurzel der Diakonie zu stärken*." Accessed September 12, 2010, at http://www.vatican.va/roman_curia/pontifical_councils/corunum/corunum_en/profilo_en/istituzione_en.html, with link there to the German. On the prominence of the *diakonic* theme in Benedict XVI's agenda, see E. Chome, "La diaconie: un bain évangelique de jouvence à notre solidarité?," *Nouvelle Revue Théologique* 132 (2010), 255–66. Such usage inevitably spills over into theological publications, as in Stefan Sander, *Das Amt des Diakons: Eine Handreichung* (Freiburg: Herder, 2008), 16–19. The Dutch volume *Diaconie in beweging: Handboek diaconiewetenschap*, H. Crijns et al., eds (Kampen: Kok, 2011), adopted Benedict XVI's statement about "the ministry of charity (*diakonia*)" being an "expression of the church's very being" (*Deus caritas est*, note 25) as its inscription.

62. Kasper, "The Diaconate," 43.

English-speaking world I do not know. Our theology of ministry and of the diaconate speaks, nonetheless, with a *diakonic* accent. Consequently, our translations of the New Testament can be as disturbingly distorted as translations in other tongues in those passages where the biblical authors used words like *diakonia* but meant something different, something unrelated to what *Diakonie* now says to us. Virtually all translations now appear to be teaching us that, in going to his death, the Son of Man was aiming to "serve people" (Mark 10:45).[63]

The constraints which this international consensus has put upon translators are a large part of the bondage we have made the center of these reflections upon "the ties that bind."

The German Whistleblower

Hans-Jürgen Benedict was a professor of theology at the revered diaconal institute, Das Rauhe Haus, founded in Hamburg in 1833 by Johann Hinrich Wichern for the rescue and nurture of the abandoned girls and boys of the city. Deeply committed to the *Diakonie* that Das Rauhe Haus was still renowned for, Benedict was made aware of the re-interpretation of *diakonia* in the course of a lecture in Finland by the Norwegian theologian Kjell Nordstokke.

On his return to Hamburg, Benedict read my 1990 research volume, *Diakonia: Re-interpreting the Ancient Sources*, was convinced by its argument, and set about advocating the re-interpretation through an article published in 2000 in the leading journal of German pastoral theology.[64] His provocative title read in part: "Does the EKD's claim about *Diakonie* rest upon a misunderstanding?"

Benedict did not mince words about the size of the problem confronting German theology of *Diakonie*. I call him the whistleblower. It turns out that he may have been whistling in the wind. On the one hand he attributed the neglect of the new research to the fact that his contemporaries were disinclined to draw their theology from foreign-language sources. On the other hand, he came to recognize that if *Diakonie* is, indeed, a

---

63. This is the translation recommended in J. P. Louw and E. A. Nida, *Greek-English Lexicon of the New Testament Based on Semantic Domains*, 2nd edn (New York 1989), section 35B.

64. Hans-Jürgen Benedict, "Beruht der Anspruch der evangelischen Diakonie auf einer Missinterpretation der antiken Quellen? John N. Collins Untersuchung 'Diakonia,'" *Pastoraltheologie* 89 (2000), 343–64.

German misnomer for what the New Testament is meaning to convey by *diakonia*, then 2006 (the year of his lecture on this issue)[65] was too late in the day to debunk the neologism. In his view, *Diakonie* is a logo too heavily embossed on German religious consciousness to be removed.[66]

The import of this paper runs counter to that. So long as the inflated and unfounded values that are associated with the German term *Diakonie* remain tied to the Greek *diakonia* of the New Testament, we will remain in bondage to a distorted view of the nature of the diaconate and be constrained to limit the scope of deacons' pastoral potential. My broad views on that potential form the concluding pages of my 2002 book, *Deacons and the Church: Making connections between old and new* (pp 128–44).

---

65. Hans-Jürgen Benedict, "Diakonie als Dazwischengehen und Beauftragung. Die Collins-Debatte aus der Sicht ihres Anstossgebers," *Barmherzigheit und Diakonie: Von der rettenden Liebe zum gelingenden Leben* (Stuttgart 2008), 129–37. See Benedict's comments on initial German scholarly attitudes to the new research, 130.

65. Ibid., 133.

Selected Publications by John N. Collins

BOOKS

2011. *Diakonia: Re-interpreting the Ancient Sources*, Oxford Scholarship Online/ Religion.

2009. *Diakonia: Re-interpreting the Ancient Sources*, pb POD (New York: Oxford University Press).

2004. *Los diáconos y la Iglesia*, trad. C. Ruiz-Garrido (Barcelona: Herder).

2002. *Deacons and the Church: Making Connections Between Old and New* (Leominster, UK: Gracewing; Harrisburg, PA: Morehouse).

1992. *Are All Christians Ministers?* (Collegeville, MN: Liturgical Press).

1990. *Diakonia: Re-interpreting the Ancient Sources* (New York: Oxford University Press).

ARTICLES

2012a. "A Monocultural Usage: διακον- Words in Classical, Hellenistic, and Patristic Sources." *Vigiliae Christianae* 66.3, 287–309.

2012b. "Theology of Ministry in the Twentieth Century: Ongoing Problems or New Orientations?" *Ecclesiology* 8.1, 11–32.

2011. [co-author Kjell Nordstokke] "Diakonia—Theory and Practice." In Kjell Nordstokke, *Liberating Diakonia* (Trondheim: Tapir), 41–47.

2010a. "Re-thinking 'Eyewitnesses' in the Light of 'Servants of the Word' (Lk 1:2)." *Expository Times* 121.9, June, 447–52.

2010b. "For Deacons It's Not a Matter of 'Either-Or' or 'Both-And.'" *New Diaconal Review* 4, November, 38–43.

2009a. "From διακονία to Diaconia Today. Historical Aspects of Interpretation." *Diakonian tutkimus* 2, 134–48. Online at www.dts.fi.

2009b. "Is the Diaconal Ministry Based on a Misunderstanding?" *Diakonian tutkimus* 2, 149–56. Online at www.dts.fi.

266 *Selected Publications*
2009c. "A German Catholic View of Diaconate and Diakonia." *New Diaconal Review* 2, May, 41–46. Review of Herbert Haslinger, *Diakonie: Grundlagen für soziale Arbeit der Kirche* (Paderborn: Schöningh, 2009).

2009d. "Re-interpreting Diakonia in Germany." *Ecclesiology* 5.1, 69–81. Review of Anni Hentschel, *Diakonia im Neuen Testament* (Tübingen: Mohr Siebeck, 2007).

2009e. Book review of Richard R. Gaillardetz, *Ecclesiology for a Global Church: A People Called and Sent* (Maryknoll, NY: Orbis Books, 2008). In *Worship* 83.2, March, 173–76.

2009f. Book review of Richard P. McBrien, *The Church: The Evolution of Catholicism* (New York: HarperCollins, 2008). In *Worship* 83.3, May, 267–72.

2008a. "Deacons—Marginal or Central?" *The Furrow* 59.6, June, 323–30.

2008b. "Deacons—Searching for an Identity." *The Pastoral Review* 4.4, July, 49–54.

2008c. Article review of James Keating, ed., *The Deacon Reader* (New York: Paulist Press, 2006). In *Bijdragen International Journal in Philosophy and Theology* 69.2, 214–19.

2008d. Article review of Gary Macy, *The Hidden History of Women's Ordination* (New York: Oxford University Press). In *Worship* 82.5, September, 463–67.

2008e. "Learning About Diaconate from Reflections of T. F. Torrance on the Eldership." *New Diaconal Review* 1.1, November, 18–21.

2008f. Review of William T. Ditewig, *The Emerging Diaconate: Servant Leaders in a Servant Church* (New York: Paulist Press, 2007). In *Worship* 82.2, March, 183–87.

2007a. "Reader Response: Deacon Words." *The Pastoral Review* 3.5, September, 38–39.

2007b. "The Embattled 'Deacon' Words." *The Pastoral Review* 3.3, May, 46–51.

2006. "Ordained and Other Ministries: Making a Difference." *Ecclesiology* 3.1, 12–32.

2005a. "Women and Ministry in the Light of 'Who Touched Me?' (Luke 8:45)." *Interface, Australian Theological Forum Inc.* 8.2, October, 125–34.

2005b. "Fitting Lay Ministries into a Theology of Ministry [Part 1], A Critique of an American Consensus." *Worship* 79.2, March, 152–67.

2005c. "Fitting Lay Ministries into a Theology of Ministry [Part 2], Making a Fit." *Worship* 79.3, May, 209–22.

2001a. Article review of Gunnel Borgegård, Olav Fanuelsen, and Christine Hall, eds, *The Ministry of the Deacon*, vol. 2, *Eccclesiological Explorations* (Uppsala: Nordic Ecumenical Council, 2000). In *International Journal for the Study of the Christian Church* 1.1, 103–06.

2001b. "Contextualising Dorothea Reininger on Women Deacons," http://www.womenpriests.org/called/collins3.htm.

2000a. "Diakoni—Teoria—Praxis." *Svensk kyrko tidning* 96.11, March 17, 107–11 (co-author Kjell Nordstokke).

2000b. "Ute Eisen on Early Women Office-Bearers." *Women-Church* 26, Autumn, 38–42.

1999. "Does Equality of Discipleship Add Up to Church? A Critique of Feminist Ekklesia-logy." *New Theology Review* 12.3, August, 48–57.

1998a. "Did Luke Intend a Disservice to Women in the Martha and Mary Story?" *Biblical Theology Bulletin* 28.3, 104–11. Paper presented to the Catholic Biblical Association of Australia, Catholic Theological College, Clayton, Melbourne, July 6, 1997.

1998b. "Letter to Catholic Women" from Letters to Deacons, http://www.women-priests.org/called/collins1.htm.

1996. "Should Roman Catholic Women Seek to be Ordained Deacons?" *Ordination of Catholic Women Newsletter* 3.1, April, 5–11. Also at http://www.womenpriests. org/called/collins2.htm.

1995a. "Many Ministries. An Unresolved Ecumenical Issue." In P. Harvey and L. Pryor, eds, *So Great a Cloud of Witnesses*. Festschrift for Lawrence D. McIntosh (Melbourne: Uniting Church Theological Hall and ANZ Theological Library Association), 220–32.

1995b. "A Ministry for Tomorrow's Church." *Journal of Ecumenical Studies* 32.2, Spring, 159–78. Keynote address, Ecumenical Summer School, St Mary's College in the University of Melbourne, Parkville, February 5, 1994.

1994a. "Gifts of God to Congregations: An Alternative Reading of 1 Corinthians 12:4–6." *Worship* 68.3, May, 242–49.

1994b. "Die Bedeutung der Diakonia—eine persönliche Erfahrung." *Diaconia Christi* 29.1/2, June, 51–71. Translation of "The Diakonia of Deacons," a paper read at the Inaugural National Conference of Australian Permanent Deacons, St Mary's Cathedral, Sydney, September 29, 1993, and at the Anglican Diocese of Melbourne Diaconal Ministry Conference, Santa Maria Centre, Northcote, February 26, 1994. The original paper was subsequently published as "The Diakonia of Deacons. A Personal Encounter" in the special English-language edition of Diaconia Christi, Sonderheft, June, 100–15.

1993. "Ministry as a Distinct Category Among Charismata (1 Corinthians 12:4–7)." *Neotestamentica* 27.1, 79–91. Paper read at the International Congress for the Study of Religion, section Society of Biblical Literature, University of Melbourne, July 1992.

1992. "The Mediatorial Aspect of Paul's Role as Diakonos." *Australian Biblical Review* 40, 34–44. Paper read at the International Meeting of the Society of Biblical Literature, Vienna, August 1990.

1991. "Once More on Ministry: Forcing a Turnover in the Linguistic Field." *One in Christ* 27.3, 234–45. Lecture at the Institute for Cultural and Ecumenical Research, Collegeville, Minnesota, October 1990.

1984. "Diakonia as an Authoritative Capacity in Sacred Affairs and as the Model of Ministry." *Compass Theology Review* 18.2, Winter, 29–34. Paper read at the conference of the Australian and New Zealand Association of Theological Schools, Ormond College, University of Melbourne.

1974. "Georgi's 'Envoys' in 2 Cor. 11:23." *Journal of Biblical Literature* 93.1, 88–96.

SOURCES OF CHAPTERS

1. *Diakonian tutkimus* 2 (2009), 134–48.
2. *Ecclesiology* 5.1 (2009), 69–81. © Koninklijke Brill NV, Leiden, 2009.
3. Previously unpublished.
4. *Are All Christians Ministers?* (1992), chapter 7.
5. *Deacons and the Church* (2002), chapter 2.
6. *Australian Biblical Review* 40 (1992), 34–44.
7. *Are All Christians Ministers?* (1992), chapter 8.
8. *Are All Christians Ministers?* (1992), chapter 9.
9. *Are All Christians Ministers?* (1992), chapter 5.
10. *Deacons and the Church* (2002), chapter 2.
11. *Ecclesiology* 8.1 (2012), 11–32. © Koninklijke Brill NV, Leiden, 2012.
12. *Ecclesiology* 3.1 (2006), 12–32. © Koninklijke Brill NV, Leiden, 2006 (originally published by SAGE).
13. *Worship* 79.2 (March, 2005), 152–67; 79.3 (May, 2005), 209–22.
14. Previously unpublished; public lecture at St John's College, Durham, Conference *"Making Connections: Exploring Diaconal Ministry,"* September 8, 2011.

Index

Early Christian Authors
anon. *De iactantia* 237
Clement Alex. *Exc. Theo.* 85 180
Eusebius *Vita* 2.29 108
Irenaeus 153
Synesios 104

Church Documents
Church of England

1 *Orientis Graeci Inscriptiones Selectae*, vol. 1, ed. W. D. Dittenberger (Leipzig, 1903).